THE GUILT PROJECT

THE GUILT PROJECT

Rape, Morality, and Law

Vanessa Place

Other Press · New York

3 10
gay

3 64.1532
PLACE, V

Copyright © 2010 Vanessa Place

Production Editor: Yvonne E. Cárdenas

Text Designer: Simon M. Sullivan

This book was set in 10.75 pt Electra by Alpha Design & Composition
of Pittsfield, New Hampshire

10 9 8 7 6 5 4 3 2 1

LIBRARY OF CONGRESS CATALOGING-IN-PUBLICATION DATA

Place, Vanessa.
The guilt project : rape, morality, and law / by Vanessa Place.
p. cm.
ISBN 978-1-59051-264-7 (hardcover) — ISBN 978-1-59051-386-6 (e-book)
1. Trials (Rape)–California 2. Rape. 3. Guilt (Law)–United States. 4. Rapists.
I. Title.
KF221.S49P58 2010
345.73'0253209794–dc22   2009041121

NOTE TO READER:
All of the quotations from witnesses in this book were taken directly
from the trial transcripts of cases that I handled on appeal. I have
changed the names of the people referred to in the book, including the
names of most of my clients, to protect their privacy.

For James A. Uyeda and Jennifer T. Mayer

CONTENTS

THE GUILT PROJECT

INTRODUCTION
A GUILTY PLEA

I AM A CRIMINAL DEFENSE APPELLATE ATTORNEY. I represent indigent sex offenders and sexually violent predators, all on appeal from felony convictions in the State of California. I have also supervised or otherwise assisted a number of other attorneys representing indigent appellate defendants. All told, I've been involved in about a thousand felony cases. Most of my clients are factually guilty by virtue of their acts; all are legally guilty by virtue of their convictions. They are the very bad men, those who trigger the question, "How can you defend people like that, knowing that they're guilty?" It's an inevitable question, though the delay between meeting me and asking the question varies according to the questioner's profile. The rich ask it sooner than the poor, the educated quicker than the unschooled. Other criminals usually don't ask it at all. Fellow cons will be the first to volunteer to crack a rapist's skull, but will never question the scumbag's right to a defense.

Once, as I was examining the superior court file in a particularly gruesome child rape case, the court clerk asked me, "How can you live with yourself?" I said that I don't.

Like a lot of abject apologies, my response was wrapped in a layer of self-righteousness, and, like a lot of self-righteousness, was also right. My job is not predicated on innocence. In our famously adversarial system of justice, we the actors play parts that are as important as the play. It's a cliché that a society is judged by how it treats its most despicable members, a cliché that mindful people accept in the abstract and reject in practice. But freedom of speech is only relevant when the opinions are vile, and due process meaningful only when applied to the daddy who rapes his son. Sex offenders are our most

1

despised citizens. To defend them without reservation, I have to absolutely accept their guilt. My job is not to defend the innocent, but to defend. My goal isn't to assure that the trial was a fair contest, but to get the bastard off, back on the street, back in the family room, back in somebody's bed. If I succeed, and if he reoffends, I can't in good conscience insist on anyone's innocence—least of all my own.

The Evolution of an Appellate Attorney

I work as a combination street sweeper and factory worker. I follow what's gone before, mopping up after the bloody mess, squaring the legal corners, assembling the lives disassembled by tragedy, and reducing reams of paper to brief-sized pellets. I read a lot, I write slightly less. I can look at almost anything, though I can't always get it out of my head. I have my own children, and I know precisely what can happen to them. When a friend noted that I'd never been raped, I answered, "Not yet." What I've learned from my job is that all of us are born mid-conversation: whatever culture we swing our hips to informs the way we frame and view our law and order. Not just because legislators and lawyers and judges and jurors watch the same TV shows as you do, or because there is a cultural loop in which news stories are consumed and regurgitated as plotlines that are consumed and regurgitated as new crimes, but because people who came of age starting in the 1970s are the legislators, lawyers, judges, and jurors of today.

We grew up believing not just that rape is an act of power and violence, but that rape implicates legal violence, as in the iconic 1988 movie *The Accused*, or the first episode of *LA Law* (1986). We were taught that rape laws needed constant strengthening because victims, always innocent, needed to be perpetually favored against defendants, who were the unproven guilty. We were told that for every molestation we knew of, there were thousands we did not, and for every rapist sentenced (to some nominal prison time) there was a worse one still skulking about. We made our laws harsher and our standards of proof easier and were surprised at the corresponding increase in crime. We now stand thigh-deep in this cultural and legal stew, and the muck is rising. If there are more rapists and molesters than before, it's not only because the laws make more of them, but because we all do.

In a democracy, the law is supposed to pour cool impartiality over hot situations, orchestrate agreements between opposites, and correct imbalances between the powerful and the voiceless. Criminal law is an acrobatic between the interests of the State in catching those who violate the rights of the citizenry, those citizens whose rights stand to be violated by getting caught, and those who stand on the sidelines and cheer. Consigned to the bottom of the criminal heap, sex offenders are the most loathed of the loathsome. We require them to register with police post-release, commit them involuntarily to mental institutions post-sentence, and add a life sentence for each illicit penetration. But robbers return to prison more regularly than rapists. There is no accurate way to diagnostically predict whether anyone will re-offend, and even torturers aren't punished for each turn of the screw.

The Evolution of Rape

In 1736, an English court called rape an accusation "easily to be made and hard to be proved, and harder to be defended by the party accused, though never so innocent."[1] To prove the charge, the law required a woman to forcibly resist and put up a "hue and cry," demonstrating his overpowering and her unwillingness. The hue and cry was a thirteenth-century common-law rule mandated for all victims of violent crime, as it was expected that victims would violently and audibly resist their attackers. Raising a hue and cry sent villagers in pursuit of villains, so proof of an element of a crime also served a practical policing function.

In the 1800s, the hue and cry was replaced in rape cases by the "fresh-complaint" doctrine. A wronged woman was expected to "make immediate complaint thereof to her mother or other confidential friend," as a New York court wrote in 1869.[2] Where there was no complaint and no obvious sign of violation, it was natural to assume that no real rape had occurred. For rape was an act of interpretation: whether forced sex was a wrong or a wooing depended on who was telling the story. And because rape has been part of romance, the literal and literary friction of sex and violence has lent itself with equal ease to comedy and tragedy. Pope's *Rape of the Lock* was a sexy trifle, Shakespeare's *The Rape of Lucrece* a sexy torment. Faulkner fused rape and race like chocolate and marshmallow in s'mores: a confection so extreme as to betray good taste, but one that sates a craving.

Used as a blunt-force tool to subjugate and assimilate another tribe or country, pervert and correct another sexuality, cement prejudice and seed family ties, take back and cede the night, sexual violation was an allegory of possession and transformation that played out the proper progress of resistance, then capitulation, then domination, like a leading lady who first slaps, then strokes her rapist's manly chest. In Ovid's *Metamorphoses*, the gods raped for release, and their victims turned into trees if they ran away or cows or crickets if they gave in. The rapists' offspring were demigods and heroes, because sex coupled with conquest is a winning combination. The victor repopulates the country he came in—*veni, vidi, vici* becomes *vidi, vici, veni*. Unlike murder, rape is irresistibly symbolic; unlike slavery, rape has better imagery in art than history.

Beginning in the 1970s, feminist and victim advocacy groups began changing these attitudes. The milestones ran from book to book and case to case, turning from cultural fringe into the fabric of society. For example, in 1975 the California Supreme Court recognized a "mistake of fact" defense in rape cases: a man might not be guilty of rape if he had a "good faith, reasonable belief" that his victim had consented.[3] The so-called *Mayberry* defense sounds like a free pass for the clueless, but it acknowledges that there are at least two truths to each rape: his and hers. And where lack of consent is at issue, her rape may not be his rape.

The 1976 paperback edition of Susan Brownmiller's book *Against Our Will: Men, Women, and Rape*[4] bears the bold-faced announcement that rape "is not a crime of lust but of violence and power." The book also toppled the myth that only evidence of the latter was proof of the former. Brownmiller's historical examination of rape as a common tool of cultural domination (in war, pogroms, slavery, and marriage itself) exploded the notion that a charge of rape, unlike robbery, needed to be specially proved by evidence of force. In 1977, the first "Take Back the Night" march was held in San Francisco, organized by Women Against Violence in Pornography. Ten years later, anti-pornography activist Andrea Dworkin's analysis of patriarchal erotics in her book *Intercourse* led to her conclusion that sex as commonly conceived could never be considered consensual.[5] Quickly nutshelled into the adage "sex is rape," this concept seemed an endgame to radical feminism and legal reform. If all heterosexual sex was rape, then reformation, like the revolution, could only be cultural.

But the law likes constraint better than liberty. Mores are easier to legislate than cultivate. As second-wave feminism rose just ahead of the Christian right, certain issues proved more amenable to a Venn diagram of codifiable righteousness. In 1979, four years after her book debuted, Susan Brownmiller advocated legislation to put pornography "back in the closet." Pornography, she wrote, "had nothing to do with the hallowed right of political dissent" as it "represents hatred of women," and "pornography's intent is to humiliate, degrade and dehumanize the female body for the purpose of erotic stimulation and pleasure."[6] By 1990, Mary Ellen Ross, writing for the *Christian Century*, cited feminist writings to damn pornography as eroticizing "violence, humiliation, degradation and other explicit forms of abuse."[7] And while right-minded people may agree that pornography eroticizes violence, both right- and left-minded people now agree that rape is a crime of violence. The pendulum has swung.

Are Rapists Multiplying?

The legal definition of rape is no longer forced sex, or sex without consent; it is sex without "affirmative and ongoing" consent. This definition is protean. It includes men who grab women off the street or seek them as they sleep, and men who have sex with drunken women who say yes or sober women who never quite manage to say no. It includes men who put knives to their wives' throats, and women who nod yes and then decide, mid-ride, no thank you.

Child molesters used to be the shadow lurkers and tot snatchers of *M* or *A Tree Grows in Brooklyn*: the stranger you weren't supposed to talk to, the man with the candy you shouldn't take. This is still the most popular cultural image. The media prefer to focus on the statistically rare tragedy of a five-year-old being kidnapped, raped, and murdered by a passerby than to report the more common horror of habitual incest. But the crime of child molestation includes not only the predatory uncle or familiar fiend, but eighteen-year-olds who have agreed-upon sex with fourteen-year-olds, eleven-year-olds who fondle ten-year-olds, and fifteen-year-olds appropriately groping each other. This categorical elasticity means there are now more rapists and molesters among us. There may be more people willing to report being raped, but there are also more behaviors classified as rape, more ways to become a rapist or molester than ever before. We think we're surrounded, but we've surrounded ourselves.

To track our bogeymen publicly, we make them register with police; to watch them privately, we post their photos and addresses online. TV shows like *Oprah*, *Law & Order: Special Victims Unit*, and especially *Dateline: To Catch a Predator* zero in on the epidemic of real and hypothetical sex offenders, turning television personalities into long-armed sheriffs, primetime viewers into armchair deputies, and crime into commercial-programming profit. Beneath this voyeur vigilantism lies the deep conviction that no law is ever tough enough, that somehow, somewhere, someone is getting off—scot-free, that is. Despite the extreme penalties doled out daily to sex offenders, lawmakers and media makers stoke the perception that these crimes are inevitably treated too lightly. And this stoking fuels all sorts of fires.

For vengeance is yours, mine, and ours. In the popular imagination, criminals were regularly hunted down by amateurs: Nancy Drew, the Hardy Boys, and Jessica Fletcher did their good deeds, serially confident that they could turn their man over to the authorities for lawful justice. In the popular reality, lynch mobs targeted the justly and the unjustly accused alike, and the sheriff left the jail cell unlocked. Still and all, law enforcement was a group effort. And as the conception of rape as a crime of violence became more ensconced in the popular imagination, so too did the notion that violence is properly met with violence, *omo a omo*. From Aerosmith's bad-daddy blasting song, "Janie's Got a Gun" to the shot in the parking lot in *Thelma & Louise* to the payback's-a-heavenly-bitch payoff of Alice Sebold's *The Lovely Bones* to the 2006 killings of two registered sex offenders in Maine, we all want to find and bury the bad guys. The common-law hue and cry is not just for victims anymore. Why wait for crime to occur when you can catch your criminals before they act and punish them straight off the bat? We want to finger the mother- (and daughter-) fuckers—and, by god, we can.

Stories for the Telling

The following chapters mirror anyone's transformation from reasonably good student with decent standardized test scores to working attorney. Armed with enough legal knowledge to fuel an opinion, you get tossed into the State-funded fray, learn the practicalities fast enough to stay afloat, then start stocking up your stories . . . stories that can be used to prove anything you like. It's easier and more popular to prove what people already believe, as it provides the comfort of constancy in what are always uncertain times. Decide who your audience is, and select accordingly. Make the molester more or less evil, calibrate his disassociation from his deeds to the sympathies of the story seekers. The rapist can be the courteous one, so clearly caught in some oedipal stew that you'll thank your own mother for the moderation of her madness, or he can be the devil incarnate, the one who considers the knife block on the kitchen counter as an improvisational prop. (I think having a knife block is like keeping a loaded .45 by the toaster.) I am a font of stories. The problem is that I've no thesis left to prove except what's told by and through my stories: that what is done in the dark by criminals is bad, but what is done by the light of the law can be worse.

This book is about how sex cases serve as cultural flashpoints and conceptual weak links. The law has too easily assimilated other disciplines and concerns in what is wrongly cast as a battle between victims and perpetrators, when it's really a tension between the person and the People. By participating in a false fight, the law, an area that must be public above all, has become increasingly vulnerable to privatization, and through privatization, to moral corruption. This rot has crept into the corners of our own morality.

The book's chapters are grouped into four sections: Guilt and Me, Guilt and Science, Guilt and Culture, and Guilt and Politics. Each chapter takes one or two of my cases as its frame. The facts of each case are only those accounts that were presented to the trial court that can be found in the appellate record, all available to the public. I have no independent knowledge as to the truth or falsity of any particular testimony or piece of evidence. I chose these particular cases because they are emblematic of that section's issues, and because, out of the thousand appeals that I've seen, these are among the stories that haunt me.

- Todd was convicted of rape based on a common interpretation of DNA evidence. Though perhaps scientifically sound, it ignores the fundamental legal principle that a man is innocent until proven guilty.
- Jonathan was a slow eighteen-year-old who had sex with a fast thirteen-year-old. He will have to register as a child molester for the rest of his life.
- George went to a party where Antoinette announced her drunken intention to fuck all the guys there; she did her best. George got life in prison.
- Francisco made a videotape of himself having sex with someone who liked to drop by for some rough sex after partying. She never complained that he raped her, but the police found the tape and arrested him. He's doing twenty-eight years.
- Patrick was a burglar/rapist who underwent a genuine religious conversion and personality change after his commitment as a sex-

ually violent predator. But having once been designated a sexually violent predator, he will probably die in the state hospital.

- MacD is a pimp. The deal on the street is that the "ho" gives the pimp her money and sex on demand, and the pimp takes care of the day-to-day. For having sex with women who had agreed to sexually service him, MacD was sentenced to 250 years, plus life.
- Two defendants—a man who tortured his wife and children, and a serial rapist of older women—both received sentences of more than a thousand years, plus multiple life terms.

These crimes, these sentences, are pointless. I am not sentimental. I am not a fool. I am not going to convince you that the guilty are innocent, or explain why people do what they do. Unlike a journalist, sociologist, or psychiatrist, I've no bent toward divination; in the discussion of the already guilty, there is little room for landing on what really happened, or sussing out deep motivation. Instead, I treat these cases exactly as they came to me, the defendant having been convicted, the facts just as contradictory and confused as they were at trial, the stories, like all stories, still open to retelling.

Again, I work for the guilty. That is, the legally guilty, those who have been convicted. I understand that my clients who are also factually guilty had no right to do what they were convicted of doing. The legal question that concerns me is, did the State have the right to take the essence of these people's lives? The moral question that concerns me is, how many lives are being sacrificed to a series of social expediencies, or to cultural arguments that have already been won?

In Sartre's book *Anti-Semite and Jew*, the Jew is cast as absolutely necessary for the anti-Semite: the figure of the Jew permits the anti-Semite to define himself by that which he is not, and that which he is not is, by definition, evil.[8] History progresses: I once went to a screening of Leni Riefenstahl's *Triumph of the Will* at UCLA. The film was introduced by a reputable historian, who condemned Riefenstahl throughout his talk, during which the audience hissed at each mention of the Holocaust. The Holocaust is an obvious evil. Condemnation of genocide

seems as gratuitous in a campus movie theater as cocktail-party condemnation of child molestation. People tell me that they can't discuss sex offenders or sex offenses because of their profound disgust
for these crimes. This repugnance to an obvious evil is presented as
a source of pride, an ethical merit badge. But the sinful pride lies in
our putting sex offenders in a category of evil that allows us to define
ourselves in opposition to them.

   Like the purveyors of genocide, sex offenders are people who have
done actual evil. And still we want to cleave to an "us" versus "them"
where the "them" acts as a repository for all evil, leaving goodness to
the rest of us. We also believe that "they" are disposable. A moral calculus is made, and the rights of "them" are deemed not worth the cost
to "us." This is wrong. Pretending that certain men are inhuman, or
that evil lies outside logic, excuses us personally and politically from
calculated mercy. At heart, mercy is simply the steady responsibility
to safeguard the humanity of all, including those we hate. There will
always be people guilty of great evil. But evil is an act, not a cultural
metaphor, not a social backdrop, and not entertainment. As a people,
we have to resist the temptation to make our morality contingent on
anybody's innocence. You might hate my clients, and you might be
right. My clients routinely disprove God. But we can't use them to
undo our own humanity.

SECTION I

GUILT AND ME

CHAPTER 1
STATEMENT OF THE CASE

If pimps and thieves were invariably sentenced, all decent
people would get to thinking they themselves were constantly
innocent, cher monsieur. And in my opinion—all right, all
right, I'm coming!—that's what must be avoided above all.
Otherwise everything would be just a joke.

—ALBERT CAMUS, *The Fall*

I WAS SUMMONED FOR JURY DUTY not long ago. After making an effort
to be excused, mainly because I knew no reasonable person would
want me on their jury, I went. Planning to read, write, look around—
anything but serve. I spent the first day in the large white-walled jury
room at the Clara Shortridge Foltz Criminal Justice Center,[1] the main
criminal court building in Los Angeles. I've often been to the clerk's
office there to look at files. The clerk's office is a large, open space full
of faint desperation and full-on hardcore bureaucracy. Every photo-
copy costs $1.50 and there's constant affirmation of the fact that peo-
ple like you and me know things by nouns, but that judicial systems
and civil servants know things by numbers. I've also frequently been
to the main Evidence Room in the basement. That's where they keep
all the evidence used in all the criminal trials in the building: bloody
clothes, nasty photos, contraband drugs, illegal weapons, and other
items that one is not supposed to own. Today, though, I'm staying up-
stairs, a regular citizen appearing for jury duty, not as a Monday-night
quarterback for the losing side, but to be judged by other lawyers to
be a judge of facts.

At 3:00 p.m., I was sent to witness the selection of a jury from
my peers. The defendant was charged with attempted burglary of a

garage, and seemed friendly enough. The attorneys had the cockiness that comes from doing trials for a couple of years, and paraded their chops, using voir dire as an opportunity for thuddingly obvious object lessons (we do not prejudge, we promise to use our absolute commonest sense) about the dullest forms of due process. Watching the lawyers galumph through their paces, I felt like a spy without a side.

But then, I've always been a bit homeless. Whether working for or against the State, the jurisprudence I hold dearest is the one I learned my first week of law school: It Depends. There's no such thing as "the law." No matter how often we refer to it in the statuesque abstract, criminal law is like clinical medicine, a more or less rough match-up of symptoms (evidence) to diagnosis (charged crime). Lack of consent + sexual intercourse = rape. Lewd intent + touching = child molestation. Each variable is composed of a constellation of statutory definitions and case law. So in rape, "lack of consent" includes saying "no!," remaining silent when confronted by a show of force, saying "yes!" under duress, saying "yes!" when too intoxicated to know what "yes!" entails, saying "yes!" then changing your mind and saying "You know, I don't think this is such a good idea." In child molestation, "touching" includes any and all touching: head, elbows, knees, and toes, as well as the private bits. If there is proof that the touching was done with the requisite lewd intent, a slap on the back or a hearty handshake becomes sexual abuse.

Doing Time with the People of California

I've spent the bulk of my working life doing criminal appeals, always for the indigent, always for the defense. But I started out on the more popular side, the one stocked with sheep and lambs—the prosecution. Twenty years ago, when I was a shiny new lawyer, I worked for the Los Angeles city attorney's office for an extraordinarily brief time: a year and change. As a deputy city attorney, I handled several teacher molestation cases involving multiple victims. The children had typically been abused over a period of years, typically in neighborhoods where the schools are public and poor, and the population transient, booming, and various shades of brown. I learned how to ask sweet-cheeked third graders if they'd been digitally penetrated, how to nod matter-of-factly at the exchange of a cloakroom grope for a brand new #2 pencil, and how to get an accurate portrait of a man's penis from a girl who didn't have any words for genitalia, including her own. I had misdemeanor cases involving thirty and forty witnesses that were all rejected for filing by the district attorney's office for insufficient proof. One of my defendants fled, was featured on, and was captured via *America's Most Wanted*. That was my triumph, twice removed, for it had nothing to do with me or my efforts.

What I remember most about this time were the hours spent talking to children in poor neighborhoods, and, once, watching a detective tell a woman that her daughter had been repeatedly raped by her fifth-grade teacher. The woman was proud and believed in God. She was wearing a carnation pink suit and a white blouse with a bow. She had a fine civil service job, what older ladies call "good hair," and lived in South-Central Los Angeles, where she'd grown up right. And her face collapsed in the middle, permanently hammered in a single blow.

Soon after that, I decided I didn't want to represent the government anymore. Too much hate. Like an abstract painting, all elements except the surface had been stripped from any situation. There was Our Side and Their Side, and ours was Pure Good and theirs was Pure Evil. Witnesses and victims rightly hated perpetrators, but prosecutors and police were merciless. Cruel as a matter of course, in the petty ways that cruelty is most easily and gratuitously expressed.

For example, in one of my cases, a professional photographer accused of child pornography was able to get a court order to have his photography equipment returned so he could work. I saw him standing on the other side of the main Evidence Room divide, watching as a sex crimes detective who evidently disagreed with the judge dropped the box holding the very best cameras to the floor. There was the inevitable shattering sound, which seemed too metaphoric. In another case, I got a junior high school teacher who had inartfully pawed some high school senior boys' groins while play-wrestling to plead to misdemeanor child annoyance. His sixteen- and seventeen-year-old victims thought it was funny. The teacher was an enormously fat man, about twenty-three, who wore black glasses and a goatee. He cried the entire time he was in court. The other people in court thought this was funny. Devil baiting is devil worship, and it made me sick.

What could I do? I reckoned the only ethically comfortable human position was powerlessness. Not passive resistance, but resistant passivity, best expressed in the childish, foot-stamping, "I won't!" But that stance is practically impossible to maintain professionally with a law degree, so the second most comfortable position is that of underdog. Underdog: the poor and alone, the chafed tremulous individual tossed against the rocks of the super-potent State. And the underbelly of the underdog is the best slot of the lot. Chaff of the chaff. Defend them all, let God sort them out, that's my motto. It's a bit of a cheat, really, particularly in my line, because if you are a defense attorney representing only indigent, felonious sex offenders and sexually violent predators on appeal—a field of non-angels fitting on pinheads—you can feel quite good about your quixotic self, tilting at windmills without worrying too much that you'll free roving bands of the clammy-handed. Mostly you lose. You fight the good fight, and you lose, and that's as it should be, for if you win, something horrible has happened at trial. Having a potentially innocent client is a queasy feeling, like hearing strange noises in your house late at night and knowing that there really is someone else inside. And so you tell yourself that it's only potential innocence that's the problem. Probable innocence is too much to bear; factual innocence is a nightmare. In any event, there's hardly ever proof positive of purity. But that's not what this book is about. This book aims at the bruises, the darker parts of the jurisprudence and culture of guilt and rape that should embarrass all of us, but haven't yet.

Raping by Degrees

To plan to kill someone and then to kill is first degree murder. To decide to kill someone on the spot is second degree. To kill someone in the heat of what's called passion is voluntary manslaughter.

Each degree of murder is progressively sanctioned: the longer you think about it, the more time you do. It's been said that rape is no less a violation than murder, though a shadowed future seems better than none at all, and that "fate worse than death" business appears to have more to do with a societal notion of damaged goods than individual trauma, no matter how tragic. The classic image of rape was the stranger rape—the dark man at the back door, through the side window, or fresh from a back alley. Yet rape, like murder, has its nuances. But unlike murder, the justice system's view of rape is not at all fine-tuned. If a woman is raped by a stranger in an alley, it is rape. If a woman agrees to have sex with her boyfriend, then changes her mind during sex, it is rape. If an adult pins a child down and rapes the child, it is forcible child molestation; if an adult is larger than a child, or occupies some special family position relative to the child, and the child consents, it is forcible child molestation by way of duress. There is no change in culpability or in sentence.

It was ever thus: even when rape didn't account for many instances of what is now unblinkingly considered rape—a husband was once thought incapable of raping his wife because her sexual consent had been secured from "I do" unto death, and a prostitute couldn't be raped by anyone, though some saw forced sex under these circumstances as a kind of theft—even then, rape was rape. There were no degrees per se. But what about the argument that other crimes function as degrees of rape, such as sexual battery, which is the unlawful touching of sensitive parts? It's not the same thing at all. Those other crimes criminalize other acts. Unlike rape, the degrees of murder all center around the same stiff; it's the intent with which the victim was undone that alters the offense.

In rape law, the only allowance for gradation of intent is its full negation. A good-faith, reasonable belief in a woman's consent— modeled after the good-faith, reasonable belief in the need for self-defense in murder cases—is an affirmative defense to rape. If you have it, you get off, so to speak. In California, that's the *Mayberry* defense.[2] By comparison, if you have its soul mate in a homicide, you are convicted of manslaughter, a lesser crime. But if the crime of rape is the crime against the woman, then the man's erroneous belief in her consent, however honestly held, should be irrelevant. To be intellectually consistent, and consistent with murder laws, there would have to be degrees of rape, with lesser penalties for rape done without the requisite wrongful intent. Why all or nothing?

Not to diminish the moral or ethical seriousness of these crimes, but some should be legally diminished. These kinds of rape and forcible molestations are being legislatively and judicially aggravated by factors that are *sui generic*—virtually every molestation involves an adult larger and stronger than the victim, and incest is more common than stranger abuse. In the workaday world of sex offenses this means that the habitually bad uncle will automatically be subject not only to a higher sentence than the bad man at the mall, but that he may also be thrown into the sexually violent predator (SVP) limbo. Even though the stranger is more apt to strike again, and with greater force, whereas the uncle may or may not be a serial abuser, and if he is, he will probably not depart from the pattern of abuse. The problem with conflating the two is that fewer people leave the State Hospital than harrow the gates of hell.

I had a client who was convicted of two counts of habitual child molestation: he molested both of his stepdaughters over the same three-year period. The question is not whether this is a criminal act: it is. The question is not whether it is a morally reprehensible act: it is. The question is whether it is the product of a mental disorder such that this person should be forever considered a sexually violent predator. Not in a street-smart, "man to look out for" kind of way, but someone whose freedom the State can preemptively take away for an inchoate, uncommitted crime.

My client was evaluated using a test called a Static-99, which tabulates factors from an individual's history that correlate to sexual offense recidivism, and scores the person's risk of reoffense. He had a score of 3, which is modest in a test that runs from 0 (no recidivism risk) to 12 (highest risk). Based on his repeated victimization of his stepdaughters, however, the State psychologists opined he qualified as an SVP. In fact, the odds of his reoffending are fairly low, and there is no legal justification for labeling someone an SVP unless there's a "substantial chance"—a realistic possibility—of reoffense. And there should be a moral hesitancy to lower this bar.

We as a society have promised to wait until harm is done before we call in the cops. It's also true that we occasionally jump the gun, as in Japanese internment camps, registered Chinese, and traitors under the Patriot Act. But normatively, and historically, the preemptive strike is crap. Laws ought be the way we want to be, unmirrored images of our better selves.[3]

Hapless Victims and Consensual Molesters

But what is the effect of treating every crime as the worst possible crime of that variety? Making rape a catchall offense belies the manifold nature of rape as everything from a momentary loss of control, akin to murder's heat of passion, to a planned predatory attack, like murder with "malice aforethought." Too, the enhancement of a crime by facts inhering in that crime falsely elevates the offense. As if child molestation weren't bad enough, each abuse must be englossed with a patina of force to underscore its heinousness. But if heinousness needs to be underscored, then abuse itself somehow becomes oddly common. There is something false in characterizing virtually every child molestation a forcible child molestation: the child is falsely absolved of his or her participation, large or small, when that participation needs to be directly addressed.

When I prosecuted the teacher–child molestations, it was the children's guilt at being complicit in their abuse that shamed them most. They knew how they had stayed after class and took the dollar bill or the Hello Kitty eraser as fair trade for a bad touch. Just as there are molesters who defend their molestation by virtue of the child's willing participation, to tell a child she was raped when she knows she traded herself for pocket change doesn't help her understand why she did what she did or how she might refuse to do it again. Or make the molester understand that consent is never the issue, because the crime of child sexual abuse is not necessarily the crime of forcible rape. So every child is gauzed in the same hapless victimhood and every consensual molester explains that she wanted it. She did want it; it's just that she didn't grasp the extent of what it was, or its consequence, or the sad range of her options. Or maybe she did. There's a system in play; you either play along or you get played.

By the same poor token, there's a qualitative difference between the man who grabs a child off the street and rapes her and the man who asks a child to touch him. There is a difference in degree in the nature of the man, the act, and the child. In his 1992 book *Child-Loving: The Erotic Child and Victorian Culture,* James Kincaid writes about the willing participation of some children in their molestation.[4] He uses this complicity to critique the knee-jerk assignment of blame—all for one, and none for all—but comes to no other conclusion. (We will revisit Kincaid's book in chapter 4.)

The banal profundity is that guilt is a sliding scale. In molestation cases in general, and incest in particular, there may well be a collusion between victim and perpetrator that is falsely denied by the stance that a rape is a rape is a rape. For example, I have represented men who threatened to kill the children they raped, and men who truly planned to marry their victims—and whose victims wanted to marry them. To paint bright lines where no lines lie abets a muzzy hysteria that admits nothing but impotence: victims are kept powerless, and offenders maintain their self-righteousness. They both know they didn't do what they're said to have done, and accept responsibility for none of it. The child doesn't grow any more competent; the situational offender sees nothing but injustice. And the State on both sides stocks a pool of perpetual victimization, encouraging perpetual dependence on the State. In order to have Safe Child programs and battered-women's shelters, you need to have unsafe children and battered women. I'm not blaming the victim, but the Victim. That doe-eyed repository of Innocence Lost that fuels minute-by-minute news bulletins, sparks ballot initiatives and public service campaigns, makes media celebs of the ruthlessly sentimental, all over the cooling remains of someone who died for no particular reason save the evil

that men do. Is innocence lost? Yes, along with Paradise. But innocence is also lost by pretending the State doesn't have its own interests
in keeping our prisons fed.

This Just In!

There's money to be made in the game, big money. Like the public
school system, the prison industry is increasingly privatized, as will be
seen in chapter 4. But crime today finds its greatest immediate reward
in the entertainment industry. Shows like *Dateline: To Catch A Predator* produce child molesters for live TV. Newspapers and cable news
networks feed off the horrible travail of the child du jour. Will she or
he be found? Maybe, says the Sheriff. Possibly, says the Legal Com-
mentator. Please, says the Mother. They've got the dogs out now, and
neighbors are fanning the woods.

This just in! It's hour sixteen, and hope is dying along with the victim, minute by agonizing minute. Meanwhile, there's a teaser for some
new show featuring Real Life Victims, Real Life Perpetrators, Real Life
Jurors and Judges and Lawyers. Real Life Suffering, Real Tears, served
fresh and hot from the cheeks of the Permanently Injured.

This just in! A new interview with the Father, his eyes swollen
from sobbing, he'd like his young one returned, followed by expert
commentary on the statelessness of the parents and the reminder
that homicidal pedophiles are no one's friend. Remember, too, to
watch that episode of *Law & Order*, and there's bound to be something similar on *Court TV*, and also tons of *CSI* to whet the armchair appetite.

This just in! Little Ill-Fated has been found in a culvert, throat cut
and underpants in a knot. And on and on it goes, through the even-
tual capture of the Monster who did it, and his trial and sentencing,
and the legislative hearings and public proclamations featuring the
Parents of the Victim, who say, as Victims now must, "Never Again,"
as if pedophilia, like fascism, is a movement that must be stopped.
But Never Again becomes Again Again as soon as a new Megan or

Brittany is snatched. And again, politicians promise a different end to the story if only Megan's or Brittany's Law is passed, a draconian law they are proud to sponsor, the way Phillip Morris once proudly sponsored *I Love Lucy*.

Does this recap feel offensive? It should. Because in all this hay-making, in which corpses and criminals serve as commercial compost, there are hardly any people. Not real people, anyway. Just a clutch of icons—those individual examples of our archetypes that stand for and against humanity, that implicate us only by way of the extremes of absolute innocence (the forever five-year-old) and ultimate evil (the soulless kiddie-raper).

I Collect Horror Pictures

I prefer purgatory. At least there's something to do. So I set to this proj-ect, what I have called my "guilt project": to argue for a morality con-ditioned, not on innocence, but on guilt. To insist on the humanity of the inhumane. And to insist that humanity be preserved with as much fidelity as we would guard all our little children, whether doe-eyed or snot-nosed. (I'm not the first to note the media preference for the snuffing of telegenic children.) Besides, it's morally superior to work for the despised, as Mother Teresa knew: to have a saint, you need a sinner—or at least a steady stream of lepers. Though I'm no saint, or even particularly pleasant, and there's more than enough guilt to gild all of us.

These seem like pretty abstract reasons for taking on this sort of job. But patriotism and religious fervor are, too. Though I come from an Army family, I'm not an unquestioning soldier. Still, you have to believe in something, whether it's the contingent sanctity of the soul or the need for a superior ground defense. In this way, I've signed on to both. I believe in the ineffably human and the inalienable rights of the citizen.

My personal constitution is stronger than most, or more calloused, or more masochistic, depending on your perception and my mood.

When I first started in these sorts of cases, I went to an FBI-sponsored seminar on serial sex crimes. The other attendees were a few male deputy district attorneys and about fifteen cops from various jurisdictions. At one point, the FBI lecturer announced that the slides accompanying the next portion of the lecture—on serial rapist/murderers— depicted victims who'd been ritually mutilated, their breasts and/or vaginas having been cut out or otherwise violently disfigured, as well as some who'd also had their eyes cut out or hands or feet chopped off. The lecturer told audience members not to look if they didn't want to, because the pictures were exceptionally gruesome. The first slide showed a naked woman of about twenty lying on her back, her breasts sliced off and a hole in place of her genitals, her arms raised and fallen to the side, her mouth agape, as if she were surprised at the state she was in. When it appeared, every cop in the room stretched, scratched, or went to fetch a fresh pencil, or made some other gesture that excused looking. I forced myself to stare as hard as I could at that image, and each of the subsequent horrors. At that time, I was also training myself to review autopsy reports and photos while eating lunch. This seemed to be the very height of professionalism.

Later, I started suspecting the height of professionalism was having the nerve to show any sign of emotional distress, however vestigial. I am a lesbian, a fact that has no particular significance to my work except that it's a fact about me, and facts about me I keep from my clients. I also have children. Like other people in my line of work, I have a talismanic fear of my children having anything to do with anything that had to do with my cases. I didn't want them using the back sides of draft briefs for drawing paper, even when they were too young to read, because it involved touching (and, I suppose, being touched by) articulated evil. I don't let them look at my computer screen while I'm working. And when I look at the exhibits I must study, I realize that I'm adding to the bad gallery in my brain, the one already overstocked with images not just of stand-alone atrocity, such as the mutilated woman, but of contextual abomination: a live five-year-old girl, dookie braids mussed, eyes puffy; the plainwrap front of a cheap apartment building, the bright chrome chain attached to the darker bars on a window; an open cut, marked by the telltale imprint of a small tooth, on my client's index finger.

Maybe I don't really know how one goes on. Maybe, like Beckett, we in the guilt trade go on because there's no point to not going on. Because great horror is as much a part of real life as great paintings, and may spring, Guernica-like, from the same screaming source — that evil in us that we don't want to acknowledge is all so human. There's something beautiful in the sheer perversity of the urge to escape ordinary humanity, something that seems as honest and right and pointless to me as our attempts to make existence itself make sense. How do I do what I do? I do not resist. I admit and capitulate to the truth of all of it: the atrocious and the altruistic. The guilty and the not-proven. Our innate rot and hard-won grace.

Faith and the Doctrine of Reasonable Doubt

The traditional jury instruction for reasonable doubt in California requires that the jurors find the defendant guilty to a "moral certainty." Implicit in this language is the assumption that the judgment of one human being by another is a fundamentally moral effort, that only an abiding faith in the guilt of the other justifies a guilty verdict. An abiding faith implies an act of faith. Faith is belief ridden bareback, that informal amalgam of intuition and cognition that represents the highest form of our collective consciousness (i.e., our collective conscience). The point I want to make is that faith is part of the equation, that there is a common understanding and acceptance of the ability of one person to pass judgment on another. Furthermore, this judgment happens out of hand and off the cuff in society at large, and has a lineage as rich as Dante's *Commedia* and as poor as the local lynch mob.

Not only do we tend to calculate the moral culpability of our fellows, but we have an obligation to do so as a matter of our own morality. To be fully human means to make moral choices, constantly and in no preordained order. Choices that are imperfect because they are human. And because they are tiny movements of hypothetical better selves in a world of pocked souls. Still, no cheating. No fixing guilt by way of divine intercession—no trial by ordeal, no walking on fire, no dunking chair—in sum, no hooking folks up to the guilt-o-meter for the final verdict, whether it's a probe seeking proof of the Devil's kiss, a polygraph, or the latest Static-99 test. The only ratified version of a communal spirit is literary: the letter of the law. If we agree to live in a land governed by laws, we must be willing to judge when those laws are being overtly rewritten and covertly misapplied.

Here is what the Massachusetts Supreme Court said in the nineteenth century about reasonable doubt:

> It is not mere possible doubt; because every thing relating to human affairs, and depending on moral evidence, is open to some possible or imaginary doubt. It is that state of the case, which, after the entire comparison and consideration of all the evidence, leaves the minds of jurors in that condition that they cannot say they feel an abiding conviction, to a moral certainty, of the truth of the charge.[5]

The United States Supreme Court approved this definition in 1994, explaining that "moral evidence" was historically understood as being different from "demonstrative evidence."[6] The distinction between moral and demonstrative evidence was described in 1790 by James Wilson, one of the Court's original justices: "Demonstrative evidence has for its subject abstract and necessary truths, or the unchangeable relations of ideas." Moral evidence, on the other hand, is Janus-faced, involving a "contrariety of proofs." In other words, "real evidence on both sides."[7]

Just as moral evidence is relational, moral certainty is relative. The belief in one interpretation of events (did it) over another (didn't do it) depends on a sliding scale of certainty involving inferential steps based on probability. As Justice Wilson put it, "[W]e rise, by an insensible gradation, from possibility to probability, and from probability to the highest degree of moral certainty." Because there is always doubt's reasonable caveat: "In a series of moral evidence, the inference drawn in the several steps is not necessary," he wrote, "nor is it impossible that the premises should be true, while the conclusion drawn from them is false." A cookie is missing from the jar; it may have been eaten, or fallen to the floor. For a thing to be proved beyond a reasonable doubt is for it to be proved in increments, each bit reckoned more probable than not, based on our human experience, experience that is also had and understood incrementally. Our moral authority is as hard wrought as our faith, and our judgments as hard-won. So we proceed slowly and with the cynicism born of a naive belief in the capacity of ordinary folks to decide metaphysical matters. Not by way of giving unblinking faith and full credit to the lads in lab coats or the boys in blue, but by subjecting each step in these moral analyses to a real moral calculus—whether each leap of faith is worthy of our belief.[8]

A Moral Calculus of Violence?

If moral certainty is the base test of morality, there can be no premade answers to moral concerns. Simply put, the story changes. William Vollman's *Rising Up and Rising Down*, a 3,298-page, seven-volume exploration of the moral calculus of violence, is an exercise in the giddy pleasures of unwon moral authority.[9] Would you kill Hitler to cut short the Holocaust? Would you snuff a small village to save a country? What's an acceptable ratio of death, assuming some are necessary to avert others? But there can be no *moral* calculus of violence, not because violence is immoral, but because violence is not calculable. There is not a unit of violence (x) for which it can be said that $x + 1 > x$. Would you kill Hitler? In a heartbeat. Would you kill his twenty-year-old nephew, the master sergeant? Maybe more quickly. Would you cut the throat of his ten-year-old niece? Perhaps. Would any Aryan do? What about gutting a plump Bavarian three-month-old—what about raping her? Enormously effective in terms of coercion. But the (x) of the violated infant is not equal to the (x) of the dead head of state. And any attempt at further refinement $[(x)^n =$

dead baby; $(x) - (x)\square^n$ = dead Führer] betrays the baseline absurdity of the value assignment $[30(x)^n$ = busload of dead children; $30(x)$ + #? = busload of dead Olympic athletes/ +/– #? for same number of Congressmen, depending on their party affiliation].

The only ratio with heft is horror to horror, and at that point, you've proved yourself to be equal to any other terror. Similarly, the pact between the aggregate Us is that justice is redress. No harm, no foul, no case, no controversy. The court will not issue advisory opinions, will not step in where there is no actual wrong done or is so close to being done that it's the swallow the summer makes. In criminal law, this means the police must detect and convict, not predict and detain. A duty lately most notable for its abrogation, both at home and abroad. Note how the preemptive moral strike cozens to the conceit of a moral calculus of violence. Note how it worsens us.

When I found myself in law school at a very young age, the result of an accelerated course of study and failure of imagination, I was surrounded by people who were far happier to be there. I embarked on a many-pronged program of disengagement, including obsessively rereading Camus' *The Fall*. Still, I learned the lesson of law school — that the law is not a medium, but a method. A tin scoop with which moral philosophy is doled out in stories. The object lesson of rape at the time of the hue and cry is that rape was a violation of all womanhood; the lesson of the raped prostitute is that rape is a violation of a woman as a subjective agent. I have learned the critical aside of morality.

The Purgatory of the Evidence Room

As I said earlier, I've often visited the Los Angeles central criminal court Evidence Room. That trip to the basement is a boat ride down the river Acheron (the river of woe in Hades; it would be easier if it were Lethe, the river of forgetfulness). To get there, you have to go to the clerk's office on the second floor, show acceptable credentials, and have one of the clerks escort you onto a special meat locker–sized elevator in the back, usually reserved for cops and people with push-carts, variously loaded with boxes of paper, stacks of manila files, and deli platters for someone's retirement party. You are taken down to the basement, which smells like a combination of car exhaust and raw potato, and abandoned outside a plain steel door with a small, thick, glass-and-mesh window. You're then buzzed into an antechamber featuring a metal detector and a gym locker with letter-sized compart-ments. After stowing any sidearms in a locker, you pass through the metal detector and press another buzzer. Someone in the back looks you over via the closed-circuit TV and buzzes you into the second antechamber. This one has a sliding frosted-glass window, a yellowing Formica counter, and two other doors. You sign the log, stating name and official business. A clerk appears and gives you another form. You fill out that form, restating name/business, adding case name/num-ber; present your identification/credentials again, now examined by the clerk, who puts down that they've been examined; then wait as the clerk goes away with what now feels like your piece of paper, leaving the sliding glass window open, allowing you to pretend not to stare into the main Evidence Room.

It's a peculiar place, staffed by nervous yet avuncular young men and older women, settled as sofas. The women sit at metal desks collaged with pictures of their children or their children's children, cheerily cynical cartoons of the "You want it *when?*" variety, and pho-tocopied messages of rosy Hope and violet Inspiration. Behind them, there are things upon things stacked on metal shelves and wooden pallets. A full car fender, dented in the middle; a chainsaw, used; a set of golf clubs, new; TVs; stereos; the business end of a lawn mower; a wilted ficus in a pot; and hundreds of cardboard boxes. Your clerk eventually returns and points you toward the door on the left, set off by drywall. You are buzzed in, and go sit in a plastic bucket of a chair facing another Formica counter and more frosted, sliding windows.

Your exhibits clerk—and she is *your* clerk now, your lone link to still-warm humanity—sits in a padded swivel chair on the other side of the divide and opens a series of marked manila envelopes. She announces each exhibit number, loudly, clearly, before forking over the item for your review. Not including the dangerous ones or those deemed contraband, though you can see photos of the relevant knives, guns, drugs, et cetera, as need be. It's a good place for a heist.

She watches you examine, or looks at you looking, which is somehow different, and more disconcerting. She sits, stone-faced, while you flip through rape kits (the medical reports taken at the hospital, featuring, like an autopsy report, a large, schematic, bold-line outline of the proto-victim, annotated with injuries, plus, unlike most autopsy reports, a large, schematic, bold-line outline of the proto-victim's privates, full frontal, a black diamond representing the vaginal opening and a series of parentheses demonstrating the labial array, and full rear as well, a small black circle for the anus, the privates pierced with arrows leading to written observations of tears, redness, untoward discharge, etc.) and pictures of the actual victim, mussed and bloodied, or the defendant, fresh from his arrest. You get to handle the victim's clothes—parts of skirts with small patches missing, cut out for DNA sampling, or the soiled headband once wrapped around a little girl's wrists.

I may be over-personalizing via use of the second person, but the only thing that really transverses the official and physical distance between me and the exhibits clerk is her palpable disapproval. Unlike me, she's no party to all this nasty. But I am.

How can I do this?

How could I not?

SECTION II

GUILT AND SCIENCE

CHAPTER 2
DNA EVIDENCE: THE CALCULUS OF GUILT

all these calculations yes explanations yes the whole story from
beginning to end yes completely false yes

—SAMUEL BECKETT, *How It Is*

THIS CHAPTER AND THE NEXT EXPLORE what constitutes proper
or sufficient proof of guilt. More specifically, what constitutes
proper or sufficient proof of guilt when the question of guilt is framed
as a matter of a scientific, rather than a moral, calculus.

We'll first look at DNA testing, whose now routine use in criminal
investigation has revolutionized the field, but may be so routine and
routinely impressive that judges and juries overlook its limitations. In
this regard, we'll discuss how the law deals with scientific evidence
generally, and how it misapprehends and misuses DNA evidence specifically. In chapter 3, we'll see how more or less scientific methods
are used to diagnose a man as a sexual predator, and (typically) keep
him locked up for life.

The problem with a DNA test is that most people think of it as
being like a pregnancy test: yes or no. Or like the verdict itself: guilty
or innocent. But the question is never guilt or innocence, not really.
You don't have to prove innocence, so the sole question at trial is
whether guilt is proved beyond a reasonable doubt, and that's a matter
of persuasion. Persuasion is the object of rhetoric, the art that makes
you vote Republican or buy what you can't believe isn't butter. Guilt
is a moral and ethical conclusion drawn by human beings responsible
for judging other human beings. Guilt is a rhetorical product. Scientific proof may be used in its assessment, but its use must be absolutely
contingent upon its absolute contingency. Science may be based on

fact, but it is not fact: fingerprint analysis is a comparison between the characteristics of two sets of fingerprints, but there is no "fact" of fingerprint analysis. The problem is not, as the California Supreme Court has said, that DNA evidence is different from other kinds of evidence; the problem is that DNA evidence is literally and metaphorically exponential—evidence raised by the power of ten. So what is imagined to be a fast train to guilt or innocence should be experienced as a local, with lots of stops, and many good reasons to get off. First, we'll look at a case, then the science, then the law, and then the science as applied to the law, and as misapplied to the law in our case.

Two Men—One Fat, One Thin

On February 15, 1999, a little after 10:00 p.m., a Hispanic couple I'll call Angelia and Javier were sitting in their pickup truck in a Los Angeles parking lot when two black men approached from either side. The one who came to the driver's side window was big and heavy and had a gun; the other man was tall and thin. The fat one said he wanted money. They gave him all they had, pocket change. The two men got into the truck. The fat man took Angelia's seat and put her in the back with the thin man. He then told Javier to drive to a bank ATM. The thin man told Angelia everything would be all right. Angelia asked them not to hurt her because she was pregnant. The thin man assured her they just wanted money.

At the bank, after Javier got out of the truck, the thin man touched Angelia's breasts and vagina, and the fat man touched her vagina. Javier returned, and gave the fat man sixty dollars. The fat man got angry, and asked if this was all they had. Javier said yes, and asked if the men were going to leave them alone; the fat man said no, and hit Javier in the face with the gun.

The fat man directed Javier to a dark, residential neighborhood, led him to the bed of the truck, told him to stay put, then returned to the cab. For the next forty-five minutes, Javier felt the truck shaking. Inside the cab, the men touched and kissed Angelia; the thin man had her orally copulate him, put his penis in her vagina, his fingers in her vagina, and his penis in her anus. The fat man had her suck his penis, and penetrated her vagina and anus with his penis. Periodically, Angelia would be made to lean over the front seat to suck the fat man's penis while the thin man put his penis in her anus. Then the positions would be reversed, and she would suck the thin man's penis while being penetrated by the fat man.

At some point, Javier was brought back inside the truck and forced to drive to another location. There, he was returned to the truck bed, and again felt the truck shaking. He thought they stayed there for about fifteen minutes, and vaguely remembered a third person appearing, a man in a red sweater. According to Angelia, the thin man resumed raping her. Then another car drove up, a short man got out, and changed places with the fat man. The fat man waited outside the truck while Angelia was assaulted by the short man and the thin man.

Everyone then drove to a third neighborhood, Javier still in the truck bed, and the man in the red sweater following in his car. They parked, Javier heard someone say, "Come on, T.," a couple of times, and the fat man told Javier they were letting him go. Inside the cab, Angelia was naked. The thin man said to Angelia, "I liked it. It was very good. You're not going to tell the cops, right? Are you sure you don't want to leave your husband and come with us?" Angelia said, "No, thank you. I have a child waiting at home for me." The fat man said something inaudible to Angelia, then told her to come closer. She did, and he hit her in the face, saying, "Did you hear what I said?" She said she had, and the three men left in the car, throwing the truck keys away.

During the assault, the truck's interior light came on several times while the thin man was next to Angelia. They looked at each other for more than an hour; Angelia later testified she got a good look at the man, and tried to memorize his face. Javier said he got a better look at the fat man than the thin one.

Angelia's sexual assault examination revealed a hickey on her neck, and scratches on her back and lower legs. Her anus was extremely swollen, and there were multiple deep lacerations at the interior base, some of which were bleeding. Both labia majora and minora were red and swollen; there were small abrasions in the area between the anus and vagina, and the hymen was bruised. Before evidence samples could be collected, Angelia went to the bathroom, wiped herself with toilet paper, rinsed out her mouth, and washed her face. The nurse got sample swabs from Angelia's vaginal canal, her external genitals, of a vaginal lavage (a rinse of the vagina) and aspirate (liquid sucked from the vagina), from her breasts, and from the hickey on her neck.

Blurry Eyewitnesses

Lyle was arrested on March 29, 1999; Angelia and Javier readily identified him as the fat man in the assault. Lyle was tried and convicted of rape. I represented Todd, arrested a month after Lyle. The question at his trial was whether Todd was the thin man.

Javier identified Todd as the thin man in a photographic lineup known as a "six pack": six pictures police put together for witnesses to choose from. But on the photo ID card, Javier wrote that he thought Todd's hair was different from the rapist's. In a live, six-person lineup, Javier identified someone other than Todd as the perpetrator. When Javier was asked at trial if he saw the thin rapist in the courtroom, he said he was "not really sure," but that Todd looked "a little" like the guy. When asked again, Javier said he was "not really too sure" that Todd was the thin man.

In the photo lineup, Angelia tentatively identified Todd as the thin man, but noted that, unlike Todd, the thin rapist didn't have a mustache, and his hair was longer. She did not identify Todd at a live lineup. Asked at trial to point out the thin rapist, Angelia gestured at Todd, while saying she wasn't sure he was the same man. When the prosecutor asked how she was able to identify Todd, Angelia said, "Because I know it's him. I have . . . I could see. He looks like him a little." The prosecutor asked if Angelia was certain; Angelia said, "I'm not sure it's him." On cross-examination, Angelia noted that one of the reasons she thought Todd was her rapist was that he was the person on trial.

At Todd's trial, his wife testified that he and Lyle had been friends in high school, and still socialized. She also testified that Todd was a very bad husband: once shortly after their child was born, he made her continue having sex after she started bleeding and she told him it hurt. A year later, Todd pled guilty to raping his Marine Corps room-mate's girlfriend: he crawled into bed with her after her boyfriend left her alone in their quarters.

Todd's family said he had been living with his mother at his broth-er's house during the winter of 1999. On the day of the assault against Angelia and Javier, Todd drove his mother to a doctor's appointment in the morning, then returned home for the rest of the day. Every-one stayed in that night. Todd's mother did laundry, and remembered that Todd was either watching television or playing computer games. Todd's brother locked the house at 11:00 p.m. as usual, and set the alarm, to which Todd didn't know the code. He also kept a watchdog outside. The alarm didn't go off, and the dog didn't bark. Every night, on his way to bed, Todd's brother passed the living room couch where Todd slept; every night, Todd was on that couch, and was still there in the morning when his brother went to work.

Analyzing the Samples

None of the rapists wore gloves. Nine sets of fingerprints were found on the truck, none of them Todd's.

The LAPD Scientific Investigation Department screened the rape kit samples and tissues, detecting sperm on a number of internal and external samples. Those samples were subject to comparative DNA analysis with blood samples taken from Javier, Angelia, Lyle, and Todd. Todd's sperm cells were not on any of the external (cloth, tis-sues) samples. The vaginal sample contained sperm and non-sperm fractions; Angelia's DNA was consistent with the DNA found in the non-sperm fraction. Both Todd and Angelia could have been con-tributors to the sperm-cell fraction: the laboratory separation of the sample was imperfect, leaving a "mixed" sample (a sample with more than one contributor).

Because of the too-mixed nature of the vaginal samples, the criminalist could not do a useful statistical analysis on those bits, leaving only the external genital sample as possible evidence. A random match probability calculation was done on the external genital mixture, resulting in a statistical match of 1 in 6,500. (An extraordinarily low number, especially in a large urban area like Los Angeles: basically, this would mean there were around 1,500 genetically qualifying rapists out of a population of ten million.)

This random match probability statistic doesn't mean that one person in every 6,500 has a certain genetic profile. Rather, it represents the chance that an unrelated person randomly picked from the population would share this donor's exact DNA profile—the odds you'd randomly choose your identical twin out of a crowd of 6,500. In other words, the chance you'd find about 5.5 copies of you in a capacity crowd at Fenway Park.

LAPD sent the sample to Cellmark, a private laboratory in Maryland, for more sophisticated testing. The Cellmark report stated the sample's non-sperm fraction matched Angelia's genetic profile; the sperm fraction was a mixture of male DNA, and female DNA consistent with Angelia. Cellmark reported that Todd "could not be excluded" as one of the contributors to the sperm fraction. According to Cellmark's first calculation, 1 in 39 quadrillion (10^{15}) unrelated individuals would share this profile with Todd. Cellmark did two more statistical analyses: the first was based on a database shift, resulting in a random match frequency of 1 in 29 quadrillion; the second used a more conservative calculation variable, leading to a ratio of 1 in 45 quadrillion. Thirteen genetic markers were tested. At some, it was more difficult to remove Angelia's DNA types but the analyst pulled out her types at a predominant number of sites, then examined what was left, calculating frequencies off those sites. A mixed-source calculation was then done to assess the frequency of any combination of any contributors to the DNA types found in the sperm-fraction sample: the final match ratio was 1 in 260 million unrelated African-Americans. Roughly 1 in the populations of France, England, and Spain, including overseas holdings. Meaning that the chance somebody other than Todd was the donor went from 1 in 6,500 to 1 in 260 million.

Todd was convicted and sentenced to thirty-nine years to life in prison. The DNA evidence was clearly persuasive. The question was, did it lead to the wrong verdict?

To understand the significance of the DNA evidence at Todd's trial, we have to discuss general DNA principles and technology. The main point is that DNA tests aren't at all like pregnancy tests. DNA tests can accurately say, "No, it isn't you," but they're dicier on the question of whether it *might* be you, and the odds that it *is* you, and not someone else. To demonstrate why DNA evidence isn't the dead-bang proof most prosecutors make it out to be requires us to delve into some biology, and a little statistics. If the science presented over the next seven pages seems difficult, note that it is the same science presented to juries, and they are expected to absorb the same principles and exceptions, in lecture format.

Technical Aspects of DNA and Its Analysis

Almost all non-reproductive human nucleated cells contain copies of deoxyribonucleic acid (DNA), which constitutes the genetic code for that person. DNA is found in microscopic chromosomes; a *chromosome* is a thread of DNA enveloped by other materials, mostly protein. A fertilized egg has forty-six chromosomes: one set of twenty-three contributed by Mother and one set of twenty-three given by Father. Twenty-two of each of the twenty-three are paired identical sets; the twenty-third set determines sex, and will either be XX chromosomes (women), or XY chromosomes (men). Because each cell contains duplicates of these forty-six parent chromosomes, each cell has the same DNA. Structurally DNA consists of two strands, coiled into the famous double helix; each strand is a string of nucleotide bases held together by a sugar-phosphate backbone.

To use the familiar image, DNA is a twisted ladder, with billions of rungs running between the sugar-phosphate strands, or the ladder's side rails, each rung composed of two nucleobases. There are four types of bases: adenine, thymine, guanine, and cytosine: A, T, G, C.

A will pair only with T, C only with G. The sequential combinations of these pairs lead to biological differentiation between species and among individuals. When a cell reproduces, the sides/strands separate, and the bases of each side then pair with complementary bases of a new strand: A will find its T, C its G, and so on. The order in which base pairs appear is an individual's genetic code, or genotype. A *gene* is a particular sequence or site located along a chromosome, ranging from a few thousand to tens of thousands of base pairs; the gene is represented by a sequence of base-type letters, which encode for amino acids, which in turn combine to form a protein. The exact function of a particular gene is determined by the order of base pairs in the gene. Of around three billion human genes, fewer than 30,000 (less than 5 percent) are protein-coding genes. Among these are the genes that are tested for forensic purposes.

The position a particular gene occupies along the DNA thread is called its *locus*. Over 99 percent of human DNA doesn't vary from person to person, but each person's DNA has certain regions where the ladder rungs differ from those of other individuals; these sites are termed *polymorphic*. The possible arrangements of base pairs that can occur in a polymorphic area are called *alleles*. Alleles can be the product of differences in base pairs, or differences in the number of base pairs: the individual genetic makeup described by the alleles is the genotype. There are two alleles at each locus, one inherited from each parent. Alleles at any given locus can be either identical (homozygous) or different (heterozygous), depending on whether the person inherited the same or different alleles from each parent.[1]

Allelic combinations in a genetic profile are represented by pairs of numbers. These numbers refer to the "size" of the alleles; size means the number of times a base pair repeats at a DNA segment. The usual analogy is to a train of boxcars on a track: the track is the allele, the segment of DNA being tested; the boxcars are made of base pairs, the model of boxcar determined by the number of base pairs it takes to make that model; and the number of times that particular boxcar model appears on that particular track is the number of repeating sequences used to classify and identify the size of the track.

The Three Steps in DNA Testing

Forensic DNA testing involves three steps. First, the DNA is extracted from an evidentiary sample such as blood or semen, and a genetic *profile* is created of the presumptive perpetrator based on that genotype. A single-source sample provides the clearest genetic snapshot. If the sample is a mixed-source sample, the perpetrator's profile may be generated in one of two ways: you can either isolate the suspect's DNA, or you can identify the victim's DNA profile and compare it with the DNA gathered from the sample. Subtract the victim's DNA from the sample, and the perpetrator's profile is what's left—so the theory goes.

Next, the defendant's DNA is analyzed for a comparison profile: if any allele differs from those in the forensic sample, the defendant is absolutely excluded from the pool of possible perpetrators. If the alleles are all the same, the defendant joins the suspect pool. Like a police artist's sketch, the genetic profile is a composite used to describe—not identify—the perpetrator. This is a calculable distinction, because the third step involves doing a statistical analysis to explain the real-world significance of the match. The goal is to see how likely it is that a randomly chosen person in the general population possesses exactly the same genetic profile as the defendant. The less likely a match, the worse things look for the defendant.

The method of DNA testing used in Todd's case was PCR/STR typing. Polymerase chain reaction (PCR) is a process that amplifies targeted loci; short tandem repeats (STRs) refer to that group of polymorphic loci used to compare and type DNA.[2] The thirteen to fifteen typically amplified STR loci are the core markers used in the Combined DNA Index System (CODIS), a national database containing DNA profiles of convicted felons. The forensic virtue of PCR amplification is that you can test very small amounts of genetic material, and test the sort of degraded samples—old samples, samples left outside, samples someone tried to destroy—common to crime scenes.

In PCR typing, the DNA strands are heated, breaking the hydrogen bonds holding the base pairs together and separating/denaturing the DNA. Denatured DNA strands form a template allowing for the manufacture of a new, completely identical strand.[3] PCR amplifies DNA essentially the way DNA replicates naturally, by self-copying. Amplification can be repeated by re-reheating the sample and repeating the denaturing process. With each cycle, the replicated DNA grows exponentially, eventually producing enough of a pure sample to permit genotyping.

After the DNA sample has been amplified, the fragments are identified according to their migration through an electric field. The primers used on STRs contain fluorescent tags, incorporated into the amplified fragments. In a process called capillary electrophoresis, the fragments go through a capillary containing a gel or liquid polymer onto a detection window. As they pass though the window, a laser fires, hitting the tags and causing them to light up; a camera detects the light and converts it into data. These data are analyzed by a software program that registers the light emitted from the tags and converts it into peaks of various sizes, printed out on an electropherogram. Size is determined by measuring the time it takes for the alleles to reach the laser window: the smaller the alleles, the faster they move.

The Trouble with Mixed Sources

There are three main problems common to PCR/STR typing: *stutter*, *dye blobs*, and *null alleles* (or allelic dropout). Stutter and dye blobs are by-products of testing. Stutter is a visual artifact on the electropherogram whose peaked shape can be mistaken for an allele; stutter occurs when a strand slips when passing through the window. Stutter can be easily excluded as a genuine allele in single-source samples because it shows up in predictable sites next to known alleles. Stutter is problematic in mixed samples because the analyst has to decide whether a peak is stutter or is an allele from another contributor. Miscalling the peak could lead to a perpetrator being wrongly excluded as a contributor, or an innocent suspect being wrongly included.

Dye blobs are the result of the primer chemical signaling the camera that it is a fluorescing entity. Analysts can usually tell blobs from alleles, though a blob could cover up a real allele. Allelic dropout occurs when an allele falls below the stochastic threshold, indicating there's not enough DNA to identify both alleles at a given locus. An allelic peak may also be so low as to be indistinguishable from what's called background noise/chatter on the bottom of the electropherogram.

Most analytically thorny, and most relevant in sex cases, is the *mixed-source sample*. The mixture is usually a mix of the victim's and the perpetrator's DNA, and is more mixed if there were multiple perpetrators, or any consensual partners. The most important part of mixed-source sample testing is separating and assigning alleles to contributors. Analysts may go one step further, assigning "major" and "minor" donor profiles based on the relative amounts of material at each locus. But whereas analysts often make the assumption that the major contributor at the majority of loci is the major contributor at all loci, there is currently no way to fully ascribe proportionate contribution, especially where a locus has shared alleles. Remember that forensic samples are often small and often degraded: amplification assumes that the genetic markers found in the sample hold true throughout the rest of the profile. But this may not be the case, because mixture proportions can vary across the sample. Testing a particularly minute or degraded sample is like grabbing a handful of colored balls from a huge basket of colored balls: though the basket has a certain percentage of red, black, blue, or white balls, the handful seized might not accurately reflect that percentage.[4]

Another common problem with mixed samples is the partial or incomplete profile. Assuming a minimum of two contributors (victim and perpetrator) at each test site, there should be four genotypes present—two from the victim and two from the perpetrator. But often only two or three genotypes "test out," leaving one or two variables open. The lack of genetic information could be because the sample is too small or too degraded—exposure to sun, damp, or certain enzymes will randomly break down DNA molecules. PCR technology can amplify minuscule amounts (>1 ng) of DNA, but extreme amplification increases the chance of allele dropout (failure to amplify), allele drop-in (additional alleles), stutter, peak imbalances, and contamination.

Inadvertent contamination is an ongoing problem, whether at the crime scene or in the lab (which is why laboratories always record their analysts' genotypes). Contamination can occur via a pre-crime contact: I happen to leave my cigarette butt just where you decide to murder someone. Or there's contamination by way of secondary transference: I pick up your DNA by touching something you've touched, then dump your DNA onto the next thing I touch, leaving the genetic misimpression you and I have touched all the same things—including the murder weapon.   ·

The Random Match Profile

Assuming the sample is a representative sample, the analyst next looks at the reference samples provided by the victim and suspect and declares a match, or declares the suspect "can't be excluded" as a possible contributor (can't say is, can't say isn't). If the suspect's reference sample and the evidence sample don't match at any one locus, the suspect must be absolutely excluded as a possible contributor. If there's no absolute exclusion, the analyst calculates the probable statistical occurrence of a particular profile. This is the random match profile (RMP) and is the final number, the one-in-so-many-million/trillion/quadrillion cited to the jury as the relatively rare odds that SODDIT—"Some Other Dude Did It."

The RMP is mathematically determined by application of the product rule (an equation representing the individual probability of two independent events occurring at the same time—such as a match at one locus), which may be modified or unmodified to account for sub-populations (populations having some common ancestry); either way, reliable statistical calculations can be made by its proper application. In figuring out the random match probability of a particular sample, the product rule is applied twice: first to determine allelic frequency at each locus, the odds of a match at that site, and then to determine the combined frequency at all loci, the odds of a match at all thirteen sites (based on a population database). The higher the number, the lower the possibility that someone randomly plucked from the population would have the identical genetic profile. Individual frequencies are multiplied together to generate a statistical probability reflecting the overall frequency of the entire multilocus profile. This combined frequency accounts for the huge ratios generated in DNA analysis. To overly simplify, if a 15-loci test was used:

$$1:10 \times 1:10 \times 1:10 \times 1:10 \times 1:10 \times 1:10 \times 1:10 \times 1:10 \times 1:10 \times 1:10 \times 1:10 \times$$
$$1:10 \times 1:10 \times 1:10 \times 1:10 = 10^{15}$$

In words, one in one quadrillion, or one in a thousand billion, a very bad number when you're the defendant in the dock.

The major statistical issues involving RMP calculation concern population substructure and database characteristics, including representivity and size: if the population/database is too small, it's not representative of the true allelic frequency in the population, and if the population/database isn't representative, the odds are wrong.[5] Within the database population, accurate application of the product rule depends on the statistical independence of each allele: statistical independence is gauged according to whether the alleles in question are at the same or different loci.[6] Assuming all calculations are accurate, the random match probability is only significant as evidence to the extent that it shows the relative rarity of such a match. The greater the frequency of a genetic profile, the less probative the possibility that profile will be found in the DNA of a randomly selected someone in the relevant population, and vice versa.[7] In other words, there is an inverse relationship between the size of the RMP and its evidentiary heft. An RMP of 1 in 2,000 is fairly useless, whereas 1 in 10^{15} is a slam dunk for the prosecution.

Likelihood, Exclusion, and Bayesian Inference

Instead of calculating random match probability as the pertinent statistic, the analyst could calculate likelihood ratio, probability of exclusion, or the Bayesian inference. Likelihood ratio represents the chance of a match if the crime scene DNA and the suspect's DNA came from the same source to the chance of a match if they came from different sources. The likelihood ratio is usually the reciprocal of the random match probability. Probability of exclusion is the relative probability the defendant committed the crime versus someone else picked from the general population.

Bayesian inference statistically accounts for information other than DNA evidence in calculating the effect of the DNA evidence. This means that the (non-DNA evidence) prior odds of the suspect being the perpetrator—based on things like proximity to the crime scene, motive, opportunity, et cetera—are multiplied by the (DNA evidence) likelihood ratio, resulting in the posterior odds that the DNA evidence came from the suspect. And this is where the real fun begins, at least for this layperson, because prior odds are admittedly subjective and impossible to pinpoint. It literally comes down to asking "what are the odds" this person would be in this place at this time with this knife and this murderous grudge, as compared to "what are the odds" it would be this person if he has no motive, or has this alibi witness.

Some experts suggest calculating posterior odds for a range of prior odds, something like 1 in 10 or 1 in 100. If the prior odds are 1 in 100, the posterior odds are 10,000 to 1.[8] In the bigger picture, this may not mean much because the higher the likelihood ratio, the higher the posterior odds, and the likelihood ratio numbers in sex offense cases are usually so very high. In Todd's case, the final likelihood ratio was one in 260,000,000 that another person would have the same genetic profile as he did, and thus be another possible source of the DNA found on the victim. In one of my serial rapist cases, the ratios ranged from one in seven trillion (10^{12}), one in 100 quintillion (10^{18}), one in nine septillion (10^{24}), and one in eight hundred forty-five septillion. In a world where holocausts are tolled in millions and hamburgers in billions, these ratios are numbers of certainty, not chance.

The Law on Science: Relevant and Reliable

Different jurisdictions have different standards for admitting scientific evidence: some more lax, favoring admission because admission of evidence is generally favored, others stricter, because scientific evidence can be over-favored by juries. The Supreme Court established standards for admitting scientific evidence in *Daubert v. Merrell Dow Pharmaceuticals* 509 U.S. 579 (1993), describing the trial judge as a "gatekeeper" who must be sure the evidence is generally accepted in the "relevant scientific community." To do so, courts are to use a four-part test to "ensure that any and all scientific testimony or evidence admitted isn't only relevant, but reliable."[9]

The four factors are:

1. whether the theory or technique can be or has been tested;
2. whether it has been subject to peer review and publication;
3. whether, in respect to a particular technique, there is a high known or potential rate of error and whether there are standards controlling the technique's operation; and
4. whether the theory or technique enjoys "general acceptance" within a "relevant scientific community."

In *Kumho Tire Co. v. Carmichael*, 526 U.S. 137 (1999), the Supreme Court extended its *Daubert* holding to all forms of expert testimony.

The federal rule sounds simple: scientific or other expert testimony is generally admissible if it is "relevant and reliable," as decided by the trial judge. Factors that may help determine the reliability of a specific scientific/expert theory include testing, peer review, error rates, and acceptability in the relevant scientific community. The California standard, by comparison, requires that the evidence pass a three-pronged test: (1) the proponent of the evidence must establish the reliability of the scientific method via witness testimony, (2) the court must qualify these witnesses as experts, and (3) there must be proof that correct scientific procedures were used in the current case.

Under both standards, *relevance* and *reliability* are key. Relevance goes to the ultimate issue of guilt: if a piece of evidence doesn't tend to prove guilt, it isn't relevant, and not admissible. Note that reliability is subject to change. A scientific technique once considered reliable can be reconsidered unreliable based on new evidence. But this runs flat into the problem of legal precedent, because a technique that has been upheld by an appellate court can't be challenged again in a trial court without compelling new evidence that the technique is no longer considered unreliable by the bulk of the scientific community. Even though a given process may have been found deeply flawed by one or several reputable sources, evidence from that process will continue to be used in court until the process is roundly discredited by the scientific rank and file.

If evidence has been wrongly admitted, a conviction won't be reversed unless that evidence unfairly affected the trial—the appellate court's working motto is "No harm, no foul." There are two standards for courts to judge whether an error in admitting evidence unfairly affected the trial: *harmless error* and *plain error*, depending on whether the exclusion involves a federal constitutional right.

If a federal constitutional right (such as the Sixth Amendment right to confront witnesses or present evidence) is involved, error is assessed under a harmless error standard: was the error harmless beyond a reasonable doubt? In the words of the Supreme Court in *Yates v. Everett*, 500 U.S. 391 (1991), was the evidence "so overwhelming as to leave it beyond a reasonable doubt that the verdict resting on that evidence would have been the same" had the error not occurred?[10] If no federal constitutional right is involved, the error is considered plain error. In that case, the conviction will only be reversed if the defendant can show that he would have gotten a different verdict (either not guilty or guilty of a lesser crime) had the error not occurred. Harmless error puts the burden on the State, plain error on the accused.[11]

The Misuse of DNA Results

Defense attorneys routinely challenge the admissibility of DNA tests, particularly when new tests are developed from old ones, or when manufacturers combine various kits to produce more comprehensive testing. But courts just as routinely approve testing protocols, usually for the same reason—the new is based on the old, the old is reliable, therefore, the new must be too. Or if kit number one is fine, and kit number two is fine, why not one plus two? The rough critique of this approach is that testing protocols and components, like skillets and sausage, may affect one another in subtle yet significant ways. Given the power of DNA evidence, each new test should be subject to independent verification before its results can be admissible at trial.

There is also a big difference between police use of DNA test results as an investigatory tool to fix suspicion on a particular person, and the prosecution's use of the same test as in-court proof of that person's guilt. If the goal is to winnow the pool of possible perpetrators, any net, no matter how wide, is good enough.[12] But if the goal is conviction, the proof had better be better than good—no dragnets allowed. Contrariwise, DNA evidence that excludes a person as a possible contributor should be absolutely admissible because there is a constitutional presumption of innocence. Note the difference between the presumption of innocence and the assumption that guilt has simply "not been proven yet," the jaded view animating many prosecutors and trial judges. The playing field isn't level. Law enforcement can and should avail itself of everything from polygraphs to psychics, but the constitutional burden of proof, the only thing that justifies taking someone's liberty, must be put to the strictest test of reason.

As a practical matter, however, the in-court fight usually focuses on some smaller issue. Were the right procedures followed in this particular case? Was the sample contaminated by the cops or the lab? The problems posed by DNA evidence should not, however, be considered purely case by case or courtroom by courtroom. Because this kind of evidence bedazzles judges and juries, and smears the line between the art of science and the art of persuasion. The deeper question is whether there should be a line between these two arts, and what ends are served by assimilating science, with its aura of impersonal certainty, into law, which trades in human convictions.

Arguing for Judicial Restraint

Science is the generally agreed upon standard of authenticity in the United States. Science tells us how often we ought to get our shots, check for rot, have our knees and teeth tapped, and whether we are biochemically compromised or just a little blue. Juries, like judges, watch *CSI*, read Kay Scarpetta mysteries, and believe what they were taught in fourth grade: that science, like evolution, moves ever forward.[13] Here is the *CSI* viewer's guide: "DNA isolated from blood, hair, skin cells, or other genetic evidence can be compared, through VTNR patterns, with the DNA of a criminal suspect to determine guilt or innocence." It's that last "or" that bothers me. Previous tests for determining guilt or innocence have included walking barefoot over hot iron, dipping a hand in boiling water, dunking witches, and eating consecrated bread (because the guilty will choke on the sacred). *Lexus ex machina—Law by machine—*though lab coats are now more fashionable than cassocks. We adore divine judgment, but like to change the face of the divinity.

DNA evidence also suits a culture that opts for the intellectual lockstep, picks its leaders off twin platforms of strength and unity, and eschews reasonable doubt as moral weakness. DNA assures us that our judgments are right, and if not right, correctable. Today, forty-two states allow some measure of post-conviction access to DNA evidence. Studies have shown that DNA evidence played a significant role in exonerating almost half of those found wrongfully convicted, and that 2.3 percent of inmates sentenced to death row from 1973 to 1989 were later exonerated. Even as the Supreme Court found there was no constitutional right to post-conviction forensic testing, it emphasized that "there is no technology comparable to DNA testing" for matching biological samples—"modern DNA testing can provide powerful new evidence unlike anything known before."[14]

According to its Web site, the Innocence Project, a nonprofit legal clinic at Yeshiva University's Benjamin N. Cardozo School of Law, "only handles cases where post-conviction DNA testing can yield conclusive proof of innocence."[15] In the case of a Tennessee man convicted of murder and rape, the Innocence Project sought a stay of execution so the defense could conduct DNA tests not available at the time of trial; the man was executed without retesting. In another Tennessee death penalty case, retesting was permitted and the prisoner fully exonerated. The Project's amicus curiae brief in the first case stated: "The power of DNA is that it can provide scientific evidence of the 'truth' in a case, the truth that provides the finality and closure that victims and families of victims need." Well, maybe. Getting the wrongfully convicted off death row and out of prison is indisputably righteous, but this sort of reification of DNA evidence suggests that *only* laboratory science should set you free.

I work for the guilt project. All of my clients have been found guilty in the eyes of the law, and most in the eyes of the Almighty. Assuming the genetic evidence used against my clients is of the strictly inculpatory variety, my practical concern is present-tense reliability. Reliability both in terms of whether some other dude did it, and whether it's fair to say that my guy did. Again, if the evidence isn't reliable, it isn't relevant, and ought not have been admitted. That is error, and error plus prejudice is what liberates the guilty. A DNA test only proves a statistical probability that someone may have contributed to a genetic sample—but contribution isn't guilt.

When attorneys in the middle of a jury trial rush to the bench at the judge's invitation, this is known as a sidebar conversation. For our purposes, a sidebar demonstration of the difference between contribution and culpability is the example of a date rape, where the presence of the accused's DNA is entirely compatible with the typical consent defense: my DNA is there because she said yes. Then there are the more exotic defenses, whose relative rarity may make them more or less successful in creating reasonable doubt. For example, the defendant has an identical, and conveniently evil, twin. Or he comes from a small village in Oaxaca where many of the inhabitants are genetically very akin, and an outpost of these immigrants happen to live near the crime scene. Or maybe it's just a fluke. In one Arizona prison study involving a thirteen-locus test, unrelated donors matched at nine STR loci, and one allele at four remaining loci. The statistical probability of such a match was remote—somewhere around 1 in 75 million. A subsequent study found three more pairs of inmates who matched at nine loci; again, the statistical probability of these matches is one in billions (the Hispanic match was 1 in 110 billion, another match 1 in 2.1 billion), thus demonstrating the gap between math and reality.[16] In December 2008, the *Los Angeles Times* reported that DNA evidence has been used to link people to crimes they didn't commit, often by way of laboratory or crime-scene contamination, sample switching, and, in cases of wrongful conviction, overreliance on underwhelming evidence. The *Times* investigation found that re-cords from five state and three county forensic laboratories showed the labs regularly made mistakes that could lead to suspects' false identification. A British council on bioethics reported that the risk of contamination has "greatly increased" with the ability of science to glean profiles from a billionth of a gram of genetic material, con-cluding that it was "vital that defendants are not convicted on a DNA match alone." And mixed-source samples were noted to be particu-larly difficult to interpret: as a scientist with Britian's Forensic Science Service has said, "If you show 10 colleagues mixture, you will prob-ably end up with 10 different answers."[17] Answers which lead to only two verdicts—guilty or not.

The only legitimate test that determines guilt or innocence is based in law, not science, and juries and judges are its constituent parts. Like most judges and jurors, I'm not a scientist, and my assessment of reliability relies on the expertise of others. On appeal, I can kick up a fuss over testing protocols and database sizes, but the technological adequacy of test kits is a question for the trial court, as is the question of raw-data interpretation, for example, whether a particular peak is an allele or an artifact.

However, the use of the statistics promulgated by the analysts involves core legal issues, the kind that make an appellate lawyer's hands go happily damp. Sex cases frequently involve vaginal, anal, and/or oral samples with multiple contributors. These usually con-tain at least two profiles: the victim and the perpetrator. If there is more than one rapist, or a consensual sexual encounter, or some other transfer of material, there will be additional contributors; most ana-lysts don't assume a maximum number of donors for testing purposes. In a heterosexual rape, one contributor will be female (the victim), and the other(s) male (the perpetrator[s]).

As I said before, if a mixed sample shows fewer than four genotypes at any one locus, analysts will statistically account for all possible allelic combinations at that locus, and use that number in the final random match probability or likelihood ratio. But this is legally wrong. What makes perfect scientific sense when in scientific doubt does not make legal sense, given reasonable doubt. As one court analogized, if a robbery victim said the robber had either red, brown, or black hair, and the defendant had black hair, the State could not argue that because the defendant had black hair, it was 33 percent more likely than not that he was the robber. "More likely than not" is not proof enough to convict—if the robber's hair is brown, the jury must acquit.

Can DNA Evidence Railroad a Defendant?

So how did all this affect Todd? In his case, seven of the thirteen tested loci were ambiguous: the analyst could only detect two or three genotypes at those sites. The LAPD crime laboratory excluded those loci; Cellmark included all possible genotypes. The LAPD random match probability ratio was 1 in 6,500; Cellmark's final ratio was 1 in 260,000,000. Cellmark's rationale for considering all genotypes was that Todd "could not be excluded" as a possible donor. This loose language neatly carts the horse, because at those loci, there wasn't any evidence *including* him, either. This is the crux of the difference between law and science: if evidence doesn't tend to prove you guiltier, it's not relevant. If it's not relevant, it shouldn't be admitted. Unless the prosecution knows what color hair the robber has, the defendant's hair color doesn't prove anything. You can't reverse-engineer guilt.

In Todd's situation, there were three possible combinations at each ambiguous locus, only one of which would have inculpated him, and two of which would have definitively exonerated him.[18] Thus the rhetoric of science—that because Todd "can't be excluded" meant he could be included—was used to obscure what became the more rhetorical nature of his guilt. This isn't horseshoes: the DNA was either Todd's or it wasn't. And odds are, it wasn't.

The scientific method is experiential and experimental, a process of quantification and observation, hypotheses and deductions, and lots of tests along the way. But courts don't work on the scientific method. Courts work on authoritarianism and precedent. The more conservative an argument, the more rooted in its antecedents, the better its chance of success. And the law looks to science for the same certainty. Lacking a Supreme Science Court, the courts have made one up, adopting the National Research Council (a private, nonprofit society administered by the National Academy of Sciences, the National Academy of Engineering, and the Institute of Medicine) as the voice of the scientific community. The California Supreme Court has stated that the NRC's opinion on the reliability of forensic DNA typing and the calculation of probability estimates, "can easily be equated with general acceptance of those methodologies in the relevant scientific community."

But the scientific community has extensively criticized both the NRC reports and courts' reliance on them. For the scientific community is neither monolithic nor monovocal. Science is set up for dissent: population geneticists, molecular biologists, forensic statisticians, probabilistic systems experts, and rank-and-file biotechnicians and criminalists may agree that DNA evidence is reliable for a variety of scientific purposes, and may also revise, refine, or refute this agreement as necessary or potentially of scientific interest, NRC be damned. The scientific worldview can turn, as with the discovery of DNA itself, on a dime. But the law is a leviathan, lumbering and a little dim, and it takes enormous effort to alter its course.

The Interpretation of Genotyping

The law's current view of mixed-source DNA evidence is that interpretation of typing results is flatly accepted by the scientific community and admissible in court. What is critical is the linguistic legerdemain here: like the courts, I've segregated "interpretation" from "results," suggesting there's a divide between mixture analysis and interpretation, and that, like a mathematical equation, results are extracted by way of analysis, and it is these results that are the subject of the analyst's interpretation in forensic DNA testing. As the NCR itself has noted, if a mixture is reliably analyzed, the results of that analysis could be reliably interpreted. But this doesn't work in reverse: just because results may be reliably interpreted doesn't mean the results themselves are reliable. But there is *no scientific difference* between result and interpretation. "[A] DNA profile generated from a sample by contemporary procedures must be understood *not as a fact about a sample but rather as an interpretation of that sample.*"[19]

Forensic Bioinformatics, a company that created a software program that automates existing DNA analysis software programs, cautions: "Interpretation of mixed DNA samples is challenging and attaching statistical significance to constituencies with DNA profiles of reference samples is difficult. A large number of alternative interpretations regarding potential contributors are possible."[20] There's no legitimate divide between technology and technician, given the admitted and absolute dependence of the former on the latter. As put by a former official at the troubled Harris County Medical Examiner's Office in Houston, Texas: "Anytime you have a mixture, you can't say it's a precise match."[21] Advises Dr. Peter Gill of the Forensic Science Service, the largest provider of forensic services to police in England and Wales: "Don't do mixture interpretations unless you have to."

The relevant question isn't whether multisource samples can be analyzed, but whether the problems inherent in that analysis (stutter, allelic drop-out, primer binding site mutation, null alleles, signal diminution, amplification artifacts, electrophoresis artifacts) have an appreciable effect on the reliability of mixture genotyping for courtroom purposes. And the answer is: they do. This has been recognized by at least five members of the Supreme Court. In *Melendez-Diaz v. Massachusetts* 557 U.S. ___ (2009), the Court held that the right to confront witnesses requires that the prosecution produce forensic analysts for cross-examination by the defense. Previously, under Massachusetts law, forensic test results could be admitted via a "certificate." The certificate, sworn before a notary public, stated that the material the police had taken from the defendant was a drug, and how much of it there was. This certificate was admissible at trial without anyone testifying as to what tests were run or how those tests were performed. A plurality of the Court found this practice violated the Sixth Amendment: a defendant has the same right to confront forensic analysts as he does every other witness against him. Justice Scalia, writing for the Court, rejected the argument that these tests were so routine the government didn't really need to bother with live witnesses. Citing various studies and reports, the Court noted the close and potentially influential working relationship between most forensic laboratories and law enforcement, the "serious deficiencies" that have been found in forensic evidence used in criminal trials, and the "wide variability" in laboratory standards and practices. The dissent, on the other hand, compared the forensic analyst's function to that of a copyist. Historically, the person who copied documents for trial did not have to testify because there was nothing to be gained by his testimony, as long as there was some certification (like a notary's seal) indicating that the copy was accurate.[22] The better comparison would have been to a translator, for though many words may have a common meaning, it is the translator who can turn Shakespeare to slop, or fob words off as twins that bear only a passing resemblance to one another. Just like an artful analyst can find matches where there are merely similarities.

DNA Shall Not Set You Free

We need a different standard for the forensic/investigative use of DNA and its evidentiary/jurisprudential use. They have different agendas and different constraints. Features that make a test reliable for determining whether someone should be a suspect are not necessarily a reliable determination of guilt. For example, in one study, a 70 percent validation rate of STR typing was reached. That means that law enforcement may have an excellent new investigative tool—a hot tip on a cold case, a way of sifting through mass casualty DNA. But just like the one in three chance that the defendant's genotype is the same as the perpetrator, a 30 percent failure to validate isn't acceptable as proof of guilt.

When the State presents astronomical mathematical odds of any-one other than the defendant having done it, this calculus relieves the jury of its primary responsibility, which is to personally decide whether the accused is guilty. But like beauty, guilt is a verdict, not a fact. The problem with RMPs and likelihood ratios is that they're quantifications of a single kind of evidence, and don't take into account other kinds, such as alibis or the absence of motive or eyewit-ness identification. Bayesian theorems are attractive because they're supposed to embrace non-DNA evidence, but they don't address the fundamental split between the world of the scientific method, a world of deduced generalities that features constant self-critique and self-correction, and the world of the law, which honors only the individ-ual, that indivisible, impenetrable unit of irrefutable Being.

DNA evidence also underscores the cultural framework within which this issue is most widely understood: television. Law is the drama of order, justice is theater. But *Law & Order* is a TV show, not a constitutional motto. The police procedural has trumped police procedure: we now have an adversarial system that pits victims against the accused, so that a win for one is a loss for the other. And no one with a heart can stand to see a victim lose.

Judgments shouldn't be expressions of an audience's warmer emo-tions, however. They should be acts of individual thought and logic. We like our laws to feel external and impersonal, like the laws of sci-ence. We want our moral precepts to be as crystalline as if animated by the same indifferent properties as those of quantum physics. The danger is that the more I see my judgment as dictated by science or any other externality, the less internalized that judgment is to me. I'm no longer part of a larger ethical system that determines the fate of my fellow, and the accused is no longer a fellow to me; rather, I am simply a cog in a cognitive machine, one animated not by Us, but by Them—the officious, amorphous, lab-coated judge-scientists. The emphasis on tests and kits and theta factors absolves us from more human calculations of guilt: whether to believe this witness, or that inference. Whether to believe that life operates not with the cause and effect of a laboratory experiment, but by acts and reactions that run through our personal fortunes as surprisingly sideways as a snake through the forest grass.

Angelia, the victim in Todd's case, couldn't positively identify him as the thin man, even though she'd spent more than an hour staring at her rapist, trying to memorize his face. In over half of the DNA loci tested, there was only a one-third statistical probability that Todd's profile matched the perpetrator's profile, and there was no other physical evidence connecting him to her rape. Given a one-third statistical probability of guilt, should Todd have been imprisoned for thirty-nine years to life? If there is a one-third chance of his guilt, should he serve one-third of those thirty-nine years? Would you?

CHAPTER 3
SEXUALLY VIOLENT PREDATORS:
THE PARAPSYCHOLOGY OF GUILT

She was in a position to fight desire which gave her pleasure.
— SISSY BOYD, *The Green Shoes*

DOES "SEXUALLY VIOLENT PREDATOR" sound like a bit part in a women's prison film? It's actually a legal classification, but can be just as dangerous a cliché: being defined as a sexually violent predator can get you locked up in a mental hospital for the rest of your life. As of this writing, seventeen states and the federal judicial system allow someone to be involuntarily committed to a state mental hospital as a sexually violent predator (SVP) after serving his sentence. In California, this means a man may be involuntarily committed for an indeterminate term if the government proves beyond a reasonable doubt that he was convicted of two or more sexually violent offenses, has a diagnosed mental disorder making him a present danger to others, and is likely to engage in sexually violent criminal behavior in the future.

Let's take these one at a time. *Likely* is supposed to have a certain empirical heft, meaning there is substantial evidence that this sort of event will reoccur. However, "likely" in everyday usage means you are more apt than not, a kind of "chances are" standard that would be very comforting if betting the trifecta, or, for that matter, preemptively locking up child molesters. The requisite *diagnosed mental disorder* can be born or bred, but must predispose the person toward criminal sexual acts of the sort that make him an actual threat to actual others: rape, sodomy, and molestation. After all, society has a duty to keep the predatory from their prey. On the other hand, the *future* is very a long time, and the only sure prophecy is a self-fulfilling one: it is absolutely certain that no one will reoffend if you never let anyone out.

Currently, sexually violent predator commitments are the functional equivalent of a sentence of life without the possibility of parole. SVP commitments are made based on psychiatric opinions that are one part misapplication of studies of sex-offender recidivism, and two parts rehashing of the person's criminal and personal history. For those who have raped, there's often a diagnosis of "rape paraphilia" — a diagnosis that has been specifically disavowed by the American Psychiatric Association. These psychiatric opinions are shortcuts in logic and law, and no one cares because the commitment standard is so low and the social danger so great. But the decision to lock a man up for life should not be simply a matter of better safe than sorry.

The Case of the Repentant Rapist

Sometime around midnight on December 20, 1977, Patrick broke into the bedroom of a woman he knew casually. He was wearing only his underwear, and his face was covered. He jumped on the woman's bed, told her that he would hurt her if she didn't shut up, and jabbed something sharp in her side. Then he pulled her nightgown over her head and raped her. During the rape, Patrick offered not to kill her children as long as she cooperated.

About nine years later, Patrick broke into the bedroom of another woman, put his hand over her mouth and a knife to her throat. He told her to roll onto her stomach and said he wouldn't hurt her. He cut off the woman's underwear and raped her. Afterward, Patrick fondled the woman's breasts, kissed her back, and rubbed the knife across her back several times.

Patrick was convicted of both rapes and sentenced to twenty-one years in state prison, serving about half that time.[1] In 1998, just before he was due to be paroled, Patrick was evaluated for involuntary civil commitment as an SVP. Part of that initial evaluation was a two-hour interview with two state psychologists, who determined that Patrick had the requisite mental disorder and was likely to reoffend if released. In 2002, after a series of legal shuffles, Patrick was up for another commitment.[2] The psychologist interviews aren't mandatory, and Patrick refused to be reinterviewed. So the state psychologists' re-evaluation consisted of reviewing Patrick's criminal record and institutional history, diagnosing a predispository mental disorder, and determining his risk of recidivism by way of an "actuarial instrument." This is a psychological test in which various factors about the patient, including his crimes, are scored, and that score ranked according to studies of sexual offense recidivism. Based on these factors, the psychologists again decided Patrick met the SVP criteria. A jury agreed with the experts' assessment, and Patrick was confined at Atascadero State Hospital.[3] Given the current state of commitment laws, Patrick will probably be confined for life.

Diagnosis: Sex Disorder

The first state psychologist diagnosed Patrick as having paraphilia, or "sex disorder," and antisocial personality disorder, as well as substantial drug and alcohol problems. *Paraphilia* is a generalized term taken from the *Diagnostic and Statistical Manual of Mental Disorders, Fourth Edition* (DSM-IV), published by the American Psychiatric Association (APA). Psychologists call it the diagnostic "dictionary" or "bible" for mental health workers, though it is more ecumenically used in billing insurance companies. The APA says the DSM's primary purpose is to provide a "convenient shorthand" for discussing patients. The manual's advantage is that diagnoses are described only in terms of symptomatologies that cluster together. Its limitation is that any such symptom-based diagnosis has nothing to do with etiology or treatment protocols. According to the APA Web site, if a diagnosis isn't in the DSM-IV, that means there weren't enough data in 1994, the date of the last major textual revision, to justify inclusion.[4]

According to the DSM-IV, *paraphilia* is an umbrella term for a number of disorder categories, including pedophilia, zoophilia, exhibitionism, and fetishes, categories whose salient characteristic is a desire for sex without consent, whether actual (an animal can't really consent) or legal (a child's consent is invalid). Patrick's paraphilia was clinically designated as Paraphilia Not Otherwise Specified (paraphilia NOS). In his case, this meant a preference for nonconsensual sex, that is, rape.

To be diagnosed with a paraphilia, someone must evidence the desire for at least six months, and the desire must cause that person "significant social discomfort." Patrick's first qualifying crime occurred in 1977, when he was twenty-one years old. His second was in 1986, when he was thirty-one. In between, he was also convicted of attempted assault to commit rape. There was another attempted rape alleged, though none of the reports gave any details apart from the accusation. The first state psychologist said Patrick's qualifying social discomfort was his negative feelings about his behavior and the disruption in his "social/occupational functioning" caused by his incarcerations: he had lost his wife and couldn't hold down a job. The psychologist felt that Patrick now recognized that rape is wrong and empathized with his victims.

The psychologist testified that whereas paraphilia alone doesn't necessarily impair emotional or volitional capabilities, Patrick's does. He doesn't want to rape, but does, is put in prison, is released, re-offends, is reincarcerated, is re-released, and offends again. Nothing seems to hinder his [in]ability to "contain himself," suggesting that Patrick "gives in to temptation" when he rapes, rather than freely choosing to rape.[5] The psychologist noted that most rapes are done by "bad people," not mentally ill offenders; the difference between a serial rapist and a garden-variety bad man is that the serial rapist works from a pattern. According to the psychologist, Patrick's pattern is that he enters his victim's bedroom around midnight, covering either his face or his victim's face, and usually uses a knife. His victims have children, making it easier for Patrick to control the women. He doesn't use excessive force, though rubbing the knife across his last victim's back showed a certain relish of violence more common in serial rapists than ordinary "bad men." That is, ordinary bad men go to prison; extra-ordinary bad men go to the state hospital.

Examining the Static-99 Test

The actuarial instrument used by the state psychologists was an updated Static-99, which tabulates factors from an individual's psychosexual history that correlate to sexual offense recidivism, scores them, then scores that person's risk of reoffense.[6] The Static-99 was designed as a predictor of sexual-offense recidivism in general, not sexually violent recidivism in particular; the original test cases reoffended by way of everything from forcible sodomy to public urination. The American Psychiatric Association disapproves of the use of such actuarial tools for predicting recidivism; the American Psychological Association doesn't.

Patrick got a high-risk total of six points: two points for having two priors, plus one point each for having more than four previous sentences, having unrelated victims, having stranger victims, and not having lived with a lover for at least two years. Patrick had lived with a woman (it was unclear whether this was his wife) for a year and eight months. Had they lasted four more months, his score would have dropped one point, and he would have gone from having a 52 percent chance of reoffending within fifteen years (more likely than not) to a 40 percent chance (arguably less likely than not). The error rate of the Static-99 is 8.4 percent for an individual in Patrick's risk category.

Patrick's score was then compared to a meta-analysis of 28,000 individuals, and the six risk factors were identified in that study, including sexual deviance and criminality. According to the state psychologists, Patrick has moderate sexual deviance based on his priors. One psychologist evidenced a dizzying ability to reduce complex penological problems to a recipe of ingredients, as if making a béarnaise sauce. He testified that there are exactly six components to criminality: (1) antisocial personality disorder, (2) a high score on the Hare psychopathy checklist, (3) poor treatment performance, (4) poor parental (i.e., maternal) relationships, (5) history of nonsexual crimes, and (6) absence of a minimum two-year cohabitation with a lover. Note the overlap between the assessed components of criminality and deviance and the Static-99 scoring factors.

Taking each component in turn, the first psychologist testified that antisocial personality disorder is evidenced by "getting in trouble on a consistent basis" and general irresponsibility. Early onset of trouble is significant: Patrick said he began using alcohol and drugs at thirteen, started stealing cars by fifteen, and had committed fourteen to twenty burglaries by the time he was sixteen. A pattern of lying is also telling: Patrick's foster stepmother said he used to steal from friends and lie, and was once arrested for forgery. Patrick's history of impulsivity and bad judgment included early drug and alcohol use, going AWOL from the Army after hitting a sergeant, a lot of short-term jobs, and two prison violations for fighting. In terms of empathy and remorse, the psychologist felt Patrick's behavior toward his victims was proof of his callousness. A score of 30 out of a possible 40 on the Hare psychopathy checklist is considered extremely indicative of recidivism; Patrick scored a so-so 22. He hasn't sought treatment at the state hospital, and has no social support group to help him, including no prospective mate, if he were to be released. According to the psychologist, the "huge" factor against Patrick was that he doesn't think he has a sexual disorder: he doesn't think he will do it again.

With regard to general self-regulation, Patrick hadn't gotten into a fight since 1995, and some of his displays of anger were "noble," such as defending a friend, or objecting to what he perceived as staff mistreatment of another patient. Patrick doesn't himself have problems with supervision, and is generally liked by male and female staff members, who describe him as quite cooperative and pleasant. Age operates in Patrick's favor because rape recidivism decreases with age, bottoming out around age sixty; Patrick was forty-seven at the time of trial. He engages in self-treatment via prayer. The Static-99 study indicated a neutral value (no points) to the effect of religious beliefs on reoffense.

Patrick had no drug or alcohol-related incidents during his confinement, though drugs and alcohol are readily available in prison and the state hospital. Throughout the first evaluation, Patrick was cooperative, pleasant, reasonable, forthcoming, and "easy to deal with." According to the second psychologist, Patrick is a "remarkably nice guy," "cooperative," "pleasant, sincere . . . a thoroughly likeable gentleman."

Psychology for the Defense

The defense put on another psychologist, one who had previously worked for the state but was now in private practice. This psychologist thought the state treatment program was largely a flop, as only about 20 percent of the patients participate. At the time of Patrick's first SVP commitment trial, no one who had participated had been returned to the community.[7] The hospital's mélange of sex offenders clinically mandates a variety of treatment modalities, from psychopharmacological interventions to cognitive-behavioral treatment—not the administration's one-size-fits-all approach to recovery. Hospital staff suffers from high turnover, and female employees are subject to a steamy gauntlet of inappropriate patient behavior, from rude comments to open masturbation to physical or sexual assault.

The psychologist testified that a lot of patient sexual transgression goes unchecked by hospital staff. Those who do not want to participate in sexual acting-out either avoid all group situations, or commit a non-sex offense in the hospital in order to be sent back to prison. Many of these men say they prefer prison to the "toxic atmosphere" at the state hospital. Either way, the field is left to the players.

According to this psychologist, SVP assessments unduly emphasize historical data, including police and probation reports, whereas a more accurate psychological evaluation would stress current functioning and adjustment. Finally, mental illness is often a biological problem, and the civil commitment process doesn't include consideration of either predicate (pre-criminal) evidence of such illness, or any real attempt at its detection and amelioration. The usual tenets of psychologist–patient confidentiality also aren't observed at the state hospital. What would usually be considered confidential communications routinely become part of patient files. This undermines treatment because patients feel the purpose of the proffered therapy is to gather information "to keep them there." No fools they: during therapy, patients are encouraged to expand and elaborate on offenses that may have transpired twenty-five years earlier, even if there is no therapeutic need for further review.

The defense psychologist evaluated Patrick six times, agreeing with the state psychologists that he was very bright, well informed, and easy to talk to. Patrick admitted his crimes to the psychologist, and expressed regret for them. He has good self-regulatory skills, though he has not received medical treatment for any psychiatric disorder. He has held a skilled job in the hospital upholstery shop for a number of years, and when he thought he was becoming overweight, began a self-developed exercise program, losing forty pounds. Patrick reads a lot and gets high marks in various educational pursuits, including paralegal school. All in all, the psychologist said, Patrick is "pretty intellectual," a "pretty serious and level-headed person."

In 1979, Patrick told a probation officer he felt nothing for his victims. However, in 1985, he was severely burned in a car accident, and physically disfigured as a result. Over time, this experience emotionally sensitized him to other people's pain. Patrick told the defense psychologist that he wished he could undo his offenses because of the pain he caused.

The psychologist pointed out that according to the APA, paraphilia NOS doesn't include rape. Rape isn't considered a mental disorder because most psychologists and psychiatrists consider rape a criminal act, which in the overwhelming majority of cases does not indicate mental disorder. According to the psychologist, adding an antisocial personality disorder to the mix doesn't transform rape into a mental disorder. There is a distinction between personality disorders and mental disorders, and although many people who come in contact with the criminal justice system have antisocial personality disorders, these aren't disorders amenable to psychological treatment.

Most individuals burn out on antisocial behavior around the age of forty (testosterone levels drop alongside levels of criminality), and the best interim treatment is confinement, not medication. By the same token, age decreases the effects of paraphilia. Paraphilia by itself doesn't predispose someone to engage in certain sorts of sexual behavior; too, the hallmark of paraphilia is compulsivity, which Patrick doesn't manifest. Paraphiliac compulsion wouldn't—couldn't—lie dormant for sixteen or seventeen years, regardless of whether someone was locked away. Even if the man didn't physically assault any-one, compulsivity would pop up in things like patient drawings of fetish objects/scenarios. Given the concentration of mentally disor-dered individuals engaging in sexual misconduct at the state hospital, it's the unusual person who has the self-control to stay within the rules of the institution. If Patrick's criminal history did support a second-ary diagnosis of antisocial personality disorder, that disorder was in remission. Patrick's greatest recidivism risk factor would be if he were to reuse drugs and alcohol, and based on his nine years' abstinence, such a relapse was unlikely.

The defense psychologist concluded that Patrick has been "proso-cial for many years," and that rape was "something [he] wanted to do, and he did it." There were no mental defenses offered to his crimes at the time, and Patrick did not claim any lack of volition, either men-tally or chemically induced. Patrick doesn't meet the SVP criteria, he doesn't have a valid DSM-IV diagnosis, and doesn't meet the legal definition of mentally disordered.

Faith, Fantasies, and Fishing

Patrick testified that when he was first convicted, he didn't feel re-morse. But at some point, he took the proverbial long hard look at himself and didn't like what he saw—a man who hated everyone. He made a decision to change, and started looking for a path; in early 1994, Patrick became the cellmate of a Christian and started read-ing the Bible, first to prove the Good Book false and his cellmate misguided, then in quest of spiritual truth. At the time, Patrick fueled his anger with cell-made "pruno," the universal prison alcohol.[8] Even-tually, Patrick saw the light and was able to shuck all his bad prison habits. He began to evidence his faith "through kindness instead of through toughness, compassion, and help if I could." In addition to his various studies and fitness programs, he and several other inmates created a Christian-based conflict-resolution support system, designed to intervene in patient disputes and help each other as needed. If someone starts a fight, Patrick or one of the other members volunteers to take the target's place, insisting they be hit instead. This turning another's cheek technique usually subverts the fight completely, because the fighting inmates have no beef with the Christian substitute.

Patrick participated in the treatment program for the first year or so of his confinement, but stopped because treatment was no longer required for him to maintain his employment level. He said he was "tired of being compared to Jeffrey Dahmer" (the state psychologists liked to compare program participants to the cannibalistic serial killer), and called the program "a farce." Once, a friend of Patrick's was asked to write a fantasy; he did, and the fantasy was returned, with instructions to write a rape fantasy. The friend complied, but the rape fantasy was also returned, with more explicit instructions as to what details had to be included, which he also dutifully did. This looked to Patrick less like valid treatment than an institutional attempt to validate state research.

Patrick declined to be reinterviewed by the state psychologists because he doesn't believe he has a mental disorder and thinks the doctors use what he says and make it mean something else. Patrick doesn't believe the SVP law is wrong, just wrongly implemented. For example, those who violently act out in the hospital are criminally charged, convicted, and go back to prison to serve their (determinate) sentences, leaving the more rule-abiding patients indefinitely confined. In one particularly egregious incident, a patient went into an educational area and beat up a female staff member during an attempted rape. This patient is now in prison, having formerly been the "poster boy" for the SVP program, a "phaser," someone who went through all the program phases. Another man repeatedly threatens suicide to be put on individual watch, enabling him to masturbate in front of female staff. The homosexual community at the hospital uses the movie theater and chapel to engage in public sex. Despite the many modes of overt sexual behavior at the hospital, Patrick doesn't take advantage of these opportunities, and has no desire to do so. Patrick never has rape fantasies. His current fantasies tend toward lake fishing.

The Law: Crazy *and* Dangerous

Because of an unhappy confluence of law and science, Patrick and men like him are trapped in legal limbo, not guilty, not free, neither at liberty to go nor sentenced to stay. In a nutshell: if they're crazy (diagnosed mental disorder) and dangerous (likely to reoffend), we can lock them up and throw away the key. And what's wrong with that? As always, it depends.

The United States Supreme Court set the general parameters of all current state and federal SVP laws in two Kansas cases. In *Kansas v. Hendricks*, 521 U.S. 346 (1997), the defendant challenged the Kansas Sexually Violent Predators Act on a number of legal grounds. The primary constitutional challenges were that the law violated principles of due process, the guarantee against double jeopardy (being twice tried for the same offense), and the prohibition against ex post facto laws (punishing someone for conduct that was lawful at the time it was done).

Writing for a plurality of the Court, Justice Clarence Thomas disagreed. Treatment, not punishment, was the genuine statutory animus for the involuntary confinement of sexual predators. Because SVP laws were civil in nature, not criminal (i.e., involving confinement in a state hospital, not incarceration in a state prison), no one was being put through the criminal wringer twice, and nothing was criminalized that hadn't been unlawful before.[9]

There are two forms of constitutionally protected due process: substantive and procedural. In the *Hendricks* decision, the Court felt that all requisite procedural process had been duly dispensed. There was an initial probable cause hearing by a judge, trial by jury, and proof beyond a reasonable doubt. To the Court's credit, this was approved as the kind of process due, despite the civil nature of the commitment, given that the person facing commitment has a significant liberty interest at stake.[10] The substantive due process challenge was based on the SVP statute only requiring proof of "mental abnormality" versus "mental illness" as the psychological predicate for involuntary commitment. Quoting a 1905 case involving a man jailed for refusing to be vaccinated against smallpox, Justice Thomas noted that an individual may be properly restrained for the common good, provided the involuntary confinement follows adequate procedures and evidentiary standards.[11] He then dismissed the abnormality/illness distinction as sans difference for legal purposes, and tossed the ball back to the states for implementation of whatever criteria they deemed appropriate in drafting their commitment statutes.[12]

As noted, the Supreme Court's opinion in *Hendricks* was a plurality, which means there was no clear majority.[13] More importantly, it means that whatever the concurrence said were the only points on which there was real judicial agreement, which are the only points that are significant for lower courts and legislatures. Justice Kennedy wrote the concurrence, emphasizing that "all Members of the Court seem to agree" the law was valid because the State has the right to confine those who "by reason of a mental disease or mental abnormality" pose a serious and continuing danger to society. In the present case, noted the Justice, the disease, pedophilia "is at least described in the DSM-IV."[14]

The dissent, written by Justice Stephen Breyer, argued the Kansas statute was really more criminal than civil, and should be treated accordingly. He agreed with the majority that Kansas's definition of mental abnormality satisfied the substantive due process requirement, and that Hendricks's serious mental disorder certainly qualified, because it was classified as such by "the psychiatric profession itself."[15] The problem, said Justice Breyer, was that the statute didn't mandate treatment, and this made it criminal in nature, not civil.[16]

Five years later, the court revisited Kansas's SVP statute in *Kansas v. Crane*, 534 U.S. 407 (2002), and this time Justice Breyer was in the majority. The Court held that although an individual may be committed absent proof of absolute lack of behavioral control, the Constitution didn't permit commitment of sexual offenders absent *any* lack-of-control determination.[17] Writing for the Court, Justice Breyer noted that Crane had been diagnosed as suffering from exhibitionism and antisocial personality disorder, as defined by the DSM-IV. The State had the power to define "the mental abnormalities and personality disorders" that render someone eligible for commitment as well as the ability to separate psychiatric ("an ever-advancing science") diagnoses from legal conclusions.[18] Although the Court declined to decide whether the State could prophylactically confine someone based solely on an "emotional" versus a "volitional" abnormality,. it affirmed that there needed to be some categorical distinction between the dangerously disordered sex offender and the "dangerous but typical recidivist."[19]

Thus, the law requires that the State prove that the man it wants to involuntarily commit is presently dangerous and likely to reoffend beyond a reasonable doubt. However, these constitutional cornerstones must be considered alongside the law's red-brick approach to expert testimony, particularly expert psychiatric opinion. The legal test for admissibility of scientific evidence outlined in the DNA chapter doesn't apply to what is prosaically called "opinion evidence." Because, in that forehead-slapping way, opinion evidence is of course a matter of opinion, and in such matters reasonable minds may, and are paid hourly to, differ. Expert evidence is frequently and famously opinion evidence. But remember: expert opinion evidence based on scientific, "technical," or "other specialized knowledge" is subject to the same sort of standards as regular old scientific evidence. According to the Supreme Court, "an expert, whether basing testimony on professional studies or personal experience, employs in the courtroom the same level of intellectual rigor that characterizes the practice of an expert in the relevant field."[20] Presumably, this means expert opinion would have as its nut a certain level of relevant-community acceptance, or at least solid peer approval—the proof of "intellectual rigor" in the pudding.[21]

The Science: Crazy *Is* Dangerous

Whether via art or science, the psychiatric diagnosis is the focal point of an SVP clinical appraisal. As was attested to in Patrick's trial, there is no DSM diagnosis of paraphilia qua paraphilia, though we can leave this for a later argument. The scoring components of the Static-99 have also been detailed. But we need to look at the test's background and subsequent history, because they contradict its current use.

Developed in 1999 by R. Karl Hanson and David Thornton of the Department of Solicitor General of Canada, the Static-99 combined features of two prior measures, producing a scale with "moderate predictive accuracy" for sexual/violent recidivism. As the name implies, the Static-99 measures only unchanging factors. Its authors consider it a descriptive work in progress, and stress that the test shouldn't be used to target people for treatment, evaluate whether treatment works, measure any changes in a person, or predict when or why someone is likely to reoffend. Hanson subsequently brought in another test—the Stable 2000/SONAR (Sex Offender Need Assessment Rating) Scale—that measured both static and dynamic indicators.[22]

In a 2004 meta-analysis of ninety-five other studies, Hanson concluded that the "strongest single indicators of sexual recidivism were (a) non-compliance with supervision . . . and (b) violation of conditional release."[23] Like the conclusions about who among the socially deviant will turn sexually criminal, this smacks of redundancy. If someone goes out and assaults someone again, that person has obviously failed to comply with supervision and violated his probation/parole. Contrariwise, if someone complies with supervision and doesn't violate his probation/parole, it's a good bet he's not raping the neighbors.

In terms of the *Daubert/Kumho* standard of community acceptance for admitting expert evidence (discussed on p. 47), the American Psychiatric Association and the American Psychological Association roundly disapprove of use of actuarial instruments in courtroom contexts. Evidencing admirable scientific caution, Hanson and Thornton themselves maintain that actuarial instruments ought not be the basis of commitment determinations, probably because the average predictive accuracy of the instruments was .58 "with significant variability across studies."[24] Excellent descriptive devices, maybe, but no more diagnostically reliable than a divining rod.

In Patrick's case, one of the state psychologists said that he found about 60 percent of the individuals he assessed met SVP criteria. Think about that for a moment. If we assume an average accuracy rate of about 60 percent, this would mean that for every 100 individuals referred for commitment, 40 would be wrongfully committed based on factors they would never be able to change.[25] Given the instruments' accuracy rates, out of 100 men locked up, there are quite a few who shouldn't be: at best sixteen, at worst, sixty-nine. Though again, the legal point about scientific evidence isn't whether the Static-99 *is* reliable (it isn't), just whether it is *considered* reliable (it isn't). But it's still used.

Yielding to "Safety First"

And here we are, wanting to preemptively put away the worst of the worst, those headline-grabbing perps who strike honest fear deep into our hearts, but without any reliable scientific basis on which to do so. The temptation to yield to "safety first" is enormous. Our tenderer ideals don't stand a chance against our protective inclinations. But my job is to spot Sisyphus, and I'm arguing for honesty and the rule of law.

Insofar as courts have glossed over application of a standardized "intellectual rigor" to SVP determinations, those cases are decided in an intellectually incorrect fashion. Insofar as they split the hair of whether SVP determinations may be based on actuarial instruments so long as that basis isn't the *sole* basis of the expert opinion, they are skirting the big point. In axiomatic terms: you ought not win if you don't play by the rules. Especially your own rules. Admittedly, this is a particular point made to a particular case. The broader issue is the instrumentation and psychologizing of crime. Let's follow the law of logic: if criminality can be qualified as a real mental disorder, then real treatment would be the protocol. This might involve medication, talk therapy, chemical castration, or involuntary confinement, depending on individual etiology, diagnosis, and prognosis.[26] If criminality is impervious to treatment, then imprisonment may be the best we can do. If individual treatment could be, but isn't, provided, then there's no point to the psychologizing, and we can skip right to shameless warehousing. If warehousing is only a stopgap between the joint and the grave, then what are we attempting to do? And if we are trying in all sincerity to address some measure of inevitable evil, what are the temptations inherent in that attempt?

As noted, the Static-99 is by definition a static assessment—risk factors don't change from the point when risk is first assessed. Once someone scores as high risk, that assessment will not and cannot be altered. Ever. Even the more recent and "more dynamic" SONAR and the SVR (Sexual Violence Risk) 20 replicate most of the Static-99 factors.[27] The only mutable factors are a postcustodial sexual relationship (forbidden in the hospital), and perhaps an adjusted attitude. Adjusted attitudes are properly viewed with suspicion because incarceration seems to provoke as many conversions as a Baptist altar call. Then again, where and who better for abrupt salvation? Similarly, the SVR 20 considers the nature of the underlying sexual offense, the degree of deviance, and the subject's attitudes toward treatment/intervention. (That the attitude *toward* treatment is taken into consideration whereas the participation *in* treatment has been shown to be a null factor is a logical cul-de-sac.[28]) In any event, the clinical analyses typically used to avoid pinning an evaluation exclusively on the Static-99 are either clinical restatements of factors embedded in the test—which is double-dipping—or similar actuarial instruments subject to the same scientific critique.

In Patrick's case, for example, one of the state psychologists used the absence of mitigating factors, such as advanced age, to aggravate Patrick's risk status, without explaining how lack of mitigation statistically equates to increased aggravation. (If your driving record is good, should your insurance company be permitted to raise your premium because the longer you drive, the greater your odds of having an accident?) Given this sort of louche logic, there is no meaningful evaluation of Patrick and other sexually violent predators apart from their actuarial assessments, self-confirmed by recasting their elements. This is bad science, frowned on by the relevant scientific community, including test author Karl Hanson himself.

Some state courts are starting to express some skepticism about the testing regime. In Illinois, an appellate court found "the better rule" mandated a hearing on the scientific acceptance of actuarial instruments, which the government failed to prove were generally accepted within the psychological/psychiatric communities. And one Florida appellate judge trenchantly noted: "The literature reflects that clinicians and other professionals in this field are currently debating many issues, including whether the actuarial approaches are superior to the clinical judgment of psychiatrists or psychologists, and, if so, why clinicians are employed to conduct the actuarial tests."[29]

But we the People like actuarial tests, because using an "instrument" sounds so much more efficacious than psychoanalysis. After all, a clinical evaluation could incorporate an analysis of historical factors that result in an increased chance of recidivism. The problem isn't the factoring in of a man's psychosexual background. The problem is the replacement of a reasoned assessment with an automatic one. By "reasoned" I mean one where there is a measure of accountability inherent in evaluation and evaluator, where the final evaluation is made on something more comprehensive than static and statistical factors, or the self-fulfilling prophylactic prophecy. If I stand in the center of Los Angeles on one foot and shout "gallimaufry" three times, it will keep away all tigers. The proof of my efficacy is that there are no nearby tigers. Of course, if SVPs were assessed clinically, the assessment would be subject to attack for subjectivity. Oversubjectivity, naturally, from the defense perspective, namely, mine. But it would be professionally harder for me to tear apart something with the sound of informed common sense than it is to go for the more vulnerable statistical vein.[30] The bottom line remains the same: What you want—what we all want—is to be right.

Quantifying Terrible Risks

I know odds are odds. I also know the decision whether to deprive someone of his freedom, even incrementally, isn't an odds game. Offenders reoffend. Some will continue to reoffend until they meet their unmakers. There's no denying that. And in the world of sex crimes, the reoffender seems particularly horrible. There's a feeling fate may have been forestalled if only we'd paid attention to what we now see as forewarning. We want our villains to be as well marked as poisonous snakes, and maintain that they are. So in both SVP determinations and sex-offender registration requirements lurks the belief that the most terrible risks can be quantified, and by its quantification, identified, and by its identification, controlled.

When we start throwing a term like "actuarial instrument" around to refer to facts that would also be considered in any clinical assessment, the line between opining and testing has been crossed with big muddy boots. I understand the use of statistical analysis as a legitimate measure of probability. But the probabilities at issue in SVP determinations can only be measured generally and retroactively. Not prospectively, not individually. And justice, above all else, must be rendered individually.

Unblinking acceptance of this type of quantification leaves no room for honest skepticism about the idea of quantification itself. We need to question the basic cultural conceit that chance should be weighed like cheese. The whole business conjures up medieval depictions of Saint Michael sitting souls on scales, sometimes measuring affinity—those that tipped toward the Virgin went thataway, and those that didn't were grapple-hooked to hell—and sometimes just weighing good against ill, souls set on the right, being of God and therefore good, and sins to the left, represented by warty toads and other noxious creatures. But there is, or should be, a more humanistic mentality at work, one that accounts for the nonaccountable, for the human problem of the nonstatistical. For the fact of Patrick.

We have to allow real rehabilitation or true conversion, the fact of the thunderclap, the lightning bolt, the heaving collapse under the awful knowledge of absolute guilt, and the ridiculous hope of one puny person's atonement, one insignificant redemption that constitutes that flash of transcendence that passes for transcendence in our drive-by lives. Do we really believe that anyone can become better than he was, and if so, what form would that take?[31] The state psychologists skitter around this, likening their -ilias to alcoholism, so though the condition is chronic, treatment protocols focus on detecting and deflecting the urge to act on the impulses created by that condition. But what about their colleagues, who apparently tried to trigger the impulse in the first instance, as demonstrated by Patrick's prison friend, whom the State's treating psychologists asked to revise his fantasy into a rape scenario? Isn't this like asking an addict to load syringes while lecturing him not to shoot up? Isn't this a set-up for his next commitment? A cynic might see the friend as just another subject in another research study, being told what to do to see if and how he does it. Poke at the lab rat, and let's see what pokes back. But given that somewhere around 90 percent of alcoholics have at least one relapse over the four-year period following treatment, the analogy is a stinker and no recommendation for SVP confinement. In *Hendricks*, Justice Kennedy warned that SVP commitment would not be constitutionally tenable if it became simply "a mechanism for retribution or general deterrence."[32] As it stands, confinement has proven nothing more than a clumsy device for both.

According to a July 16, 2006 *Los Angeles Times* article, Timothy Lee Boggs, convicted in the 1980s of molesting several nine-year-old boys, was to be released in May 2005 after completing a treatment program. The state did not do so because it could not find a place for Boggs to live, despite making 269 tries. The government argued that Boggs shouldn't be freed because no one wanted him; the trial court acknowledged that although there was a "significant" danger Boggs would reoffend, "[on] the other hand, he has paid his debt to society, and then some." You can almost hear the heavy-crowned sigh echoing the chambers. Parenthetically, the article noted that Boggs was the sixth SVP to "win" release from the state hospital in ten years.[33]

There are molesters and rapists and ever shall be, and repeat offending is a dead certainty. And still, it is true that we don't assess murderers to see if they are likely to kill again, or probe the anger management strategies of those convicted of beating their wives and neighbors, or require robbers to take actuarial exams though those men are certainly ripe to reoffend, at least statisically. Too, sometimes we take a chance on someone's metaphysical makeover not because it is a statistical guarantee but because we are the better for our better beliefs. It has always been paradoxical that the most conservative of Christians tend to believe least in the power of Christ to save the worst of us, and liberals would throw away the hospital key in the name of collective security. Because the worst of us lie and manipulate, rape and take, destroying yet another life, ending someone else's innocence, and we wish we could isolate this segment of the population. What if we could do a preventative sweep at eighteen, scoring for "personality disorders" alongside the driver's license test? We could throw in a PET scan of the brain and see what bits light up best, for the brains of the dangerously deranged are different than yours and mine, particularly yours.

Patrick will never get out of the hospital, though he should. I've represented a number of sexually violent predators. Some, like Patrick, are kept just for the sake of keeping, the "better safe than sorry" set. Some make me shrug and say I'm glad I'm not on that jury. And some are proof of the wisdom of involuntary civil commitment—if I could believe in the wisdom of involuntary civil commitment. But I can't. It appeals to the desire to shove nightmares into the closet and bolt the door, but suffers from a nagging absence of intellectual rigor. To sign on to SVP commitment would be to feign belief in a science that doesn't yet exist in hopes of a solution that is too cynical for me. I still think actions should be punished, not men. These men may be more or less monsters, but if their monstrosity is grounds for caging them in perpetuity, then their monstrosity should be measured in human terms. It should be done very clinically and very currently, with the ability to recognize that most statistical deviation—the monster who becomes a man.

GUILT AND CULTURE

CHAPTER 4
TEEN SEX: THE WAGING OF GUILT

I vow and promise to protect every living thing that God has put
on this earth. I'll protect butterflies and flowers. Children rich
and poor. Hmph! I'll even protect crab lice!
— BROTHER GLACKIN, *The Boys of St. Vincent* (1992)

A THIRTEEN-YEAR-OLD GIRL SKIPS SCHOOL, gets drunk, and has sex
with an eighteen-year-old boy she thinks is cute. He is convicted
of child molestation. Does that mean crime is on the rise? Teenage
trysts, once punished by a good long grounding, are being prosecuted
as felonies. Lesser crimes, like statutory rape, have become greater offenses. It's easier to be a rapist these days, not because of lax security
or looser mores, but because the definition of rape is broader. And the
sentences commensurately longer. Our tough-on-crime culture leads
to more people in prisons for more years. Luckily, the private sector
is more than happy to step up to the plate. Or the trough. The prison
system is a growth industry, for all the wrong reasons.

This chapter is about the failure of the law to keep pace with the
culture: the law gets more puritanical as the culture goes wilder. So
the law becomes a dragnet for those criminalized by the culture. Or
it's about how the law keeps pace with the culture: the law gets more
draconian the more the culture transgresses. So the law is there to
scoop up the products of a world gone mad. Or maybe it's about how
we like to have our crime and punishment in equal bittersweet measure, like coffee with cream. But even if the law allows for all these
contradictory possibilities, we should not. In Dante's *Inferno*, one of
the damned, a friar, describes how he counseled his Pope on how
to betray his enemies, but only after the Pope absolved him of this

treachery before he committed it. When a devil came to collect the friar at his death, the devil pointed out that it was impossible to repent and sin concurrently. "Perhaps you didn't reckon I'd be versed in logic."[1]

The Case: Heidi and Jonathan's Day Off

In May 2001, thirteen-year-old Heidi and her friend Irene, fifteen, called Jonathan and told him they were going to skip school. They arranged to meet at a nearby park. Jonathan was eighteen and a special education student in high school. He later testified that he thought Heidi and Irene were in the eighth grade. Though Heidi was only thirteen, she was fully developed physically. She liked Jonathan. She'd gotten his phone number and called him every day for about a month. She told him she liked to drink, and asked him to ditch school with her.

That May day, the three met as planned, and decided to go to Jonathan's friend Hector's house, walking there by way of the wide concrete gully known as the Los Angeles River. The four then retired to Hector's bedroom, Jonathan and Hector lying on one bed, the girls on another. They were very bored. Jonathan went to the store and bought soda for Heidi and Irene and two 40-ounce bottles of 211 Steel Reserve beer for Hector and himself. Heidi wanted beer, so Jonathan let her have some of his.

Jonathan got drunk. Heidi felt sick; she threw up twice. The boys also smoked a joint; Hector offered it to the girls, but they refused. By this point, Jonathan and Heidi were lying on one bed, and Hector and Irene on the other. Irene told Jonathan and Heidi to kiss. They began kissing; Hector videotaped Heidi and Jonathan kissing. After a while, they all went to Jonathan's house. Heidi said she was feeling dizzy.

At Jonathan's house, they watched television for a while in the living room. Jonathan had another beer, Heidi went to the bathroom, threw up again, returned, grabbed Jonathan's hands, and led him to his bedroom. They began kissing and giving one another hickies. Jonathan later said that he was so drunk the room was spinning. They had sex, returned to the living room, watched a little more TV, and went back to frolic in the park. That night, Heidi told her mother she'd ditched school. She did not tell her mother she'd had sex. Heidi had never ditched before, and was afraid she was going to get into trouble. She was afraid her mother would be even angrier about the sex.

The next day, Heidi's principal lectured her about skipping school. During their conversation, the principal asked Heidi where she had gone; Heidi said she went to Hector's house. After further prodding, Heidi told the principal she'd had sex with Jonathan, and he called the police, who arrested Jonathan.

During Heidi's sexual abuse examination at the hospital, she told the nurse that she had done "some kissing" with Jonathan and had consensual intercourse. At trial, Heidi testified she did not "like" Jonathan: she just wanted to have sex with him.

Jonathan's defense was simple: Heidi had not only been willing to have sex with him, she started it. But legally, this was not only irrelevant, it was a confession. Jonathan was convicted of child molestation and sentenced to six years in prison. He will have to register as a sex offender for the rest of his life.

The Law: All or Nothing at All

Every crime is composed of an act (*actus reus*, or the act done) coupled with a thought (*mens rea*). For example, the crime of theft is composed of the taking (*actus reus*) plus the intent to permanently deprive (*mens rea*). Smaller crimes are connected to greater crimes in one of two ways. One is as lesser *included* offenses; the other is as lesser *related* offenses. Whether a crime is a lesser included or a lesser related offense depends on that crime's particular composition of thought and intent as compared to its greater offense.

Like Russian nesting dolls, lesser included offenses are contained within greater crimes. You can't commit a battery without committing an assault. Battery is the use of unlawful force on someone else; it includes assault, which is the unlawful attempt and present ability to use that force on someone. (I was standing next to you and I punched you.) Assault is a lesser included offense of battery. A lesser offense doesn't necessarily contain all the elements of the greater; you can commit a lesser offense without satisfying all the elements of the greater. (I tried to punch you, but missed; I'm guilty of assault, but not of battery.) Conversely, you can't commit a greater offense without committing the lesser. (A battery is a completed assault: if I fondle a sleeping woman, I've necessarily assaulted her.)

Defendants have a right to have their jury instructed on lesser included offenses on the theory that they could be found not guilty of the charged crime, but guilty of the lesser included offense. It gives the jury a means to moot prosecutorial over-charging, to bring the verdict in line with the actual offense. ("He swung, but he missed, for God's sake.") Naturally, it's better to be found guilty of a lesser, as the lesser will typically carry a shorter sentence, make you eligible for parole, or have some otherwise diminished penal consequence.

The second group is the lesser *related* offenses. These are not by definition included in the more serious crime. Not all the elements in the lesser are found in the greater, for example, but the lesser crimes are considered close enough to be thought some part of the greater — like a small dining area off an open kitchen. Statutory rape and child molestation both involve sexual activity with someone below the age of consent. Statutory rape is legally defined as "an act of sexual intercourse" with a minor, provided the minor is not one's spouse (Cal. Penal Code § 261.5). Child molestation, by comparison, is any touching of a child with "lewd and lascivious" intent (Cal. Penal Code § 288[a]). Statutory rape is a lesser related offense to child molestation, and is the lower-register charge traditionally pled to when grown-ups dated teenagers, or the default verdict when juries disapproved, but didn't flat-out condemn such liaisons.

Instructions on lesser related offenses were once required when requested by a defendant. But in *Hopkins v. Reeves*, the Supreme Court held that any obligation to instruct on lesser related offenses impermissibly interferes with the State's "prerogative to structure its criminal law."[2] In California, the rationale for losing lesser relateds was that the obligation violated the separation of powers doctrine.

The executive branch (the prosecutor) has the power to "select and propose" criminal charges, and the judicial branch (the court) has the power to dispose of them.[3] Any rule compelling the court to instruct on lesser related offenses would involve the judiciary poaching on the executive's province. Courts still have a duty to instruct the jury on lesser included offenses if there is enough evidence to warrant consideration on whether the defendant is guilty of the lesser offense; there is no obligation to instruct on lesser included offenses if there is no evidence that the offense was less than that charged. If you are charged with child molestation, and you have touched a child with a lewd intent, your jury will not be instructed to consider whether you are also guilty of battery or statutory rape. In other words, the jury has no choice but to convict you of the greatest possible offense.

The Sexy Child Argument

Is Jonathan a child molester? Is he the one who makes you grill the children, bolt the door, or scrutinize the soccer coach? Younger teenage girls who angle for older teenage boys, older teenage boys who sport with younger teenage girls: these are archetypes, and their angling and sporting are rites of passage. There's no wall separating childhood and adulthood—and their attendant sexualities—though the law pretends at one.

James Kincaid argues in his book *Child-Loving* that much of the current fuss over child molestation is humbug. His thesis is that the child (i.e., the concept of The Child in post-Victorian Western Culture) has been fashioned "so as to make its eroticism necessary," that the erotic child is culturally significant, and that denial of the child's core eroticism is erotic in itself, and dangerous in practice. Kincaid lovingly traces figure of the erotic and eroticized child, coming to the conclusion that children are sexual, that the relationship between child and adult is necessarily erotic, and that in the vast majority of adult/child sexual encounters there's no harm done. So Kincaid would have us take away authoritarian presumptions/proscriptions and go "into play,"a freed sense of childhood sexuality.[4] He doesn't think that going from power to play would facilitate abuse, but does believe it would allow for positive child/adult sexual relationships. The ones where the pedophile loves the child, and the child the pedophile. No harm, he says. But the foul remains.

Many of Kincaid's arguments are elegant recapitulations of pitches that have been made by everyone from Humbert Humbert in *Lolita* to the North American Man/Boy Love Association. I don't buy them. I don't think that the relationship between child and adult being necessarily erotic is true, and certainly not true in any rigorous sense. Any analysis is suspect that insists that because a certain perspective exists (or persists), it must have a legitimate point. Particularly when the perspective inherently involves power differentials. Saying that there has always been adult/child eroticism, and therefore adult/child eroticism is natural, is very different in this way from saying that homosexuality is natural. The more apt analogy would be to say that master/slave sexual relations are natural. The fact that adults sexualize children — along a sliding spectrum from cute bathtub photos to child prostitution — isn't the same thing as a fundamental sexual relationship between children and adults. It *may* be from the point of view of the adult, but there isn't much evidence that children sit around and sexualize adults. There's no proof that unmolested children, left to their own devices, would seek out sex with grown-ups. Children might want to peek at naked people and touch their own and their little friends' private parts, but the hard-core stuff is prompted by pedophiliac adults.[5]

But I do agree that eroticism more easily and properly bridges certain genders and ages. Part of the problem with the usual pro-child sex argument is that its proponents cherry-pick their examples. Kincaid's paradisiacal adult/child paradigm is the man/oldish boy relationship, that stalwart of initiation rites and the mythopoetic mentor, the stuff of daddy/boy porn and the really cool high school coach.

By comparison, the stereotypical seduction of the older boy by the mature woman, invariably cast as a sun-dappled, vineyard-heavy marvel of sexual initiation, carries no comparable sense of intellectual mentoring or social education. I'm thinking of all those Italian-French-Spanish films that begin with a boy in blue shorts on a black bicycle and quickly cut to a young widow doing something barefoot and lip-bitten, in *décolletage et déshabillé*.[6] The male naïf is a budding philosopher, the female a *prêt-à-prendre*. Post-seduction, there's no more use for the Woman, as there's nothing more she can teach the now-Man. Contrariwise, in Kincaid's Wonderland, the older man can go on disseminating his pearled wisdom to his protégé.

When the seduced is female, there's no such tender mentoring/initiation to be had, for the girl-woman serves primarily as an erotic-nostalgic shot in the arm for the graying man. And there's little older/younger female sexual iconography aside from a few tropes taken from female prisons or girls' boarding schools.[7]

There are legitimate feminist questions about power imbalances in inter-age relationships, exacerbated in inter-gender relationships, including the aforementioned staple of the middle-aged man/teenage girl.[8] There are cultural and historical thickets such as men having made women the responsible repository for male sexuality—the adolescent girl is handed faux reins and told, like Icarus, to steady the drive of the sun—and base realities such as teenage pregnancy and an anti-abortion, anti-childcare, anti-welfare State. The difficulty is not that child molestation laws inhibit natural childhood sexuality, but that their application to natural childhood sexuality may be unnatural.[9]

A Disposable Generation

To prosecute an eighteen-year-old for child molestation based on consensual sex with a thirteen-year-old perverts the concept of perversion. To prosecute a fourteen-year-old for messing about with a thirteen-year-old is a farce wrapped around a tragedy. These are fundamentally interchild relationships. Those who defend adult/child sex want a childhood sexuality that involves indisputable adults, with mortgage balloons and retirement plans, bad gums, worse knees and memories, foreseeable futures, and a fear of aging unto dying. Childhood sexuality exists, now, before, and ever after, amen, but there's no prudishness in believing it should exist only among children. Play doctor, play nurse, play pantless, grope each other madly and often in the rumpus and romper room, wonder at the metamorphosis of soft bits and sneak sex like sips of your parents' locked-up liquor, and worry, worry, worry about the consequences. All this seems perfectly reasonable as a manifestation of Nature.

In addition to helping build a false generational wall, the law furthers the idea that everyone under the age of consent must be absolved from all sexual responsibility. There is a creepy puritanism here, a feeling that sex itself is wrong, and that, in terms of underage sex, there are only two sexual roles: victim and perpetrator. The State officially approves abstinence, and where abstinence fails, official criminalization follows. Strictly applied molestation laws are one aspect of this dynamic, but it also plays out in policies to restrict or proscribe teenage abortion, and the move toward laws that would require parental consent for teenagers to get birth control. According to Planned Parenthood, forty-four states legally require parental notification or consent for a minor to obtain an abortion; as of 2008, thirty-five laws are in official effect. However, most states have abandoned all attempts at enforcement. Laws requiring similar notification/consent for birth control exist in two states (Texas and Utah), and have been introduced by several other state legislatures (including Kentucky, Minnesota, and Virginia) and in both the House and Senate ("Parent's Right to Know Act").

Most of this legislation has run face first into the minor's constitutional right to privacy, protected by Title X and Medicaid, and Supreme Court suggestions that official denial of contraception is not a proper way to limit sexual activity. Still, a number of faith-based organizations and faith-based politicians advocate amending Title X to mandate parental notification for contraception. Adolescents said they'd rather not ask Mom and Dad; a survey of teenage girls published in the January 19, 2005 edition of the *Journal of the American Medical Association* indicated that only 1 percent would forego sex altogether if parental notification were mandatory, whereas 18 percent would opt for unsafe sex. If states cannot enforce abortion notification laws, their ability to enforce contraception notification laws would seem unlikely, given the greater state interest in protecting the health of pregnant minors and their progeny.

The Puritan condemned, and there remains an American penchant for condemnation, an internecine urge that claims generations of disposable young men. The Jonathans of this world—young, with no future but time—are not anybody's concern except the family that bears them. There's as yet no New Deal workfare, no Civilian Conservation Corps, Works Progress Administration, Tennessee Valley Authority, little straight-up welfare, no Great Society pledge to give a leg up or a handout. There aren't even Union workhouses, the Treadmill, or the Poor Law. But there are still prisons. And prisons must be populated, and it is a popular thing to populate prisons. Voters, as the phrase goes, "overwhelmingly" support any crackdown on crime. This makes it easy to criminalize, or increase the criminality of, offensive behavior. (Let us leave aside what constitutes offensive behavior, though the category is evidently procrustean, sized according to social mores that are deemed morals [e.g., marrying whites and Negroes, renting to one when the building was mostly occupied by the other, two people of any sex and race fornicating extramaritally].) The building and running of prisons is one of the last growth industries in many states, including California. A fair number of corporations employ inmates, and inmates earn between about eight and forty cents an hour.

In its 2007–2008 budget, California was to spend $9.8 billion a year on its prison system, about 6.7 percent of the total State expenditures (as compared to a 6 percent national average).[10] And it still can't keep up with demand. As of 2006, California had some of the "toughest" sex offender laws "in the country."[11] A claim coveted by other states: 2006 also saw a federal trial in Kansas litigate whether state law mandated that health care providers and educators report *any* sexual activity by anyone under sixteen.[12] "Any sexual activity" would include fondling, or "heavy petting," as the old folks say, and maybe even really good kissing. Federal District Judge J. Thomas

Marten ultimately decided that the law only required reporting non-consensual or abusive sex by those under sixteen, and any sex involving those under twelve. Although the court carefully noted that "all underage sex should be discouraged," therapists, doctors, teachers, et cetera, retained the discretion whether to report teen lovers. (Kansas Attorney General Phill Kline had been attempting to take reporting laws that one step further back; perhaps there could be a Wee-Tip hotline for those who spy small hands creeping under the covers or a too-lingering glance in the high school shower.)

California's penal code was further strengthened in 2006, when Proposition 83 passed with a 70 percent majority. The ballot referendum raised all sentences for child rape to twenty-five years to life, turned possession of child pornography from a misdemeanor to a felony, extended parole for violent sex offenders to ten years (the start of parole may also be tolled another five years for anyone considered for SVP commitment), and required registered sex offenders to wear electronic monitoring devices/global positioning systems for life. It also originally prohibited registered offenders from living within two thousand feet of any park or school "where children regularly gather," but that part of the law was struck down in late 2008. Local ordinances may fashion further residential restrictions. Prop 83 is known as "Jessica's Law" because the lamb shall be known only by her sacrifice, and represented a clutch of desperate measures for artificially desperate times. (We'll discuss offender registration and revisit those one thousand– and two thousand–foot buffer zones in a later chapter.)

On Child Pornography

The elevation of the crime of child pornography was not quite so great as press and politicians made out: the offense went from a straight-up misdemeanor to what's called a "wobbler," a felony that can be sentenced either as a misdemeanor or a felony, depending on the judge. The sacrificial-lamb motivation and justification for making possession a potential felony was provided by the parents of "Courtney," a twelve-year-old who was raped and murdered six years earlier. The killer had been involved in child pornography, and, the logic goes, had he been arrested on (and presumably convicted of) that charge (as a felony) he might not have gotten to the kidnap-rape-murder stage of sex offending. The same rationale was once used for felonizing possession of marijuana—that it would stunt the future crop of dope fiends. Let's agree that child pornography—real child pornography, the stuff that differs from its adult version only in levels of body hair and the size of the protuberances—is an abomination. Its production a crime in itself, as its creation documents a molestation, and its dissemination exponentially furthers the abuse. But possession, purely private possession, of something called child pornography may be something else. And that something else may be a concern for us as a society, but may not be something we want to feed our state prisons with.

Let's also clarify terms: child pornography in the popular cultural imagination is a seven-year-old shown giving a man a blow job, that is, hard-core porn involving young children. Child pornography as statutorily defined in California is any medium depicting someone under the age of eighteen "personally engaging in or simulating sexual conduct," sexual conduct defined as intercourse, any vaginal/rectal penetration by any item, masturbation "for the purpose of sexual stimulation of the viewer," sadomasochistic abuse for that same purpose, "exhibition of the genitals or the pubic or rectal area of any person for the sexual stimulation of the viewer," defecation/urination for the purpose, et cetera.[13] Possession of child pornography is having the stuff and knowing the person depicted is under eighteen. This has led, on more than one occasion, to police experts testifying about the relative ages of male Thai actors, and medical doctors testifying about buds versus non-buds, and stop-motion analyses of pubic development. Though it would seem that if you're counting hairs, the issue of knowledge of the actor's majority is up for grabs. (But please note the cutoff age is *eighteen*. Legally, kiddie porn also includes the murkier area of money shots involving fifteen-, sixteen-, or seventeen-year-olds.)

The "exhibition of genitals" provision is the most problematic, or used to be, back when film kiosks were forever turning in photos of four-year-old Billy's bum arched enticingly skyward as he showed off his pantless cartwheel, or three-year-old Anyesha standing spread leg–proud staring at the camera in her Mama's (too cute) bra top and no panties. Depending on the camera eye level, the cops would visit the parents and, depending on the home creep factor, (a) hook them up and toss them into the grinning maw of justice; (b) scare them silly with the possibility of (a); (c) scare them silly with the possibility that unscrupulous photo-kiosk employees could be hawking snaps of Billy/Anyesha to the salivating pedophile community; (d) explain to them patiently the facts of life relative to (b) and (c), and back in the squad car, wonder "What the hell were these people thinking?"

The fact is, there is very little commercial hard-core child porn produced these days. Most of the gunk your spam filter catches consists of young-looking young women and men dressed or undressed up as youth with titles that fabricate their minority. (My quick Google search for "teen porn" results in 4.12 million hits, "teen girl porn" 2.01 million hits, "virgin porn" 1.65 million, "schoolgirl porn" 1.39 million, and the catchall, "young girl porn" 4.90 million.) So the average kiddie porn connoisseur is a ham-handed fellow with a generous imagination and a willingness to go along for the ride. Whereas the hard-core kiddie porn connoisseur is hooked up via the Internet to private file sharing featuring real live little girls and boys.

A fair amount of the hardest child pornography involves certain photos that have been circulating and recirculating for years, and the bulk of the new porn is homemade. Anyone with a taste for molestation, a digital camera, and a computer can become a child pornographer, which is why the kiddie-porn connoisseur is hardly ever nabbed for simple possession. Like the dope fiend, there's another reason he comes to the attention of law enforcement, and it's usually the nastier allegation of sexual abuse, or production/dissemination of child pornography.[14] So the possession charge is almost always an ancillary charge, enabling prosecutors to plea-bargain a bit, or allowing the State to slap on an extra three years per image onto that twenty-five-to-life sentence. And if kiddie-porn possession was the only charge of conviction, there's no reason in the world to believe that conviction would deter a murder. There are many shoplifters. There are many, though not as many, robbers. There are some robbers who, after taking the till, put the barrel of the gun beneath the chin of the store clerk, and shoot. There are some who rape them first. There are some who do worse. There are monsters, and monsters aren't deterred by a three-year hop in the joint. The only way a felony kiddie-porn rap is going to stop a potential child kidnapper/rapist/killer from becoming a child kidnapper/rapist/killer is if someone happens to shank him in the shower.

But let's say the freshly buffed State really does roll up its soft, cotton sleeves and takes on private possession of child pornography. Let's also imagine that there is some social profit to this enterprise. How would this prosecution work? Would police be given a free ride to trace the flow of tot-traffic across the Internet? For some reason, the World Wide Web believes that I have an unflagging interest in enlarging my penis, upping its staying power, and, that done, provides me a steady stream of eager sex partners.[15]

My computer's spam filter is set on high, but even so, these messages slip easily into my inbox. If I had such tastes, I could download a batch and leisurely scroll through them, deleting those I found *de trop*, saving the ones I liked for later. It's as if a great bundle of magazines arrived daily at my door, some with the good American fun of *Playboy*, *Penthouse*, or *Hustler*, perfectly legal, and perfectly culturally acceptable, some slightly more intense, such as *Juggs*, *Swank*, and *Barely Legal*, and some that cross all lines of taste and morality, making even the devotees of *Playboy*, *Penthouse*, and *Hustler* and even *Juggs* and *Swank* call their congressmen. And what if the good men of the federal or state government were to come around before I could get rid of the stuff I disapprove of? Though who's to say I didn't have my single-handed pleasures before disposing of the evidence? It's a big net. Many may be caught. As a defense attorney, this gives me job security.

Back to terms. As noted above, Proposition 83 upped the sentence for "child rape" to twenty-five years to life, the same sentence as first-degree, premeditated murder. (By comparison, second-degree murder only gets you fifteen to life.) "Child rape" is a hot-button redundancy. Rape is sex without consent. Because children are incapable of legally consenting to sex, any sexual activity with a child is rape. What Prop 83 did was increase the penalty for vaginal or anal intercourse, or oral copulation of a child, to twenty-five years to life. Previously, it was possible to be sentenced to three, six, or eight years for child molestation involving significant sexual contact, depending on the circumstances of the offense (for example, having multiple acts of intercourse or multiple victims triggers an alternate sentencing scheme, resulting in terms of fifteen or twenty-five years to life). Note that under Prop 83, Jonathan would have gotten an automatic life sentence.

The U.S. Supreme Court weighed in on the highest penalty in 2008 with *Kennedy v. Louisiana*. The case involved a man slated to die under a 1995 Louisiana statute imposing the death penalty for rape of a child under thirteen. The Court ruled that the Eighth Amendment's prohibition against cruel and unusual punishment forbids putting someone to death when the crime itself did not result in a death. The Court wrote that the crime "was one that cannot be recounted in these pages in a way sufficient to capture in full the hurt and horror inflicted on his victim or to convey the revulsion society, and the jury that represents it, sought to express by sentencing petitioner to death." Though a child's rape could well be a fate worse than death ("the victim's fright, the sense of betrayal, and the nature of her injuries caused more prolonged physical and mental suffering than, say, a sudden killing by an unseen assassin"), "it is not at all evident that the child rape victim's hurt is lessened when the law permits the death of the perpetrator."[16]

We Are Growing Prisoners

There are now more people in prisons than ever before. In 2005, the Department of Justice's Bureau of Justice Statistics reported 491 inmates per 100,000 of the general population, including children.[17] There were 2.2 million incarcerated adults. Seven million U.S. adults were under some sort of correctional supervision, constituting 3 percent of the adult population; that is, one in thirty-two American adults was either in prison, jail, on probation, or parole. As of 2007, the U.S. prison population topped three million, about 1 percent of the whole.

Two-thirds of new inmates are in for new crimes, one-third for parole violations. Recidivism is the primary cause for prison overcrowding. Recidivism not based on a new criminal offense, but on parole violations, specifically technical parole violations, like failed drug tests. And prisons seem to have no function beyond human storage. A June 2006 report issued by the Commission on Safety and Abuse in America's Prisons concluded that our prisons are a failure, cement copses of violence and boredom, in which disease runs unchecked and mental illness grows murderously deeper, where severe social isolation is the norm, and recidivism the only possible correctional outcome.[18]

Here's a story: A friend I'll call Portia became a Superior Court judge here in California a couple of years ago. As part of becoming a judge, you must visit one of the maximum-security facilities in the emptier parts of the state. The visit is a group affair; new judges are brought in en masse to see where they'll be sending people. Portia said the guard who let them into the prison reception area was a day or two away from retirement, and felt no public relations pressure. The reception area is where they put inmates awaiting their housing assignment; an inmate can spend months in reception, given housing shortages and the particular needs of certain inmates.[19] This particular reception area featured a small antechamber leading to one of those enormous tiered cellblocks, where rows of bars stretch out and up like some Escher sketch, shadowed with puppet people and smelling of men. Portia said it was noisy when they stepped into the antechamber—the sounds of people shouting, talking, flushing, walking amplified by the tiers and the hollow center. When her group stepped from the antechamber into full view, there was a moment of absolute silence, then an enormous roar which built up and out from the lowest, nearest cells to wall the entire arena, full-throated, full-throttled screams of delighted rage. The old guard turned to the new judges and said, "*You* are their entertainment."

There are no books in reception, no television, no radio, no work. No legitimate stimulation, but plenty of raw appetite. I won't debate the humanity of this; either you like the tang of cold blood or you don't. But we agree to turn our prisons into meatpacking plants by lengthening terms for some existing offenses, broadening the definitions of guilt for others, and refusing to allow for conviction on lesser offenses with shorter sentences even for those who deserve leniency. Jonathan, like too many young men, became yet another body to be processed by an already overwhelmed system.

The Private Sector Steps In

Enter the private sector. There are whole books on the phenomenon of private prison building, and private prison running, readily available—we can confine ourselves to a more general critique.[20] The core problem with applying capitalist principles to incarceration is the self-perpetuating effect of an ever-expanding penal system. According to Bureau of Justice Statistics reports, there were 7.2 million adults (one in every thirty-one) in prison/jail or under probation/parole in 2007. Private prison facilities held 7.4 percent of federal and state inmates (up 0.4 percent from the year before); at midyear, this totaled 118,239 inmates, up from 112,134 the previous year. About 28 percent of privately held inmates are held for the federal system, and prison populations overall are expanding at the same rate as the prisons themselves. Given that the prison population is steadily increasing, the number of warm bodies to be privatized is obviously on the rise.[21]

Though the rate of privatization moves faster in some jurisdictions than others. The federal prison system has the largest number of inmates in the country.[22] According to the Bureau of Justice Statistics 2007 report, there were 196,804 federal inmates in total; about 14 percent are in privately held prisons or community correction centers. According to my interpretation of Department of Justice statistics and those provided by the California Department of Corrections, though the largest public prison systems have the most bodies promised to the private sector, the smaller systems pledge the largest inmate percentages.[23] This means the increase in privately held prisoners will occur at a greater rate than any prisoner increase nationwide. In the simplest, roundest, flattest numbers, if about 7.5 percent of all inmates are privately held, then the private prison system is the third largest prison system in the United States, behind the federal system and California.[24]

It's been a growth industry, and promises to continue to be, despite the vicissitudes of the economy. Correctional Corporation of America (CCA), headquartered in Nashville, is the biggest private prison company in the United States. According to a 2001 federal audit report, CCA held 53 percent of the federal prisoners in private facilities. According to its own Web site, CCA held approximately 80,000 inmates in 2008, and "partners with all three federal corrections agencies (The Federal Bureau of Prisons, the U.S. Marshals Service, and Immigration and Customs Enforcement), nearly half of all states and more than a dozen local municipalities." The GEO Group, the second biggest private prison company, had 24 percent of privately held prisoners, and the third largest company, The Cornell Companies, about 14 percent of the market. CCA's 2005 earnings were $1.19 billion, there was about a 30 percent jump in revenue and stock prices in 2006, and profits were on the rise even in the troubled times of late 2008. The GEO Group was similarly thriving. As the head of CCA said in a 2008 interview, "There is going to be a larger opportunity for us in the future."[25]

These figures are historical, not prognostic, but the physical market reliably expands. As of 2001, there were 18,000 privately held federal prisoners, but no contingency plan for their housing if these corporations were suddenly unable to meet their contractual obligations. By 2005, the number of privately held federal prisoners had grown to about 27,200; there was still no contingency plan. Meanwhile, prison policy experts anticipate inmate populations in ten states to increase by 25 percent between 2006 and 2011.[26]

Inmates are being individually outsourced as well; two contracts were awarded in 2006 to the GEO Group and CCA to "temporarily" house 2,260 California inmates in four other states. The GEO Group will house 1,260 inmates in Indiana for $28.7 million per year for three years; CCA will house 1,000 inmates in Phoenix, Oklahoma, and Tennessee for $22.9 million per year for three years. As of November 2008, California contracted out more than 5,100 individual inmates to facilities "accredited by the American Correctional Association."[27] These figures are well above the inmate population percentages we've been working with, indicating the futility (and stupidity) of any claim of a constant rate of privatization.[28]

So there is the famous "prison-industrial complex," as coined by activist Angela Davis in 1998. But it's an unfortunate moniker, because it suggests a grand conspiracy rather than a field of neglect, ineptitude, and opportunism. And in the course of human events, neglect, ineptitude, and opportunism will trump the well-oiled conspiracy every time. Because in addition to the various corporations that are slicing off pieces of the prison pie, private prison running is not an all or nothing proposition: private contracts cover everything in the joint from who sells whose prisoner "bonaroos" (good clothes) to who gets to tinfoil their teeth.

California spends about $800 million for contracted-out prison health care services and has yet to meet constitutional standards of care. As of July 2005, America Service Group, parent corporation of Prison Health Services (PHS) and Correctional Health Services, had contracts in twenty-eight states, actively providing medical care for 237,000 inmates. In October 2006, the Florida Department of Corrections announced that PHS submitted the only qualifying bid for its $800 million, ten-year health care services contract, despite problems with services provided under its previous contract, effectively sealing the ongoing deal. In 2009, the company served 174 jail and prison sites (180,000 inmates) in twenty-three states, providing care for over 7 percent of inmates in the United States. Meanwhile, the *New York Times* and the *Los Angeles Times* regularly publish investigative reports on the awfulness of inmate health care, with epileptics fitted into vegetative states, diabetics deprived of begged-for medication, the mentally ill made mentally iller.

Faith Shall Set You Free—For a Price

There has also been money for very private concerns, including funds for "faith-based" rehabilitation programs, such as the evangelical Inner-Change, run by Prison Fellowship Ministries (PFM). For a time, Iowa paid $1.5 million a year to InnerChange, which gave inmates who participated in its diet of weekly revival meetings, daily prayer, worship services, and Bible-study and religion classes the more earthly rewards of better cells and special visitation privileges. The federal judge who slapped down the program on First Amendment grounds wrote, "For all practical purposes, the state has literally established an Evangelical Christian congregation within the walls of one of its penal institutions, giving the leaders of that congregation, that is, InnerChange employees, authority to control the spiritual, emotional, and physical lives of hundreds of Iowa inmates." The federal appellate court, including retired Justice Sandra Day O'Connor, affirmed the ruling, finding that the program's religious instruction was unconstitutional indoctrination. However, there is no constitutional bar to the state permitting faith-based programs not paid for by the state.[29]

In June 2006, the Federal Bureau of Prisons suspended religious treatment programs in six prisons,[30] while Prison Fellowship Ministries contracted with CCA in March 2006 to launch a four-step "faith-based Re-Entry and Aftercare Program" designed to "teach inmates fundamental principles for leading successful and happy lives." CCA also partners with Good News Jail & Prison Ministry, the Institute in Basic Life Principles, School of Christ International, and Champions for Life, all, according to CCA, providing "non-denominational guidance." Non-denominational apparently means Christianity Not Otherwise Specified. Good News Jail & Prison Ministry is an evangelical Christian organization whose CEO lauds its growth from a one-chaplain-one-jail notion to a nonprofit corporation serving 360 institutions in twenty-four states, nineteen countries, and one U.S. territory. The Institute in Basic Life Principles calls itself a nonsectarian group while announcing glad tidings of "Sharing the Light of Christ in Mexico," and stating that it was "established for the purpose of introducing people to the Lord Jesus Christ."[31] School of Christ International is self-explanatory; the evangelical achievements of Bill Glass's Champions for Life are bullet-pointed on its "About" page.[32]

Whatever federal restrictions there may be on giving direct aid to a single religion, those guidelines may be harder to enforce against a private-prison corporation that funds an evangelical rehabilitation program. Note that these funds are in addition to the federal money that was already given or promised to those faith-based community organizations (FBCOs) subject to federal oversight. It's the new E(vangelical)-based economy. There are no atheists in foxholes, and no non-evangelical Christians in the hole.[33]

There are federal guidelines for giving faith-based organizations actual and direct tax dollars, but, again, states can avoid the First Amendment church/state bullet by receiving spiritual aid free. For example, the California Institute for Women and the Prison Industry Authority "in cooperation with a nationally recognized faith-based prisoner re-entry program"—later identified as Alpha USA Divisions of Prisons & Re-Entry—started a pilot rehabilitation program designed to facilitate California's female inmates' return to society. The program includes a "curriculum of study based on Biblical principles" pre-release, and continuing assistance post-release. The State was not reimbursing its collaborator for services or curriculum. According to Prison Industry Authority general manager Matt Powers, the "life skills that are taught in the Alpha Project can greatly assist inmates in successfully transitioning back into society." Plans are also in place for a second pilot program at (all-male) Folsom State Prison.

Alpha USA Divisions of Prisons & Re-Entry is part of Alpha USA, whose primary product is a ten-week course designed to "explore the validity and relevance of the Christian faith to your life today."[34] The basic course involves meeting other Alpha humans over a meal, which includes a Talk and Small Discussion, and a get-away weekend devoted to such "life skills." Alpha's Web site says there is no cost for the course, though "you might be asked to make a donation toward the cost of the meal and the weekend away." Course materials are available for purchase, and there's a seven- or eight-step plan for going forth and running courses for others. But the plan will cost you, in conference fees and follow-up materials. Like the perfect pyramid scheme, all profit goes straight to the top, avoiding any messy and un-Christian distribution of lesser wealth.[35]

I don't want to look a gift in-depth analysis of the human condition in the mouth, but it does seem that part of the community re-entry program is to enlist a new crop of Alpha females to spread the Word via Course Materials. And although there is most certainly a spiritual need in stir, there are other ways of tending to the pent soul: Alcoholics Anonymous, for example, sends members to almost every prison and jail in the country to talk and hold meetings. Not a dime changes hands. As proved by our SVP, faith can be had without recourse to a set of DVDs or bullet-point proof of the majesty of the Message.

But I've gotten all caught up in a synecdoche, for there's far more and far more direct money to be made off the Big House. California's Prison Industry Authority (PIA) was established in 1983 to "improve enterprises employing prison inmates." As of July 1995, the PIA oversaw thirty-one types of business at twenty-three of California's then-thirty-one prisons, employing about 7,000 inmates in "such varied product and service lines as license plates, dairies, meat cutting, optical goods, and specialty printing." Annual sales, mostly limited to public agencies, ran about $152 million, and the agency netted about $10 million.[36] Though there may be a good argument for the state keeping its inmates busy (and productive) working for the state, the PIA is not the sole conduit for inmate labor: a number of private corporations have been making inroads in all kinds of ventures, from the manufacture of gangsta-wear (the former Prison Blues), to telemarketing for AT&T, to taking phone reservations for major airlines. Overhead is low and, as noted, salaries management-sweet. And though America has censured China for using unpaid prison labor, our condemnation is based on an eight- to forty-cent hourly wage differential. A Little Debbie snack cake at the prison commissary costs about forty cents. They sell them individually, out of a $3.50-for-twelve cake box. If you want something larger, like a TV, you can order directly from private companies such as Amarak or Access Catalogue. Access Catalogue charges $120.99 for a Clear 13-inch KTV television; 13-inch color televisions run about $80 on the street. Prison privatization has evolved from the State leasing out able-bodied cons to corporations to the State and the corporations profiting off warm bodies, sick bodies, bored bodies, and just plain bodies. These days, the field hands don't even have to go to the field to turn somebody else a dollar—they just have to watch TV.

Short Term, Fast Track

As I've said before, I don't believe in grand conspiracies, because I don't believe people are capable of maintaining the social-insect focus necessary to envision, construct, and maintain such structures. This is not incompatible with a belief that market forces will, like ants to a wall crack, rush in to seek the sugar, and once the sugar's found, make a track whose eradication is practically impossible. Private prisons are a short-term, fast-track solution for everyone: they infuse money into the private-sector economy, create private-sector jobs, and "temporarily" solve prison overcrowding. They do not address the government's obligation toward those it chooses to imprison, or the social costs of choosing to imprison so many. Private companies are, if not amoral, not charged with morality—they owe nothing but paid service to the State. The State, contrarily, owes something to its People, who permit it to be the State.

This isn't about capitalism, pro or con. This is about capitalism, heads or tails. We live in a capitalist society. As a capitalist society, we can make decisions about what things we want to subject to the market and what things we do not. Spare kidneys, for example, seem to be things we do not believe ought to go to the highest bidder. Fire departments shouldn't really drive faster to the largest houses with the fewest people. We'd be upset if our local hospital opened a business-class ICU or stocked better blood for the well-heeled.

What is the State's responsibility to the people it decides to incarcerate? What was the State's responsibility to Jonathan, the slow 18-year-old? How much education did he warrant? How much employment?

What sort of wage? How much was the State willing to spend on him before it was willing to spend $63 a day to have a private corporation take him away? What constitutes more governmental interference — the nannyism of a welfare state or the Big Daddyism of mass incarceratons? In his convict lease essay of 1893, Frederick Douglass wrote, "Men talk of the Negro problem. There is no Negro problem. The problem is whether the American people have honesty enough, loyalty enough, honor enough, patriotism enough to live up to their own Constitution." Today, there is no prison problem.

The people Karl Marx believed would compose the revolutionary "reserve army of the unemployed" are being culled from the fields and put to work in the Big House. The market needs of late capitalism dovetail too neatly with the cultural need to self-sanctify. And so we have come to live in a society swimming in private porn of the "drunktweensuxcox" variety and public porn of the true-stories-of-true-crimes variety, and still find some common thrill in the trill of moral condemnation while we rent out our surplus population. Which seems far more morally offensive than what happened between Jonathan and Heidi.

CHAPTER 5
SEX-OFFENDER REGISTRATION:
TRUTH AND SOCIAL CONSEQUENCE

Sentence first, verdict afterwards.

— THE RED QUEEN, *Alice in Wonderland*

W E ARE A COUNTRY that denies stink and believes in sanitizing guilt. We'd like to make bad better by way of clear labeling and clearer segregation: Identify the guilty and excise them from the community. If you can't excise them from the community, segregate them within the community. If you can't segregate them within the community, hang a sign around their necks and cry "Unclean!" as they pass. If you can't secure neck or sign, post their photos online and on telephone poles and make them announce themselves wherever they go. When it comes to sex offenders, we try to rope them off, like dogs, and bell them, like cats. We want to make them easy to find, identify, and exclude. As a result, laws aimed at controlling the movements of sex offenders after release from custody have been blooming like American Beauties. Some can be attacked as unfair or unworkable, but they're a hardy and thorny species.

Before we get into the details of offender registration and global positioning system (GPS) ankle bracelets, let's yield the floor to some right-minded chest thumping. With the passage of Proposition 83 in 2006, the *Los Angeles Times* announced that California had "overwhelmingly" enacted the "toughest" sex offense laws in the country. As Governor Arnold Schwarzenegger said, "I am sponsoring this legislation to give California the strictest laws and toughest penalties for the worst crimes."[1] But even for the "Governator," it's tough to be toughest, for competition is fierce. In New Mexico, Governor Bill Richardson "proposed toughening New Mexico's sex offender laws to the toughest level in the country."[2] A New York assemblyman also promised to "do all that I can to ensure that New York State has the toughest sex offender laws in the country—our children deserve no less."[3] And in its passage of a sex-offender law in 2005, Iowa combined molester fear with down-home boosterism. As one state senator put it: "Florida claims to have the toughest sex offender laws. Iowa should be number one in the nation. That's the thing we ought to lead with, along with corn and beans."[4]

Offender Registration Limbo

In every state, sex offenders are required to register their post-prison residence with local law enforcement. I practice law in California, so I'll focus on that state's rules. They are echoed in other jurisdictions, but if you're in Maine, Nebraska, or Idaho, your mileage may vary. (NB: If you find reading about the following rules exhausting, think how much more exhausting it must be to actually follow them.)

California's registration laws oblige a person convicted of a specified sex offense who lives, works, or goes to school in California to register as a sex offender with local law enforcement for the rest of his life. The registration rules are daunting and all encompassing. If you have more than one address, you register both. If you are homeless, you register any place you're at for five consecutive working days; if you don't have a new address after five consecutive working days, you have to register wherever you are on that fifth day. Transients must register any address where they sleep, eat, work, "frequent, and engage in leisure activities."

If you move out of California, you must register in the new state within five working days, and the officials in that state have to notify California that you've registered with them. Anyone who lives out of state but works in California, with or without compensation, for more than fourteen consecutive days, or a total of thirty days a year, must register in the state. Anyone who goes to school in California part or full time must register his address and his school's address. Transients have to re-register every thirty days. Anyone who has been determined to be a sexually violent predator has to re-register every ninety days after being released from the hospital. Everyone has to re-register annually, within five working days of his birthday. All registration requirements apply to subsequent re-registration.

Qualifying offenses include rape; sexual battery (touching an "intimate part" without consent); forcible sodomy; child molestation; "annoying" a child (the misdemeanor version of child molestation, also includes having sex with someone over the age of eighteen who you believe to be under the age of eighteen at the time—the wannabe molester); forcible oral copulation; penetration with a foreign object (includes fingers); sexual penetration under false pretenses; pimping, pandering, procuring a minor; contributing to the delinquency of a minor when said delinquency involves any lewd or lascivious conduct; incest (marriage and sex with those "within the degrees of [forbidden] consanguinity"); child pornography (sending, making, selling, having); sending "harmful matter" (including telephone messages) to a minor with the intent to seduce the minor; meeting a minor for the purpose of genital exposure (either party); communication with a minor with the intent to commit a sex offense; indecent exposure; solicitation of rape, sodomy, forcible oral copulation, penetration with a foreign object, or child molestation; conspiring to commit a qualifying offense; and any conviction for murder, kidnap, or assault related to the attempted perpetration or perpetration of any of the enumerated sex offenses. Any person ordered to register as a sex offender anywhere else has to register in California, as does any person found not guilty by reason of insanity of committing a qualifying offense.

Off With Their Heads!

As a general rule, each individual act committed during a single criminal episode is grounds for a separate charge, conviction, and sentence. Failure to comply with any one part of the registration requirements is a separate felony offense. All felonies in California are subject to the three-strikes laws: if you commit a felony with one prior conviction, your sentence is doubled; if you commit a felony with two prior convictions, your sentence is twenty-five years to life, and your sentence on each count is twenty-five years to life, to be served consecutively. All registered sex offenders would have at least one prior conviction, namely, the grounds for their registration.

In sex-offender hell, felonies can multiply like rabbits. One example is that violations of the registration requirement may be charged under their separate subdivisions. This means that someone could be convicted for failing to file an initial registration, failing to file an annual re-registration, *and* failing to file a change of address. Given the three-strike laws, this could result in a sentence of seventy-five years to life without the person having committed a new offense. And has, although late in 2008 the Ninth Circuit Court of Appeal struck down one twenty-eight-years-to-life sentence for failing to register as cruel and unusual punishment in violation of the Eighth Amendment: the man had registered, but registered three months late.[5]

Registered sex offenders must wear a GPS device for life, and must pay its costs unless the Department of Corrections finds they are unable to pay. Registered sex offenders can't work with minors, or live within 2,000 feet—almost half a mile—of "any public or private school, or park where children regularly gather." The GPS device signals whenever an offender gets too close to a forbidden zone.

Imagine for a moment that Los Angeles has a center, and choose as this center an area populated by a variety of socioeconomic and cultural groups: Hollywood. By that, I mean the *real* Hollywood, humble. home to Russians, Armenians, Koreans, Thais, Mexicans, Filipinos, and all manner of folks on the move, some up and coming, some down and out—City Council District 13, where 250,000 of our fellow citizens already belong. As its city councilman's Web site proclaims, the 13.3-square-mile area of District 13,"has it all," including thirty-five public schools and fourteen public parks. There are twenty more private schools in the relevant zip codes. What half mile do you imagine lies outside all these places where children routinely gather?

Striking a blow for common sense, a California court in 2008 ruled that the 2,000-foot residency limit was unfairly restrictive. On November 19, 2008, the Fourth District Court of Appeal became the first California court to find that the residency restrictions in Proposition 83 are not just public safety measures but also punish ex-offenders by forcing them out of their homes. As reported in the November 21, 2008 *San Francisco Chronicle*,[6] the appellate ruling leaves the law in effect, but limits its application. The sex offender who initially sued to keep the state from forcing him to move pursuant to Proposition 83 had lived a law-abiding life in his home within the 2,000-foot zone for twenty years. Another man had been convicted in the 1980s for molesting his daughter, served his five years, and was sixty-nine years old and incident free when he got the letter telling him that his home violated the new law.

Registration on My Mind

Georgia, no statutory slouch, passed a law in 2006 prohibiting sex offenders from living within one thousand feet of a slew of places, including schools and churches. That may have been overreaching. In July 2008, a federal judge blocked the part of the law that prohibited offenders from living or working within a thousand feet of school bus stops. One of the plaintiffs in that case had been convicted of statutory rape because she didn't stop her teenage daughter from having sex with her teenage boyfriend.[7] Another was living in a hospice and unable to walk; another had Alzheimer's. The lead plaintiff had been convicted of consensual oral sex with her fifteen-year-old boyfriend when she was seventeen; in November 2008, she sued to be declassified as a sex offender.

As the result of this litigation, and several other lawsuits, a few Georgia sheriffs agreed not to enforce retroactive application of the registration law to elderly or disabled sex offenders. But these exemptions applied only to named plaintiffs or those exempted by the kindness of local law enforcement. Georgia's other sex offenders still have to get out and keep moving.[8]

When Iowa enacted its version of the 2,000-foot residency limit in 2005, many local governments added further restrictions.[9] For example, Des Moines added libraries, swimming pools, and bike trails, which put 98 percent of the city off-limits to registered sex offenders. Subsequent offender housing shortages have resulted in so many absconsions (in the first six months of the legislation, three times as many offenders were considered missing as before the law's passage) that the Iowa State Sheriffs' and Deputies' Association, Prevent Child Abuse Iowa, and The Iowa Coalition Against Sexual Assault, among others, have urged repeal of the residency restrictions in favor of "child safety zones," areas where sex offenders would not be allowed to enter, like schools and day-care centers.

Sex offenders who don't just take off and/or start living in cars and tents, in parking lots and under bridges (homeless shelters often fall within the outlawed two thousand feet) have crowded registration-compliant motels and trailer parks, turning rural areas into hotbeds of uprooted and rootless abusers. An Iowa farmer interviewed by the *New York Times* in 2006 complained that his children couldn't remember all the mug shots supplied by the local sheriff every few weeks.[10]

According to a 2007 *USA Today* study, two-thirds of states permit non-specific registration (including registering as homeless, registering a shelter address, or an inexact location such as "woods behind Wal-Mart"), and thousands of sex offenders are listed as transient, primarily because of residency restrictions.[11] Some local governments have cut to the chase, banishing registered sex offenders entirely. One subdivision in Amarillo, Texas, banned convicted sex offenders from owning or living in new homes. The homeowners association plans to periodically check the state database for those violating the deed restriction.[12]

The Sex-Offender Shuttle

So now that we're making more rapists/molesters, where do we put them? In California, officials have tried to block the parole of sex offenders because they have no place to house them. They have bedded ex-offenders on office cots while trying to find registration-compliant housing, let them hang around the sheriff's station, and shuffled them among low-rent motels before the five-day mark to avoid registration.

Any registration-compliant motel willing to take sex offenders long term can make a nice profit from the new laws, charging $200 for the first week's residence, $300 for the next week, and $350 for the third. Victims can compound the problem by requesting that a particular offender be housed at least thirty-five miles from their home. This has an odd unintended consequence, as it gives the offender a general idea where his victim lives, information that is otherwise kept secret.

California Assemblyman Rudy Bermudez of Norwalk complained that he had received reports of molesters being moved every four days between a group of hotels and motels near Disneyland. An Anaheim Convention Bureau spokesperson said the sex offenders weren't really all that close to the Happiest Place on Earth. Bermudez's claim was denied by Department of Corrections officials.[13] Besides, said the parole administration, the men were wearing their global positioning devices. Left unanswered: What happens when they run into children walking down the hall to the Coke machine?

In short, the guilty continue to live among us, and we continue to be unfree. Is the only practical solution to keep sex offenders locked up? Sexually violent predator commitments continue "indefinitely," and indefinitely is a long time. Given how easy it is to violate registration/residency provisions, and how easier still to charge multiple violations, sex-offense laws become Möbius strips, all but guaranteeing a steady stream of ex-offenders into the great maw of the prison-industrial complex.

I know automatic registration requires too much of too many. I feel no more secure knowing that someone like Jonathan, Heidi's onetime playmate whom we met in chapter 4, is registered and globally tracked. I'm also not convinced of the social utility of keeping constant tabs on someone convicted of misdemeanor child annoyance. I'm certainly not convinced it's worth some portion of $100 million a year of my tax dollars. The oft-repeated justification for rigorous offender tracking schema ("If this legislation saves even one child . . .")

is bizarrely illogical. In a capitalist universe, dropping another $100 million annually into education or health care would be a more utilitarian way of demonstrating Love of The Children.

In a pre-Proposition 83 *Los Angeles Times* op-ed piece, the co-director of the Violence Reporting Project lauded legislation prohibiting a judge from giving probation to someone convicted of incest.[14] Though the author acknowledged that prosecutors rarely sought such a sentence, she stated that judges "often granted it just the same," saying "it's not clear how many child sex abusers walked free" because of a grant of probation. Something here needs straightening out—for it seems awfully important to find out roughly how many "walked free" and who they might be before publicly complaining. Too, the complaint doesn't make sense.

First, probation isn't exactly an unencumbered stroll; there is supervision, with the prospect of prison dangling over the probationer's head. Second, the incest provisions can apply to underage cousins, if someone chooses to prosecute, and I'm not sure that hard time is needed in that situation. Third, if the "how many" is one, or two, or 743, that might make a wee bit of difference in my calculus of guilt, and thus, my sense of just punishment. Acting as though our collective house is on fire is not a good guide to social policy. Probation may well fit the facts of a particular case and of a particular defendant, and I think I'd rather have a member of the judiciary decide that on a case-by-case basis than have a member of the State Assembly do so as to all cases, as to all time.

The original intent of the registration requirement was to facilitate police tracking of known sex offenders, the theory being that if a sex offense was committed, it would help to know what bad men lived thereabouts. The problems seem to have started as the People were let in on the information. Megan's Law began as a general heads-up: you could go online and see roughly where someone who registered lived, but couldn't get an exact address or identification, or details as to the predicate offense. But then it became precise public knowledge, leading to such absurdities as the Page One column in the *Los Angeles Times* about the staff writer finding out his Altadena neighbor was a registered offender.[15] The neighbors posted the man's name, picture, street address, and offense on trashcans and tree trunks, and staked similar signs on lawns, sent fliers around titled "Registered Sex Offender Movement Alert," and were planning on picketing. The fifty-three-year-old man had been convicted of sexually abusing his daughter beginning when she was six or seven. (She reported him in 1993, when she was sixteen, and he admitted molesting her.) He served three years in state prison. He lived 850 feet from a park, complete with playing children. The neighbors said they wanted to ostracize the man, "drive him out" of the neighborhood. They said they were worried about property values. One retired couple, the first black couple to move onto the street thirty years previously, declined to post the signs; the husband wondered if the mood could turn lynch-like.

Or vigilante-like. In Lakeport, California, a registered sex offender was stabbed to death in November 2007 by a neighbor who apparently misunderstood the online postings. In jail, the alleged killer said he took "evasive" action against the man, whose offenses as listed on the Megan's Law Web site could have been interpreted as involving molestation. The murder victim, however, had been convicted of raping adult women. Leaving the question whether this distinction regarding the man's guilt makes any moral difference in his murder.[16]

When the man with the *Los Angeles Times* neighbor was interviewed, he said he knew the molestation was wrong. It had been precipitated by his wife's suicide, he said: he had improperly turned to his daughter as a surrogate. He said he was not generally attracted to children. The man has had no arrests since his release from prison. Still, the columnist was disturbed by the man's lack of remorse. Or insight. Or what remorse and insight the columnist felt he should have. The columnist felt the man "ought to outwardly display torment. Forever."[17]

Pervs on the Loose?

Unlike the *Times* columnist, if a sex offender lives in my neighborhood, I am far less interested in breast-beating displays of regret than

I am in the ongoing cease and desist. I've seen plenty of cases where ongoing remorse accompanies ongoing molestation. Admitting the evils of alcoholism isn't worth jack if you continue to drink. But the obvious problem of sex-offender registration is its utter failure as a preventative measure. As far as I can tell, there is no single child saved, no matter how many buckets of dollars are tossed at global positioning systems or new supervisory agencies, or roving bands of registration enforcers.

In every registration case I've had involving a subsequent conviction of child molestation, the woman whose child the sex offender was offending knew full well of his registration status.[18] Similarly, there's little utility to employers backgrounding new hires, regardless of the workplace relevance of the prior offense. Or ChildSafe Network's online offer of a sex-offender search engine—the lead reads: "Protect your most valuable assets! Does a registered sex offender live next door? Around the corner? On the way to the playground?" Then the copy: "Sign up for the FREE Sex Offender Search Engine and keep on top of who lives in your neighborhood," accompanied by a medallion stating "All This FREE," and the closer—"Register today and receive a FREE Child Identification Kit! The kit helps you record all the information, hair samples and fingerprints necessary to find your child if he/she is ever abducted." There is a picture of a young blond woman kissing the cheek of a blond teenager, smiling at the camera. (I believe we are to assume the young woman is the teenager's mother.)

Preliminarily, someone who views a child as an "asset" may have more in common with molesters than is comfortable to note. Too, on the odd chance your child is abducted, you'll have hair samples and fingerprints where the child left them, right there on the hairbrush and the doorjamb. And finally, you're not helping to find either the child or the abductor, just to identify remains. The truly ugly truth is there's nothing here to protect anyone from anyone or anything. Except, possibly, the estranged spouse who makes off with the child and takes up a new life under new names. Or a Humbert whose American dream involves taking a road trip and setting up a picket-fence existence with his beloved Lolita. But that's got nothing to do with what we're really worried about, does it? It's the use of the bogeyman to scare the bejesus out of us that deeply offends, or should. We ought take care of our children not by taking reference samples from them, but by teaching them how to live in a world where good comes along as often as evil, though evil on a smaller scale.

Rules to Live By

The Parents for Megan's Law Web site is full of good and useful information, such as abuse prevention tips (molester "tricks"), the reminder that most abuse is committed by someone the child has some other sort of relationship with (friend/family), and behavioral/physical signs of abuse (changes in mood, school performance, sleep/eating patterns). But it is also strangely hysterical, with headlines that read like tabloid headlines:

> *Loopholes in Perv list (600 worst sickos left off registry)*
> *Thousands of Pervs on Loose: Study*
> *Halloween Fiend Watch (Cops track pervs)*
> *"Banished" Pervs Sue Over Law*

Look at the language. The group is dedicated to The Child. The Child as Innocent. The Child as Lamb. And against the Lamb lies the Wolf, the Beast, the Sicko, and the Perv. But the wolf and perv exist in a world where children are also chicken and jailbait, and women are cunts and ho's. We're surrounded in equal measure by glass houses and folks with rocks. The only ex-offenders who can disprove the need for strictest registration/residency requirements are those who die incident free.

I'm not sure how I feel about sex-offender registration, to be honest. It does have curbside appeal, at least in terms of the habitual rapist or the molester who is a stranger.[19] But most molesters are the boyfriend or the uncle or the boy next door, and most habitual rapists, being habitual, have a better chance of being in the slammer than on the street. And I'll be no safer knowing there's a registered sex offender around the corner than I would without this knowledge, provided I live by the common-sense paranoia we all ought to live by.

Here are my personal rules: I don't let nice men help me from public to private spaces, and I don't help them; I don't open the front door without peeking; I don't send my kids outside alone; I teach them not to be obliging to adults looking for lost kittens, puppies, or directions to the nearest Dairy Queen. They do not automatically defer to authority, or believe that anyone wants to make them actors or fashion models. They should never go to a second location with someone they've safely met but don't really know. I believe most adults shouldn't find children other than their own especially fascinating, and shouldn't precipitously volunteer to take them camping, teach them chess, go boogie-boarding, or call them up just to chat. I sleep with my windows locked and the doors double-bolted, I don't curry favor with those I do not know, and will cross the street to avoid passing a solitary stranger. I honor my vague feelings of creepiness. I protect myself and those I love, and I do it without feeling guilt or recrimination. Specifically, I reject the logic that would have a woman risk her own safety rather than appear racist, make the male stranger feel bad, or, most idiotic, appear not to be afraid. In sum, I play the same bad-luck lottery we all play, and just try to worsen my chance of winning.

CHAPTER 6

THE FUTURE OF SEX-OFFENSE LEGISLATION: PRONGS OF THE PITCHFORK

Right or wrong, weak or strong, I don't make the rules . . .

—ERYKAH BADU, "DANGER"

WHEN AMERICANS GET FRIGHTENED, we bolt the door, go to war, and pass laws to help us lock and load. The fear sparked by sex offenders has produced lots of door bolting, wars on pornography, Internet predators, and repeat offenders, and many laws designed to identify the guilty, past, present, and future. The three-part focus of those laws: online identity, lie detectors, and your very own DNA.

On December 11, 2006, the *New York Times* reported that New York and Virginia were planning new modes of "tightening oversight" of sex offenders. The Virginia attorney general wanted online IDs and e-mail address registration. New York wanted to use polygraphs when asking parolees about their whereabouts, Internet use, and anything else indicating a potential violation. At first, New York wanted unlimited use of lie detectors, but a federal appellate court made the state promise to use the test only in inquiries related to parole supervision, case monitoring, and treatment. Senators Chuck Schumer of New York and John McCain of Arizona said they were going to sponsor federal legislation similar to the Virginia law. As subsequently enacted, the Virginia statute requires e-mail addresses plus "any instant message, chat or other Internet communication name or identity information that the person uses or intends to use . . ."[1] On October 13, 2008, two federal statutes were signed into law requiring, among other things, that sex offenders provide Internet identifiers to state sex-offender registries, and authorizing the Justice Department to enable social networking sites to compare these identifiers with those on the National Sex Offender Registry. Failure to register or update online information is punishable by ten years in prison.[2]

Liars and the Liars Who Test Them

For those who've never seen the right police procedural, polygraphs, commonly known as lie detectors, are machines that use sensors to measure a subject's physical responses to questioning, such as breathing rate, pulse, blood pressure, and perspiration. Fluctuations in those responses are registered on a graph, monitored by a polygraph examiner. The examiner asks the subject a series of innocuous or benign questions (name, address, date of birth, et cetera) then proceeds to more accusatorial matters. Sudden changes provoked by more pointed questions are chalked up to the anxiety born of lying, or its companion, fear of getting caught.

Polygraphs are routinely used by employers and police, but they have a mixed record of success. The tests don't work well with those already under significant stress, those too sociopathic to register anxiety when lying, or those too psychotic to recognize that they are lying (and perhaps in this, they're not).

Polygraph evidence, including the offer or refusal to take a test, is not allowed in California courtrooms unless both parties agree to its admission. Twenty other states allow polygraph evidence only by party agreement; the others don't allow it at all. Most federal courts permit polygraph evidence via party agreement or at the judge's discretion. It is inadmissible in military courts. The Supreme Court has ruled that automatic exclusion of polygraph evidence doesn't violate a defendant's Fifth or Sixth Amendment rights to present a defense.

Polygraph evidence isn't universally allowed because there's no scientific agreement on the reliability of the procedure. Some studies show the test is a good test; others say it's no better than a coin toss, having an accuracy rate of about 50 percent. Some Supreme Court justices have criticized governmental entities that use polygraphs to justify hiring or firing their employees (including police), but object to a defendant trying to introduce positive test results on his own behalf. Police like polygraphs because they spook suspects. There's no winning with a lie detector. If you take the test and pass, it's not admissible, and won't help in your defense. If you take it and fail, the cops will lean on you more, armed with this further, albeit suspect, proof. If you refuse to take the test, that seems suspect in itself. New York officials recognize that the test is fairly bogus, saying it primarily provides "an incentive to tell the truth" for those afraid to lie to a machine. The science is fiction, but the fiction of the science can produce fact.

Protecting the Virtual Playground

I'm not sure what the government wants with online IDs and e-mail addresses, except as another way to violate sex offenders. Certainly there isn't a real-world thought that registration of electronic identifiers would cause the least little hitch in an Internet predator's activities. E-mail accounts are common as squirrels, and run about as freely; e-mail addresses can be routed and rerouted, and changed at the drop of a dime. Online IDs aren't worth the paper they're not printed on. Moreover, the focus seems all wrong, predicated on a false sense of time-space wherein the online is like some place that can be secured in real time. But others feel much differently.

When the Virginia legislation was first proposed, MySpace's chief security officer, Hemanshu Nigam, remarked that the law was "an important recognition that the Internet has become a community as real as any other neighborhood and is in need of similar safeguards."[3] Along with Facebook and Yahoo, MySpace supported similar legislation proposed by New York's attorney general in January 2008. The Electronic Security and Targeting of Online Predators Act (e-STOP) requires convicted sex offenders to register their e-mail addresses, instant-message screen names, and any other online identifiers with the New York State Division of Criminal Justice Services. Those data are then made available to social-networking companies and other online services so that they can block access to sexual offenders and remove them from their sites.[4]

For online social-networking sites, there is obvious marketing appeal in online socializing being seen as the same as joining the gang at the mall or bellying up to a neighborhood bar. But MySpace and Facebook are not neighborhoods, or neighborhood hangouts, not even metaphorically. They are anonymous public forums, great stoae in which the only illumination comes from the content of the communication, not the purported identity of the speaker.

In the most abstract sense, this is the beauty and crux of Internet speech: truth lies only in language. There's no *real* fifteen-year-old girl online, any more than there is a real meeting of real minds. There are messages sent into the home; some are stories, packaged as such, some are based on a true story, some are pretty close to what passed for the facts at the time they were typed. Though each of these is more tailor-made than those stories pitched by your TV, they are all messages. All just words. All absolutely free, all the time. The Internet is still the only soapbox secured for the Little Man, even when he is calling himself Hailey Sue and swearing he's got beautiful blonde hair and is almost fifteen. There's no protecting anyone from false free speech, except by teaching them how to sniff it out. And this is perhaps how the Internet does resemble the common pub or more common TGIF, because you can't believe everything you hear in those places, either.

We don't expect our government to step in and demand background information from the patrons, telling her that the him she's been chatting up is married, with a penchant for drunken sex, or that the one showing the one next to him a picture of his daughter is her habitual molester, or that the guy who says he just loves kids is telling God's honest truth. My analogy is faulty in that children don't usually hang out in bars, but they do hang around other watering holes. Public forums are distressingly public; those who want to protect their children from the street mammer jammers have to keep an eye on them while they're little and teach them to look both ways when they get older. For the other problem is that there's a new bad man born every minute, mostly spawned from the brain of another battered lamb.

Inflating DNA Databases

States have also been rushing to fill up the DNA databank for a good long while now. All states require DNA samples from those convicted of sex crimes or murder; forty-four states require DNA samples from all convicted felons. As of October 2009, twenty-one states, including California, have approved collecting samples from those arrested for specified offenses, primarily burglary and serious felonies. Virginia began collecting DNA from those arrested for violent felonies in 2003, California began collecting from all suspected felons and some misdemeanor arrestees beginning in 2009, the federal government currently collects from all its arrestees, and North Carolina lawmakers are considering a bill mandating sampling from anyone arrested for any crime. *Any* crime—including shoplifting, tax fraud, and tipping Holsteins. Crimes involving absolutely no forensic relationship between anyone's DNA and the criminal offense at hand. And that's *arrested*—not convicted, not even charged. Just hooked up by the local blueboys, an experience more common in the poorer parts of town, most common in the brownest parts of town, though many pale and upright citizens have felt the pinch of the cuffs for driving under the influence, or exercising their constitutional right to amass in protest. The bottom line is that any arrest—even a potentially bogus one—gives the state access to, and control over, all your genetic information. And you can't refuse to provide the sample.

In January 2008, California dramatically pushed the use of DNA investigation from exact genetic matches to near matches.[5] As reported in the *San Francisco Chronicle*, Attorney General Jerry Brown announced that the state Department of Justice would start scanning its million-sample database for a near match to crime scene DNA samples when an attempt to find an exact genetic match failed. A partial match could suggest to police that the person they're looking for is a relative of a past lawbreaker whose genes are already in the system. Brown stressed that sharing partial DNA matches would provide only investigative leads. These would have to be buttressed by normal police evidence gathering before charges could be brought against a family member of the DNA donor in the database. But dismayed civil libertarians claimed that the new program would expose innocent family members—or even total strangers—to police surveillance and investigation. Given that California is taking DNA samples from anyone arrested in a felony case, the state is accumulating a permanent store of DNA from people who may never be convicted of any crime.

Protecting the Private Parties

The civil libertarians cry foul at this indiscriminate gleaning, conjuring up the threat of government misuse of such data—though they're a little vague on exactly how. DNA databank supporters (let's call them "civil totalitarians") say that DNA is "the fingerprint of the future," and the broadest databank would be useful for both crime solving and crime absolving. Supporters say that anyone found not guilty could petition to have their genetic information expunged. Remember that the European Court of Human Rights struck down similarly broad databanking in Britain based on the European Convention's right to privacy, a right not strictly codified in the United States Constitution.[6]

However, among our Bill of Rights, the Fourth Amendment protects against unreasonable searches and seizures. The Fifth Amendment protects against compelled self-incrimination. As a rule, most body fluids, and any information contained therein, can be taken without running afoul of either constitutional guarantee because whatever your blood or sperm says about you, it's not being made to "say" it, any more than your bloodshot and pupil-bouncing eyes testify to your bar hop. And a search and seizure is not unreasonable as long as there's probable cause for the cops to pry. You seem drunk to me, and you're driving, so I have probable cause to take a sample of something—breath, blood, or urine—to prove the DUI. Similarly, if the constitutionality of DNA gathering is predicated on having probable cause to arrest, then a not-guilty verdict, which simply means there was not proof beyond a reasonable doubt, would not necessarily be enough to get his nibs out of the state's bio-coffers. You have to petition to have your DNA removed from a database. But this petition process could upend the presumption of innocence because the petitioner would have to prove that he didn't do it, or at least didn't do it in a way that would eliminate any justification for the state keeping his genetic profile on record.

Like the civil libertarians, I'm not sure to what nefarious purpose the government could put a mammoth DNA database. I suppose it could lease the data to insurance companies, so that those with genetic predispositions for cancer or diabetes or procreating a disabled child could be culled from the herd. Or perhaps big drug companies would bid for the information, anonymously and in bulk, so as to know when the demand for certain drugs might be peaking, and to structure their protocols and public offerings accordingly. Or maybe something simpler, like targeting products to those who fit the genetic demographic. Diet companies could direct mail people with soon-to-be-fat DNA. Nursing homes could line up their Alzheimer's patients earlier on, before the mind goes. There's money to be made, and it will most certainly be made.

But let's say we believe what the government says, that such a stockpile of genetic profiles would be enormously helpful in the statistically insignificant but emotionally enormous serial rape or rape-murder scenario, or in any case in which a cold hit could work swifter justice (police find a genetic sample at the crime scene and run it through the database, fingers crossed, and the convicted burglar is nailed for a murder/rape). Or even, if such a thing could be proved, preventative justice (the serial killer caught before going on to his next victim). And let's pretend, despite what we now know, that DNA is the fingerprint of the future, that it's not overly subject to interpretation or statistical manipulation, but is dead-bang proof in any and all cases.

This has at least two unintended, yet not unwelcome, consequences. First, we might learn that there are more statistically improbable matches than heretofore suspected, thereby providing defense attorneys with good ammunition for cross-examination. Second, we might also be able to better challenge what is termed a match, given that we don't know what will turn up as databanks are filled with the criminally or poverty inclined. There may be some statistical reconfigurations based on—what? Strange kinships or kindred genomic natures? The push and pull of finer-tuned theta factors? Or some additional information like that unbelievable yet true nine-loci match between the two unrelated Arizona inmates mentioned in the DNA chapter? And what happens to precedence based in science then?

There is also the question of privacy. Not in the way of an abstraction, but in the American way. I remember as a child reading a biography of Daniel Boone, pride of Kentucky and exemplar of westward expansion. He left the Bluegrass state for Missouri, paddling past Cincinnati with the complaint that his home state had gotten "too crowded." My book was illustrated with black ink drawings, one of him in profile, set against a pine forest, the smallest black spiral trailing from the farthest grove. The book said he moved farther west whenever a neighbor moved close enough that he could see their chimney smoke.

As a people, we still shudder at the sight of our neighbor's smoke, and can't abide his smell. We like big houses on bigger lots, blocking off many square feet of air to no purpose but buffer. We throw our arms open to the world and keep our hearts and minds strictly to ourselves. We don't much like the idea of anyone knowing who we are, not exactly, which is part of the reason we eschew the public intellectual, or any spokesperson beyond the Hollywood or Washington celebrity, because we understand they are neither entirely real nor representative. Even the promise of salvation and life everlasting is a private promise, for we are a private people.

The free-floating willingness to subject the privatest part of one's self to public scrutiny is contrary to our nature. To the extent this willingness has been bought, it's been bought on the backs of the sex offenders, the burglars—Them, not Us. But as the pool of the Them gets bigger, it starts to include more of the Us. Your sexual orientation may be genetic; your employer may care. Your wife may, sadly, be prone to ovarian cancer; your insurer would be interested. Your brain may be allelically programmed to slowly slip away; your children should be warned. You may share more things with others of your kind than you would like to know, or have known. They are us. Your e-mail address is mine, if I want it. Your online identification also applies to me. Do I have a right to hook you up to a lie detector and ask if you've ever harbored any lascivious thoughts about the baby? What about the sitter? When would you like to say when?

CHAPTER 7

DRUNKEN SEX AND HOMEMADE MOVIES:
WHO'S GUILTY NOW?

Two things fill the mind with ever new and increasing admiration and awe, the oftener and the more steadily we reflect on them: the starry heavens above and the moral law within.
—IMMANUEL KANT, *Critique of Practical Reason* (1788)

GUILTY IS AS GUILTY DOES: if I do something the law deems a sin, I'm a sinner. If I do something the law ignores, I'm not. There is a kind of offense that is purely cultural. You can euthanize a dog you don't like, but you can't grill it for dinner. You can keep your children under lock and key, depending on the size of the container: houses are all right, cages are not. It's a mortal sin but not a statutory offense to have sex with your neighbor's wife, as long as you're both stone cold sober, but things get sticky if she's drunk.

This chapter details what happens when the law decides that having sex with a drunken woman is not just a violation of the gentleman's rule, but a crime to be prosecuted to the fullest extent of the law. Whether the victim likes it or not. After all, being tough on crime sometimes means being tough on victims, too.

Case #1: Antoinette Loves Mexicans
In 2003, a young Asian woman I'll call Antoinette was eighteen years old, recently graduated from high school, and living at home with her parents. At trial, her demeanor was subdued, and she portrayed herself (according to trial counsel's motion for new trial) as meek and somewhat inexperienced. But people are sometimes inconsistent. One spring afternoon Antoinette and her boyfriend, "Bobby," went

out, first to the beach, then to a male friend's house, and eventually to a house party in the projects in Carson, a working-class suburb a dozen miles south of downtown Los Angeles. By the time she got to the party, Antoinette had drunk one or two 40-ounce bottles of malt liquor and a can of Budweiser, and kissed someone who was not her boyfriend because, as she later told police, she gets "frisky" when she drinks, and thought the guy was cute. As she told her boyfriend at the time, she was "feeling good."

When they got to the house party, Antoinette started socializing heavily. According to several witnesses, including Bobby, she started hugging different men and letting them kiss her, telling them, "I want to fuck you." According to these same witnesses, Antoinette also said that she wanted to have sex with "all nine Mexicans" at the party. She stumbled and fell down once, a couple of hours after they arrived. Shortly after her fall, a police patrol car drove by, and everyone scattered. Antoinette testified that she ran behind one of the houses with another male friend and two other guys. The friend pushed Antoinette onto the dirt, and raped her in front of the others. Antoinette testified that she didn't hit him or scream because she was too scared. She said she felt groggy, "like I was blacking out." She didn't remember whether she had anything more to drink, or if she spoke to anyone. She did remember seeing a white SUV parked near the houses, but not how she ended up inside the car with a group of guys. She also didn't remember telling the police that she was holding the friend's hand as she got into the car because she was feeling "frisky."

My client, "George," was a man in his thirties, with no criminal record. He was the driver of the SUV; he drove first to a liquor store, and then to a Motel 6. The next thing Antoinette said she remembered was being raped by George. She testified that she was in a motel room with six or seven men, half of them naked. Antoinette said she was "just scared." She didn't know what to do, so she didn't do anything. She didn't cry, didn't tell George to stop, didn't push him away, didn't try to free or excuse herself. After George climbed off Antoinette, another man got on top of her. About six men had sex with Antoinette that night. One of them was George's co-defendant, "Earl."

Antoinette didn't recall seeing Earl before he raped her. While Earl was raping Antoinette, another man poured a cup of water on her vagina for more lubrication. At some point, Antoinette did a line of methamphetamine with George because she was falling asleep during sex. By morning, only George and the two men from the alley were left in the room with Antoinette.[1]

The motel's checkout time was noon, and the group left in George's SUV. Antoinette didn't attempt to run away; she testified that she didn't know why not. The group returned to the housing projects where the party had been held, dropping Antoinette off at someone's house. She didn't ask to go home because she was missing her cell phone, purse, and twenty dollars. She went to another house to try and get her belongings back; at trial, she said a man at that house forced her to orally copulate him in exchange for her property. She later told police that two men raped her at the house, but that when she told one of them to stop, he did. Someone eventually gave her the purse, but her cash and cell phone were not returned. No one threatened her, or told her not to report what had happened. She asked to be taken home, and a neighbor gave her a ride.

Antoinette arrived home around 5:00 p.m. to find her parents anxious and weeping. Ten minutes later, her uncle arrived with a police officer. During those ten minutes, Antoinette didn't tell her parents she'd been assaulted. Antoinette told the cop just that she remembered being at a Motel 6 and "having sex" with some men. Taken to a hospital for a medical examination, she told the sexual assault nurse that she had voluntarily ingested drugs in the ninety-six hours before the exam, and drugs and alcohol between the time of the assault and the time of the exam. She had not changed her clothes. The nurse testified that Antoinette looked clean and "well-groomed."

George and Earl were later arrested and charged with rape.

George's basic defense strategy was to argue that Antoinette was a willing participant in the sex. His most useful witness was a woman named "Heaven" who lived in the project with her boyfriend, whose brother "Angel" was nineteen or twenty years old. Heaven said she saw about forty people at that party, five of them women. One woman, who matched Antoinette's description, was "slap-boxing" or "playing around" with Earl, the co-defendant. A few minutes later, this woman was hanging on Earl "like if she were a baby," her legs around his waist and her arms around his neck. Earl was carrying her; the woman looked happy, as if she'd had a few drinks.

Heaven testified that the next morning, she and her boyfriend's brother Angel were in their garage when the same woman came by with two other men and asked for a place to have sex. Heaven told them they couldn't have sex in her house. As the group walked away, Heaven heard the woman say, "Where are we going to fuck?" Heaven felt disrespected by the woman, who she thought was misbehaving. She testified that she wanted to "whip her ass."

Another neighbor said he saw Antoinette walking with Angel and another couple, and told his wife that it looked like Angel had a girlfriend.

Angel and two other men later pleaded guilty to raping Antoinette.

A teenage girl neighbor testified to seeing Antoinette "acting up," "jumping on top of guys," hugging them, and being too loud. She also jumped atop a white car and started dancing; the teenager said she'd never seen a girl act like that. At some point, the teenager asked the woman if she needed help. The woman said, "No, I'm fine. I just want to get fucked some more by these guys." There were three or four men present. The girl said she later saw the woman having sex with one man, standing up. The girl and Heaven didn't talk about the case, except to say that Antoinette "gives girls a bad name."

Blood, Alcohol, and Bad Behavior

According to the experts who testified at George and Earl's joint trial, a woman of Antoinette's size who ate and drank what she said she ate and drank would have had a blood alcohol level of between 0.19 and 0.21 at midnight. If she drank what her boyfriend, Bobby, said she drank, her blood alcohol level would be between .07 and .08. Either way, all alcohol would have been eliminated from her body by morning.

As noted, Antoinette's blood alcohol level was somewhere between a low of .07 and a high of .21 or .08, depending on whose testimony you believe. The defense pointed out that people can function at .19 and .21. Functioning is related to alcohol tolerance, and tolerance is acquired either through exposure to drinking or as a matter of natural biological ability. Most people in the .19 and .20 range are able to drive a car, though not very safely. If a woman ingested a line of methamphetamine between midnight and 5:00 a.m., she would be in a heightened state of alertness. "Blackouts" are distinguishable from unconsciousness as a phenomenon of short-term memory loss, and an altered recollection of events, rather than a loss of consciousness itself.

Impaired memory would be expected at Antoinette's blood alcohol level, assuming normal tolerance. At a blood alcohol level of .10 and above, some memory impairment might occur, including short-term memory loss or misinterpretation of events. If memory loss occurs, it is permanent. Eighty ounces of beer consumed over a period of time by someone Antoinette's size could cause drowsiness by 11:00 p.m.; someone with a moderate drinking pattern would be judgment-impaired at a 0.20. You wouldn't do something really dangerous, but you might decide to tell your boss what you really think of him.

The Story the Jury Didn't Hear

George was convicted and sentenced to twenty-eight years to life. After the trial, the defense located a number of witnesses who told a much richer story than the one the jury heard, and who subsequently testified at the defense motion for a new trial.

These witnesses included Heaven's boyfriend's brother Angel, who said that he pleaded guilty before George's trial, but that his plea was a mistake. According to Angel, Antoinette and another guy came to his house the day after the party, and Antoinette led the two to a bedroom and invited them to have sex. They accepted the invitation, as did a third man who showed up with some of her things.

Another neighbor said she saw someone matching Antoinette's description at the party, lifting her dress and "letting guys touch her."

When Antoinette hoisted her skirt and started "climbing on top" of some of the men, the neighbor told Antoinette that maybe it was time she left, and offered her a ride home. Antoinette said she didn't need a ride and wanted to stay. The neighbor took Antoinette's arm and tried to walk her away from the men, but Antoinette pulled away and said to leave her alone. Antoinette also said she was "going to do all these guys" because she was "partying." The neighbor took this to mean Antoinette was going to have sex with the men. She thought Antoinette was under the influence, but not drunk or unable to take care of herself: "She seemed to know what she was doing and what she wanted." A little later, Earl came to the neighbor's door and asked her to drive Antoinette home. The neighbor said she'd already offered, but that if he could convince Antoinette to leave, she'd take her home. Neither Earl nor Antoinette returned to the neighbor's house.

Then there was "Leo," who testified that on the night of the party, he heard that there was a "girl party" under way at the Motel 6. About 2:00 a.m., Leo and a friend drove over there, but the friend ditched him at the motel. Leo saw three men lying on the bed and two others walking around. Antoinette, wearing a towel, came out of the bathroom with two guys. She got on the bed, took the towel off, looked at Leo and started touching him. He was kind of excited until another man started kissing her and laying her down. Antoinette didn't seem to be forced to have sex: when men asked her to orally copulate them, she did.

Leo also testified that while having intercourse with one man, Antoinette moaned: "Give it more, harder," "I like it." She sniped at some of the others, saying, "You're a pussy, you can't perform, you can't get it up." Antoinette invited Leo to have sex, but he declined; she touched his chest and upper thigh, asking why he wasn't interested. He said he didn't find her attractive. She asked what was wrong with her, and if he was gay. Leo testified that he didn't feel right. He decided he was shy, he testified, and thought what she was doing was disgusting. Leo said he kind of enjoyed watching at first, because it was "like porno." But by the time *Good Morning, LA* came on the motel television, Leo was bored, going out of the room to smoke and look for his friend.

When no one else wanted to have sex, Antoinette also grew bored, and Leo and she talked. She asked Leo if he thought she was cute, and if he liked her. When Leo said he didn't want to have sex with her, she examined her legs and said, "Look at all these bruises on my legs. What am I going to tell my mom?" Leo suggested she tell her mother she fell down the stairs. When Antoinette responded, "No, that's dumb," Leo told her to make up her own damn excuse.

A female relative of one of the motel employees testified that she walked by the room and saw Antoinette sitting on top of a man with her skirt up, wearing a tube top and no underwear. Other men were grabbing her, "feeling all over her" while she kissed the man beneath and gave him a "lap dance." The witness was also prepared to testify at a new trial that she had seen Antoinette doing the same thing on another date with other guys. This could have impeached Antoinette's credibility, given her portrayal of herself as inexperienced, but the court found the proposed testimony irrelevant on the issue of consent.

The motion for a new trial was denied on grounds that these witnesses' testimony wouldn't have changed the guilty verdict. The Court of Appeal agreed. Because Antoinette was legally drunk, it didn't matter whether she was a willing participant—whether she actually consented—or not. But I think it did, or should. And you'll see why more clearly in the next case.

Case #2: Rough Sex, Lies, and Videotape

"Francisco" and a female friend went barhopping with another friend, "Barbara." Barbara came back to Francisco's apartment, passed out, and he had sex with her while she was more and less unconscious. A few days later, Francisco was arrested and charged with date rape. While investigating the date rape, police searched Francisco's home pursuant to a warrant that authorized the police to seize any videotapes "related to the case." The police took a tape from a video camera in a bedroom. Barbara did not mention seeing a camera, or a tape, and there was nothing in the affidavit that indicated the police thought there might be a videotape related to the case. The second half of the tape showed Francisco having sex with his girlfriend, "Cheryl." The first half, however, showed Francisco having sex with a very drunk woman, later identified as "Zeina." This portion of the tape depicted some slapping and some repeated articulations of "No," along with a few echoes of "Oh, god," and "More." The taped session with Zeina ended in mutual giggling. In addition to the date rape of Barbara, Francisco was charged with raping Zeina.

At the trial, the prosecutor argued that although there were sounds of sexual pleasure throughout the tape, Zeina's display of sexual satisfaction was an involuntary physical reaction, akin to wakening with an erection or having a wet dream. (Zeina did not appear at the trial, or provide a statement to police: the evidence in this portion of the case came solely from the video.)

In his defense, Francisco testified he had dated Zeina a few years back. Though she came from a strict Ethiopian family, she was a "party girl." She liked to show up at his apartment after hours, drunk and eager for sex—aggressive and rough sex, as demonstrated by the tape. After a few months, the two stopped seeing each other, and eventually lost contact.

Francisco's girlfriend, Cheryl, testified that she was the woman on the other half of the tape. Some of the same sort of behavior, including slapping and name-calling, appeared in her segment as well. She and Francisco had an open relationship, and she remembered Zeina, who would periodically show up drunk at Francisco's apartment. Zeina once tried to instigate a ménage à trois, but Cheryl refused.

Francisco was acquitted of the date rape, but convicted of rape of an intoxicated person: Zeina.

After the trial, Francisco's friends were able to locate Zeina, but she refused to get involved. She said that her sexual encounters with Francisco were now in her past, and she was putting the relationship behind her. Francisco's appeal and request for a new trial were denied.

So there you have it: two women, Antoinette and Zeina, one with a demonstrated preference for drunken sex, another with a more ad hoc engagement. One woman wanting nothing to do with her former partner, whether for or against his interests, the other feeling some sort of morning-after regret. Both women were adults, and both were, according to witnesses, willing participants. The law says they were both raped.   ·

The Law on Consent

As noted in chapter 4, every crime is composed of an act (*actus reus*) coupled with a thought (*mens rea*). So taking something (*actus reus*) + the intent to permanently deprive someone of it (*mens rea*) = theft.

There are basically two types of intent: general and specific. General intent is the intent to do the act: if I deliberately punch you, I'm guilty of battery. Specific intent is some intent beyond the intent to merely do the act. If I touch a child with a lewd and lascivious intent, I am guilty of child molestation, even if I only touch her kneecap. But if I diaper a child with no such intent, I've not committed any crime, even though I definitely touched her privates.

Every criminal defense is predicated on the failure or excuse of either act or intent: you either didn't do it, or if you did it, you didn't do it with the requisite intent. Or, you did do it, and with the requisite intent, but some other thing negates or excuses that intent. For example, let's suppose I want to kill you. I sneak into your backyard, see you sunbathing, and shoot you. What I don't know is that an hour earlier you died of heat stroke. So I am not guilty of murder because you couldn't actually be killed when I acted on my cold-blooded intent.

The *actus reus* of rape is sexual intercourse. Rape is a general intent crime with a footnote: the requisite intent is the intent to have *unlawful* sex. Unlawful sex includes nonconsensual sex with an adult and consensual sex with someone who can't legally consent, such as a child or what the law gently calls an "idiot." Unlawful sex refers to a legal category, not to anyone's specific intent to rape. If I intend to have sex with someone who is sixteen years old, and that person agrees to have sex with me, I am guilty of statutory rape in many U.S. jurisdictions. Unlawful sex is statutorily defined as sex without *affirmative ongoing consent*: Any "No" slipped in flagrante delicto must stop the proceedings. Any intervening incapacity turns "I will" to "I won't." If

I change my state of mind during sex, whether by saying so or by falling asleep, my consent is no longer continuous, and my partner had better desist and cease. To be perfectly clear: I withdraw consent by indicating "Stop." But the law says my consent is also revoked if I fall asleep or pass out.

Rape by Intoxication

In California (as in most states and Britain), it is against the law to have sex with someone who is so drunk or drugged out that, according to the standard jury instruction, that person was "prevented from resisting the act by an intoxicating or any controlled substance." The relevant California jury instructions specify that "prevented from resisting" means the victim lacked the legal capacity to give consent. "Legal capacity is the ability to exercise reasonable judgment, that is, to understand and weigh not only the physical nature of the act, but also its moral and probable consequences."[2]

For actual consent to have legal significance, the person consenting must have "sufficient capacity" to consent. Insufficient capacity includes mental incompetence, which can be permanent, such as mental disability, or temporary, such as being a child or being drunk. Intoxication can be voluntary or involuntary. Some states' rape-by-intoxication laws only apply if the defendant himself administered the intoxicant. Easiest scenario: the man puts a date-rape drug in the woman's cosmopolitan. Thornier scenario: the man pours that extra glass of champagne that prompts the candlelit "Yes," especially when the "Yes" is slurred, and the male host equally tanked.

How the intoxicant was administered will dictate whether the victim's intoxication was voluntary or involuntary (e.g., was she *forced* to do the last Jell-O shot?), and whether the subsequent sex was rape.

Like statutory rape, rape-by-intoxication is a legal construct—a fiction that substitutes for fact. There can be consent aplenty, but *actual* (or factual) consent is negated because the intoxicated woman is incapable of giving *legal* consent. Resistance is presumed. This is the legal fiction that had the woman not been intoxicated, she would not have consented, and therefore any consent given while intoxicated is void. Because it doesn't matter whether the woman actually consented, it's also irrelevant whether the man believed she consented, or whether that belief was reasonable (the champagne was flowing, as were our clothes, and happiness reared its ugly head). The only factual question becomes did the man know the woman was too drunk to legally consent?

It's always easy to chop off the most extreme situations—the passed-out partner is too drunk, and the one who had a single glass of cotillion punch not drunk enough. Beyond that, it's anyone's game. Unlike the crime of driving under the influence, there is as yet no blood alcohol level short of unconsciousness at which it could be presumed beyond a reasonable doubt that someone's consent was not the product of reasonable judgment. The British are settling the question based on a statutory presumption of intoxication. Police take a blood or urine sample from the woman, fix her blood alcohol limit at the time of testing, then—as was done with Antoinette—deduce the woman's blood alcohol level at the time of the assault, given a constant burn-off rate for alcohol. If the woman's blood alcohol level during the encounter was above a certain amount, her consent will be legally irrelevant.

Obviously, there is a slew of factual problems in this approach. First, as demonstrated by Antoinette, accurately deducing someone's blood alcohol level depends on that person being tested relatively soon after the encounter. If the woman waits until the next day to report the rape, there will be no current blood alcohol level to extrapolate from. Second, blood alcohol levels provide only a rough guide to real-life inebriation: as the expert in George and Earl's case testified, someone who drinks often and lots will be much more functional at a higher blood alcohol level than someone with less experience with booze. Judgment may be impaired, but it's not gone missing. So instead of trying to prove that the woman was a slut, the defense will try to show that she was a sot—a difference whose distinction may be of little comfort to the woman.

More interesting are the legal issues, as they contain a moral and
ethical morass that makes the factual problems seem like a moonlit
stroll in a good neighborhood. But definitions first, and first is the
definition of *consent*. California law defines consent as "ongoing and
continuous affirmation" to sex. Yes must be "Yes-yes-yes." If any one
yes is followed by no, or "Maybe this isn't such a good idea"—or any
other statement, gesture, or pregnant silence meant to signal a change
of heart—the woman's yes is withdrawn, as he should be. This is significant in rape-by-intoxication cases because a sober yes does not
carry through to a drunken yes. The "Yes-yes-yes" chain of consent is
presumptively cut off by the "no" furnished by her intoxication.

Let's suppose I'm a premeditated-fun sort of gal. This morning,
I'm feeling especially bright-eyed and cogent. I decide that tonight
I'm going to go out and get thoroughly and variously plowed. I now
soberly tell my nearest and dearest of this intention, including identifying my future sex partner (so there's no mistake there). I happily
carry out my plan in the evening, getting drunk and having sex with
said partner. I have still been raped, even though I wanted it all, soup
to nuts. My yes became a no without any alteration by me except for
my blood alcohol level. That's because my subjective intent is legally
overridden by my objective intoxication.

The definition of *legal capacity* is like color on a canvas: its presence defines its absence. The "reasonable judgment" standard seems
to mean that a defendant can only defend by showing that the conduct agreed to was not the product of a lack of rationality. Logically,
the defense will try to show either that the conduct assented to was
objectively reasonable, or that it was the sort of conduct this victim
would consider subjectively reasonable even if she weren't drunk.

Under an objectively reasonable standard, a defendant could theoretically present some sort of sociological evidence, or obscenity-like
community-standard testimony, something to prove that women of a
certain age who frequent certain social circles or come from a specified geography or demographic consider drunken sexual encounters
objectively reasonable. Or that this particular victim, given her peculiar sociopsychological makeup, would consider the alleged acts to
have no adverse moral connotations: she and her kind adore getting

drunk and having sex with a bunch of strangers/a steady boyfriend/ that bit of beef from the motor pool.

Subjectivity, Sociology, and Shields

In her 1794 book on the French Revolution, Mary Wollstonecraft writes, "Every political good carried to the extreme must be productive of evil."[3] Laws passed with good intentions and historic justification may snap together to create a legal terror. You can't argue that "she wanted it," even if she did. Evidence of a woman's subjective makeup is inadmissible: courts can't order psychiatric examinations of sex-offense victims to assess credibility. Expert testimony on the psychological profile of a particular victim—"She's a masochist; she's a sex addict; she just likes a few cold ones to warm up"—is considered too speculative in terms of how this particular victim may or may not have acted in this particular situation. "She may be a masochistic alcoholic suffering from a DSM-diagnosed hypersexuality, but she still said no."[4]

Sociological or group-based evidence suffers from the logical-legal problem that consent, as a manifestation of individual judgment, can't be reasonably inferred from group mores. But which cultural norm is the relevant one? Is the community standard that of civic-minded jurors, fraternity brothers, a neighborhood party girl? Which neighborhood would be significant? Are the cultural mores of South Los Angeles different from those of East Los Angeles? Different from Beverly Hills? Different from Des Moines? What if the woman was from one cultural background, the man from another, and the sex took place in a third environment? Finally, what transcendent body would decide which of these standards were "reasonable" as applied to any given victim, who may or may not be in step with the cultural norm?

In any event, a defendant is also usually precluded from producing proof of the victim's subjectivity, or at least that subjectivity as manifest by her history. Every state has a rape shield law, which bars evidence of a victim's sexual history for purposes of proving actual or legal consent. Consensual sexual conduct on one occasion is deemed irrelevant to prove consent on another. These laws were designed to curb the defense practice of assailing the sexual mores of rape victims as a way of defending against the charge of rape. This mode of defense has been culturally memorialized from *Law & Order* to *The Accused*, and also was manifest in the allegations made in 2006 by the exotic dancer against those nice lacrosse players from Duke—although it seemed the victim could be rightly blamed in the Duke case, given that the accused were fully exonerated. Though it is also a perfectly reasonable defense: if I have like to have sex with strangers, isn't that relevant to a determination of whether I did this with the defendant?

There is both the reality and the cliché of the rape victim revictimized by the trial. Not that long ago, my morning paper carried another story about a rape prosecution in which the head of a victim advocacy group said: "Despite all the laws passed that give victims more rights in criminal cases, in most cases, the person on trial in the courtroom in a rape case is the victim."[5] This is dangerously reductionist, and dangerously foolish. A rape victim is no more on trial than a robbery victim. In every criminal prosecution, it is not the victim, but the state that is on trial—the state chooses to prosecute a person, and the state must be put to its proof. If the rape victim is questioned forcefully about the identity of her assailant, or the accuracy of her description, or whether she might not have been all that drunk, or her sex and drinking habits, it is because the stakes are high. If she's wrong, and she's just identifying this defendant because he is the guy on trial, or because he looks sort of like the guy, and probably is him, or because she is so ashamed of what she did that she'll say anything to shift the focus from her to him, and what's he ever done for her anyway? As much as *The Accused* is an accurate portrayal of a certain kind of callousness in the treatment of rape victims, *To Kill a Mockingbird* documents another social horror: the innocent accused. Or the man who is only culturally guilty. The stakes are the same for both defendants, for at the end of every successful prosecution, it's just the guy in the dock who actually gets locked up.[6]

In any event, the rape shield law is an imperfect proscription. First, some states allow admission of otherwise shielded evidence if necessary to protect the defendant's constitutional rights. The shield is therefore more porous than is generally thought—and I have no problem with that. Second, the shield is predicated on a fairly straightforward sexual assault scenario in which the he-said-she-said is limited to the facts at hand, such as in a date rape. (Though I've had cases where the defendant tried to convince the jury that the woman that he waylaid in an alley or parking garage was game for sex on the spot, evidence of her severe injuries notwithstanding.) Third, a good defense attorney may be able to find some way around the ban, because it's unfair to keep out evidence that's legitimately critical to a fair trial, as the Sixth Amendment recognizes. This works out less often than I believe it should. I understand the arguments for protecting a victim's privacy and saving her from the secondary trauma of a really nasty cross-examination, but still, the fairness of a criminal trial seems more pressing, more fundamental, more infinite a concern than any one prosecution.

The conceptual problem is that rape shield laws preclude proof of any number of acts, which, though frowned upon by the general populace, might be gladly agreed to by the alleged victim in her day-to-day life. In George's case, this could include Antoinette's interest in drunken group sex (which a number of witnesses testified to both at trial and in the unsuccessful attempt to get George a new trial). In Francisco's case, it included defense evidence that his former date Zeina liked being spanked and otherwise physically dominated, liked having drunk sex or rough sex, and didn't mind being videotaped during sex (evidence that was apparently presumed relevant or at least was not objected to at trial).

One appellate court explained rape shield laws by analogizing rape to robbery, saying that just because someone had given someone else money, this doesn't prove the person hadn't been robbed by the defendant. But if someone has the habit of handing out money, then it seems terribly relevant to the issue of whether booty was bestowed, as the defense claims, or taken, as the victim insists. So if a person is in the habit of drunkenly pressing money into other people's hands, and if that person has never complained of being robbed, the conceit that no one in his right mind would be so prodigal is not a legitimate reason for the State to prosecute the recipient of his largesse. Similarly, in Francisco's case, if a woman freely had drunken sex, including somewhat rough drunken sex, and hasn't complained of rape, the State shouldn't lock up her partner for his bad-boy behavior.

At Francisco's trial, the rape shield law acted as an evidentiary sword against the defense, because the government could freely argue that nothing was really known about the victim. With nothing being known about the victim, all sorts of things, including her resistance, could be presumed. (For example, the prosecutor argued that Francisco and Zeina couldn't have had a consensual encounter because no black woman would put up with calling a man "master," as Francisco ordered Zeina to do on tape. The prosecutor overlooked the fact that Zeina was African, not African-American, and that Francisco was Mexican-American, a cultural combination that might not involve the same legacy of oppression. And some people simply like to transgress. But nothing beyond what Francisco testified to could be known about Zeina, not legally, and not to Francisco's jury. The combination of laws creates a bubble of presumptions around the intoxicated woman that can only be pierced by showing that she wasn't all that intoxicated.

In George's case, his own sobriety or lack thereof wasn't relevant to his appreciation of Antoinette's diminished capacity—all he needed to be was sober enough to physically have sex, and she had to be sober enough to intellectually appreciate the "moral and probable consequences" of agreeing to have sex. Demonstrating the anomalous situation in which two people, equally loaded, agree to have sex, and one of the two is legally relieved of the effect of her consent by virtue of her voluntary intoxication, whereas the other is fully responsible for the effect of both parties' agreement.[7] At the risk of sounding ungrateful, there's no feminist purpose served by allowing only one side full agency, even as that agency is temporarily impaired. Sauced goose should also be sauce for the gander—shouldn't it?

Who Is Shielded, and from What?

In *Wardius v. Oregon*, the Supreme Court held that the due process clause of the Fourteenth Amendment incorporates a guarantee of reciprocity. As famously put by Justice Thurgood Marshall, due process speaks "to the balance of forces between the accused and his accuser."[8] This assurance of a level playing field would seem to mean that if a defendant is not permitted to present evidence of his own intoxication or mental disability to negate his wrongful intent to commit a rape (by negating his capacity for wrongful intent), then the State can't introduce this same evidence to negate an adult victim's capacity for legal consent. Unless—and it's a big caveat—different treatment is specifically authorized by statute, and the authorization serves a compelling state purpose.

Rape shield laws serve the compelling state purpose of encouraging rape victims to report and help prosecute their rape without fear that their characters and personal histories will become the subject of a public trial. But rape shield laws that don't allow for admission of significant defense evidence unfairly keep one salient set of facts from the jury while allowing another. Is it important to know that the defendant has a prior date-rape conviction when he is accused of raping a woman he just met? If so, it's also important to know that the victim has a history of having quick sex with men hot off the street.

The rape-by-intoxication instruction given to juries also turns the consent standard from whether the victim was able to appreciate the "the act, its nature, and possible consequences," to whether her appreciation was unreasonable. But unreasonable as measured by what? The mores of twelve jurors? Larger social convention? Is there a community standard that needs to be set for what constitutes a failure of reasonable judgment after a few beers or too much Veuve Clicquot? To decide to pop in on someone you're sort of dating for a round of post-partying sex or choose to do all the guys at the party may be an absolutely unreasonable exercise of judgment, but may also be absolutely appreciated for what it is—in act, nature, and consequence—at the time the decision is made. It seems beyond paternalism for the State to decide that an adult, who could and presumably would complain of violation had violation been had, has, in fact, been had. And it seems beyond comprehension that a videotape of slaps and moans, groans and giggles, could be used to convict a man of rape and sentence him to twenty-eight years in state prison. And yet it was.

The rape-by-intoxication statute says that the woman is "prevented from resisting" because of her intoxication. This language should not by itself be used to vitiate a woman's prior consent, unless the law means to say that every actual yes given over a few too many drinks isn't just a false yes, a yes not to be trusted, but an affirmative resistance to the ensuing sex. So that in the language of old-school feminism, no means no, and yes does too. And, in fact, this is what the law has said. But this is Orwellian stuff, not the stuff criminal convictions ought to be made of.

This brings up a larger topic: what do we want from our criminal laws? What is the point of them, and how do we further that point by the laws we enact, and the cases we choose to prosecute? And if furthering this point is too great an agenda, is there a smaller point that can serve as a kind of legend, so we can understand why certain acts are illegal because everyone historically agrees they should be (like raping the baby) and other acts are illegal because we've decided we should live in a world where such things ought be (like boffing the drunken lady)? And why there are still other acts that we think should be censured, but not criminalized, no matter how achingly annoying (like men telling random women on the street to "Smile!"). This is a great and serious topic, for while we've been talking in some ways about points on pinheads, these points and the perspective they propound are found in everything from our treatment of terrorists and other enemies, foreign and domestic, to the way we address the effects of our history of sitting on the poor and mostly dark heads of those not of the ruling class, and our sporadic commitment to baseline social welfare.

Sex, Videotape, and a Nation of Laws

One of the problems with being a nation of immigrants is that we can shrug off the facts of our national history while wrapping ourselves in the mantle of its rewards. Slavery's got nothing to do with me, says the man whose family crossed over in 1903, yet you can't tell him from his neighbor, the one whose family has been here since the Revolution, and Jim Crow worked long term to the advantage of both. Cotton picked in Georgia warmed the backs of Boston, and white privilege isn't contingent on having had a Pilgrim in the woodpile. It's a big-picture mess, to be certain, far too grand a topic to tackle here, but we can discuss, from a bit of distance, the perspectives that might tether one precept to an apparently faraway other. Our stance on acts like having drunken sex shows how we see ourselves as individuals, and how we are as a nation, and how we might have ourselves really be.

No harm, no foul. Did harm occur in our two cases? Was Antoinette harmed by having sex with "all nine Mexicans," as she wanted? Antoinette may have suffered harm, but was it harm she freely took on? Did Francisco's date suffer from her habits? I don't know, and neither do you. If you think about it, the only one who violated Francisco's date was the State, which played a private sex tape publicly and repeatedly. The focus of that jury's inquiry became not the effect of intoxication on that woman's powers of resistance, but on her powers of judgment. No moral woman would say yes, the argument goes, so this woman could not say yes.

As a rule, we reserve the right to make decisions about our private lives, including our right to make the most potentially disastrous decisions, such as whom to marry and whether to procreate. In tort law, the assumption-of-risk doctrine states that if you voluntarily engage in activities that carry certain risks, you can't sue when the threatened harm comes true. If you go skydiving and your chute fails to open, your heirs are pretty much stuck with the fallout from your choice. Shouldn't the same be true in certain criminal-law situations? Voluntarily engaging in inherently dangerous activity could preclude criminal liability for foreseeable harms. If you're a woman and decide to go to a bar and get drunk and then opt to sample the fresh bit you've just met, he ought not be liable for your rape. This is a delicate proposition, and we could carefully circumscribe the limits of the risk assumed: he should not be liable for your rape unless you withdraw your consent and he does not comply. He should also be liable for any other harm caused by the encounter—things not within the sphere of risk initially contemplated. So if he drunkenly drives you both into a tree beforehand or beats you up afterward, he's guilty and good riddance.

This concept is quite common in aiding-and-abetting law, and the doctrine of liability for "reasonable and foreseeable consequences" of joining in a conspiracy. In short, if I agree to help you rob the liquor store, I am liable if you cap the clerk, as that is the sort of thing that might naturally happen during a stick-up. But I'm not liable for your sophisticated Lotto counterfeiting scam using the tickets you tore from the clerk's hands as templates. The idea is to limit criminal responsibility to those things that the defendant could have, should have, would have seen coming. And to let him off the hook for those unpleasant and untoward surprises.

The legal negation of actual consent does two things, both bad. First, it turns every successful frat party into a crime scene. Second, it completely abrogates female sexual responsibility, and, by extension, female sexuality itself. Despite the quasi-official mores embodied in these laws, there are still different strokes for different folks. One woman's righteous outrage may be another's rocking good time. Absent any real evidence that a woman would not have consented had she not been intoxicated, a man should not be held to have committed the acts with the requisite intent—a knowing lack of consent.

What Are We Guilty Of?

There are real victims. There are women who go to parties and end up under the table and the host with no intention of doing either. The pernicious specter in all this is not the rapist. The real snake is the thesis that women are like children, and like children, must be protected from themselves. Alternatively, women must be protected from man's inherently predatory nature—a nature they cannot resist. As Sylvia Plath wrote in her poem "Daddy": "Every woman adores a Fascist . . ." With these laws, we created a Dr. Doolittle pushmi-pullyu world where a woman's penchant for victimization is assumed as natural as a man's for penetration and predation. Either women are the moral tit, supplying conscience for the culture, or they are the bodies it composts. We don't seem to have a fully human view of sexuality, where bad happens and it's damn good, and good sometimes goes bump in the night. Social conservatives condemn what they see as a liberal "victim culture," but they work overtime to create more crimes, and thereby more cultural victims. Liberals join in, and thus is knit the snuggly cover of nannyism. There's a collusion here, and to what end? We all want to believe the very best of ourselves, and will seize any opportunity to see the reflected us in better moral light. The morning after, previously hallmarked by the normal aches and pains of guilt and recrimination (and the red-eyed vow, "God, I'll *never* do *that* again!") has now become an opportunity to recast oneself as victim, and one's partner as perpetrator.

This is quick commodification of a pre-packaged morality, born of the need to keep intact our innocence despite our wet-thighed experiences to the contrary. Americans fancy that our moral precepts cannot be elided or cut to suit current trends. Like old family photographs, they are supposed to be preserved whole or not at all. But like the antique photo, our moral precepts are more apt to hold an idealized black-and-white image of ourselves rather than the colorful truth. Our insistence on our own purity begins in the intimate and steamrolls out, becoming more common the further it goes from the private to the public sphere. And in our apple-cheeked desire to keep our precepts inviolate and ourselves guilt free worms the deeper lie. We know what we're capable of, and this guilty knowledge lets us sell ourselves the need for constant surveillance of ourselves—via the mall security camera or the roving wiretap—and instantly redress others' transgressions, via greater criminalization, harsher sentences, and the preemptive strike. If we were less guilt ridden, perhaps we'd be more guilt free.

We codify the right to a fair trial in the Constitution because all we have is time. To incarcerate someone is to take away that person's time, just as to kill someone robs that person of their lifespan. We don't diminish murder on the grounds that the victim's life wasn't worth living; killers of gangbangers and Aryan nationals are to be locked away as tightly as killers of sweet-cheeked infants. To allow our government to imprison people—even very bad people—without making sure that the imprisonment is justified, cheapens our own mortality. In his *Critique of Practical Reason*, Kant wrote of "the starry heavens above and the moral law within." And even in this abyss, there are heavens above and humans below, and our Constitution is the sublime horizon.

CHAPTER 8
THE BALLAD OF MAC THE PIMP

> Those in darkness drop from sight.
>
> —BRECHT AND WEILL, "MACK THE KNIFE"

THERE ARE PIMPS and there are ho's. There are rules to the game these players play, and one of the rules is cash at hand and sex on demand. There are rules to the game that prosecutes these players, and one of the rules is that what counts as consent gets to be determined courtside. An expert can testify that pimp–ho sex is nonconsensual by definition, thus turning every sexual transaction into a sex crime. Like Antoinette the partying girl and Zeina the late-night date, those who go pro lose their sexual autonomy—on both sides of the legal divide. For on this point, judge and pimp agree: only the uninebriated and the unpaid are allowed to freely choose to have sex.

The law in every state says if you earn any part of a living by an act of prostitution, you are a pimp. And if you force someone to orally copulate you, you are guilty of forcible oral copulation.

MacD was a pimp in Los Angeles. In 2003, he was arrested and charged with pimping, pandering, and, because he took sex from his prostitutes, forcible oral copulation. He was also charged with kidnapping one of his prostitutes. Though he took his prostitutes' money, he was not charged with robbery.

At trial, the prosecution put on Rickie and Dakota, two of MacD's ho's, as his victims. Their situations were very different. MacD treated Rickie brutally, and she tried hard to get away from him. Dakota, by contrast, endured some abuse but seemed generally happy to stand by her man.

The defense's main witness was a third prostitute named Tee, who testified that Rickie had plenty of opportunities to get away from MacD, and could have easily gone if she'd chosen to. Tee also said that she had never seen MacD mistreat Dakota, whom she called a liar. Finally—and this goes to the heart of the pimp–ho relationship—Tee claimed that a ho is always free to choose: leave or stay, work in a stable or go solo.

The prosecution had a court-appointed expert in prostitution and pimping named Lois Lee testify that MacD used a number of pimping strategies to lure women into "the game," and so dominated the women in his employ to destroy their free will. So in this view, for example, when Dakota orally copulated MacD—which she did often—Lee testified that it couldn't have been consensual because ho's are incapable of genuine consent.

I find Lee's testimony dubious and—given that her expertise is both self-created and self-vetted—self-serving, but her testimony was apparently persuasive enough to the jury, and her expertise has been thoroughly approved by the Court of Appeal. MacD was convicted of a number of counts, and sentenced to seventy-seven years and eight months; he will be eligible for parole after sixty-five years. Having lived by one set of rules, he was jailed by another.

The Rules of the Game

Prostitutes are raped with soul-numbing regularity. Like apples in the street grocer's bin, they're handy and tempting, and even the beat cop has been known to help himself for free.[1] Similarly, we know that pimps are bad men who take advantage of a bad situation: the prostitute hooks up with the pimp for a whole host of historical reasons, both cultural and personal. The pimp can also be psychosocially analyzed with more or less ease. Neither is innocent, both are guilty. The question is what happens legally when worlds of guilt collide.

Three themes run through MacD's case, and pimp cases generally: (1) criminal law is primarily and properly charged with redressing the violation of the rights of those who could not or would not enforce their own; (2) the law serves, properly or improperly, as a general tonic for purely social ills; and (3) the law inevitably embodies stories that are exported to the culture at large, which then feeds them back into the legal system, thereby reinforcing all three themes, plus the prides and prejudices they obligingly animate.[2]

MacD is a pimp. A pimp has ho's. The terms of the pimp–ho agreement include ho loyalty to the pimp, manifested by not skimming money or slacking off, as well as providing sex on demand. Ho's are also not permitted to talk to, or make eye contact with, a black man on the street, because all black men are presumed to be rival pimps. If a ho interacts with any pimp in any way, she has agreed to be his ho. In fact, it's amazingly easy for a ho to hook up with a pimp and sometimes happens almost by accident.

A pimp and his ho's are referred to as a family, with the attendant dysfunction. The pimp is called "Daddy," and sister ho's will compete for his trust and affection. The top ho is called the "bottom bitch." The bottom bitch may be allowed to serve as second in command, especially in training new ho's.

Ho's frequently work "tracks," specific geographic locations well known as hotbeds of street prostitution. Before hitting the track, ho's are taught what constitutes a reasonable price list and how to detect undercover cops.[3] In Los Angeles, a pimp typically drives a ho to a job site (whether a track, private party, or house call), drops her off, and waits for the ho to call him to pick up the money. This reduces the chance a ho will be robbed by another pimp, customer, or unethical cop. Other places are more pedestrian friendly. When tracks get hot (too many cops), a pimp may take his best ho's on the road. From Los Angeles, favorite destinations include San Francisco, Las Vegas, Atlantic City, and Washington DC. Ho's are not allowed to keep any money they earn. They don't need to: pimps buy ho's their clothes and sundries and pay for their room and board at various low-budget motels. Ho's who don't abide by the terms of the pimp/ho agreement are subject to discipline by the pimp. Discipline can include beatings or rapes. Discipline is often done in front of the rest of the family, to impress the lesson of unwavering loyalty. Pimps who rely heavily on discipline to keep their ho's in line are known as "gorilla pimps," and considered somewhat déclassé.

Rickie: Split Lip, Cold Bath

At trial, Rickie testified that she hooked up with MacD while turning tricks for a different pimp at a bus stop. A black woman, she and MacD made eye contact as he drove by in a bright green Caddy. MacD took Rickie to a hotel, where they drank brandy and shared job histories. MacD hit Rickie once at the hotel, slapping her face when she couldn't remember a toast he was trying to teach her. Rickie then orally copulated him at his request. MacD told Rickie that he'd drive her to the Sunset Boulevard track, and that if she "took care of" him, he'd "take care of" her. Rickie began prostituting for MacD, making $100 to $500 a night. Work started between 11:00 p.m. and 1:00 a.m., and continued until she'd made some money, sometimes going until 5:00 a.m. Like MacD, she slept during the day at whatever motel they were staying in. MacD periodically shared Rickie's room, but mostly she was alone. She didn't leave because she didn't feel she needed to, she said. "There wasn't really a problem. I was comfortable, and I felt like I was safe."

At the trial, Rickie testified that a couple of days after she started working for MacD, they went to Oakland because MacD had a court appearance in San Francisco. He showed her the Oakland tracks, then dropped her off at a hotel: she would work, and he'd be back later. She worked for the next three days without seeing MacD. The first night she was raped by a date, who hit her in the face and kept her for three hours before dropping her off on the street. At some point, Rickie called MacD and told him about the rape. MacD said that sort of thing didn't happen in Oakland and was upset that the man had taken Rickie's money.

On day three, MacD returned, and he and Rickie picked up another woman, Tee (who would later testify for the defense). While alone in the car, Rickie found papers in the glove compartment with

MacD's real name. Until then, Rickie had only known him as "Mac-Daddy," or "D the P[imp]." Rickie wrote down MacD's name on a scrap of paper, then tore up the paper; MacD and Tee returned, and MacD found the bits of paper. Rickie said it was a trick's name. MacD closed the car door, and he and Tee stood outside, talking. MacD did not seem upset when he got back in the car, or as they drove back to Tee's apartment.

Once inside, MacD told Tee to put trash bags on the living and dining room carpets. She did, and he took Rickie into the kitchen and began hitting her in the face and stomach, punching her in her nose and opening her lip. For the first time, Rickie wanted to quit MacD. MacD next poured alcohol on Rickie's cuts, put her in a cold bath, pointed a gun at her, and told her to give him three good reasons why he shouldn't kill her. He then took her to the emergency room to be treated for her rape injuries.

Rickie told the E.R. personnel that she'd been raped. She didn't say she was a prostitute, or that she'd been beaten or a gun held to her head. Her nose wasn't broken, and her lip went untreated. She never mentioned MacD. Rickie and MacD returned to Los Angeles the next day, and she went back to work. Why didn't she take the money and run? Because, she testified, "It's like I wanted to leave, but I didn't want to." A week later, knowing that MacD would be back in San Francisco, Rickie moved in with a friend. Another week passed; Rickie stayed hidden.

One day, Rickie and her friend went to a large swap meet. As the two women were loading the friend's trunk, MacD pulled up behind them, blocking their way. MacD told Rickie to get in his car; she agreed, and said she was just going to get her purse. MacD jumped out of his car, pushing the friend out of the way. He slammed Rickie on the hood of his car, denting the hood and hurting her back; he then threw her into his back seat. A pregnant woman was sitting in the front, laughing. A police car came up beside them as they drove out of the lot; MacD told Rickie, "You can yell, but before they get here, you'll be dead." Rickie sat in the back, crying. (As you'll see, Tee told the story very differently at trial.)

MacD asked Rickie why she hadn't phoned. She said she'd been in the hospital and had asked the hospital to call him. He said she should have called after her release. MacD took the pregnant woman to a store, locking Rickie in the car. Rickie could have escaped through the front doors, but figured they'd be back before she could get very far.

Next, they all drove to a Comfort Inn in Hollywood. Once inside the suite, MacD again asked Rickie why she hadn't called, and slapped her. She fell to the floor. MacD told Rickie that she had to get him money because she'd been gone for a week; she agreed, and orally copulated him. At trial, Rickie testified she orally copulated MacD in the past because she wanted to make him happy because he was her friend. During their brief relationship, Rickie orally copulated MacD about ten times. When they had vaginal intercourse, she chose not to use a condom; Rickie had feelings for MacD and thought she could change him.

Rickie testified that she didn't want to orally copulate MacD at the motel. She didn't tell MacD because she "knew how he would react." She testified that she was "frightened in her mind" of MacD, and orally copulated him this time only because he'd hit her. Afterward, MacD took Rickie out for a drink before dropping her off at the Sunset track.

Rickie was soon stopped by the cops; she told them she'd been kidnapped, but they just took her picture (for their "prostitute book," a photo log kept for easy identification) and told her to go home, saying if they saw her again, they'd arrest her. Rickie called MacD and told him she had to leave because the vice squad was "sweating me." He picked her up, and they returned to their suite. The pregnant woman was asleep; MacD woke her up and took her and Rickie back to the track. Rickie worked until 6:30 a.m., then called MacD to be taken home. After she'd showered and rested, Rickie said she wanted to get back to work. It was a lie: she was going to leave. After getting something to eat, MacD took Rickie to a track down by the airport, but there were too many police. Instead, they went to the Figueroa track, in southern downtown Los Angeles. He left her to work while he got his hair braided. She stopped a car and got a ride to her friend's house. The friend called the police.

Rickie was given immunity in exchange for her testimony against MacD, and was glad to get it. At the time of trial, she was on probation for stealing and forging checks, and hadn't complied with the terms of her probation.

Dakota: Junior Year a Broad

As noted, MacD was also charged with crimes against another of his prostitutes, a white woman I'll call Dakota. She testified at trial that she met MacD about three years before trial, when she was nineteen years old and living on her own. Dakota had dropped out of college, had no money, and testified at trial that she "was trying to establish my independence" from her parents, who had been paying for school and treating her "like an overprotected child." She prostituted for a couple of pimps before meeting MacD in Oakland.

When Dakota got into his car, MacD said, "Bitch, my name is MacDaddy," and added: "You've just gotten in a pimp's car, and you've chosen up." Dakota knew what it meant to choose up a pimp, but hadn't intended to do so at that moment; rather, she got in MacD's car "to interview him." Dakota gave MacD her pimp's phone number, and he "called and served" her former pimp, saying Dakota had chosen up with him. To choose up a pimp is to decide to work under a particular pimp. The prostitute must pay the chosen pimp a fee. MacD's fee was normally $300, but Dakota was to pay $500 because she was white. (Rarer, and therefore more valuable, on the street.)

When MacD drove onto the freeway, Dakota started to panic and protest, realizing he was serious; MacD pulled to the shoulder and asked her if she was going to get out. As Dakota opened the door, he grabbed her hair and pulled her back into the car and sped off. He called her a stupid bitch, telling her she'd already chosen up and was behaving "totally out-of-pocket" (disrespectfully). Dakota gave MacD $40, all she had. MacD drove to the small town of Novato, where they got a hotel room. Dakota did not try to leave because she was scared. MacD told her he'd get her things and everything would be all right. He said she would be safe with him, he would take care of her, and, as long as she made money, she could have whatever she wanted.

The next night, MacD took Dakota back to the Oakland track, where she made $200, which she gave to MacD. He had instructed Dakota to keep her head down at work and not to look at black men because "they are all pimps on the street," warning her that looking at another pimp would be going "out-of-pocket" and grounds for discipline. That night, Dakota got into a car with a black man she thought was a client because he offered her $100 for sex. But as they drove off, the man said he was a pimp, and, over the next four hours, robbed and raped Dakota, then put her on the street to work for him.

Dakota called MacD. When he came and picked her up, he was angry that she had no money; he didn't believe she'd been robbed and raped. He took her back to the hotel room, and sent the other women to Denny's, telling them not to return for three hours. MacD locked the door and had Dakota undress as he drank a bottle of Hennessy. He told Dakota to crawl to him, and as she did, he told her that a good bitch would never lie to her pimp and that she was going to be his loyal bitch and obey him and make money for him. MacD slapped Dakota's face, first on the right side, then the left. She began crying; he said, "Real bitches don't cry," and punched her. He punched her whenever he saw a tear, to teach her not to cry. MacD told Dakota to answer, "Yes, Daddy," to everything he said. Then he said, "You're going to be my white slave. Your people have enslaved my people for hundreds of years, and now it's your turn to pay. You're going to be my slave, and you're going to worship me, and you're going to serve me."

When she was first interviewed by the police, Dakota didn't tell them about stripping, or crawling, or that she'd been punched for each tear shed.

After beating Dakota for half an hour, MacD unbuttoned his pants and told Dakota to serve him. He pulled her face to his crotch and forced her to orally copulate him while telling her she was going to be his slave, to obey him, to be a "good white bitch" and make him lots of money. MacD told Dakota to get on the bed on all fours. Dakota said,

"No, please don't, don't do anything to me." When MacD sodomized Dakota, she screamed and jumped; he grabbed her by the hair, pulled her back, and continued raping her for the next three hours until he passed out and the other women returned. Dakota did not try to leave.

A week later, MacD drove his women down to Los Angeles because there were too many police on the Oakland track, Dakota had been arrested, and the Sunset track was a better market for a white blonde. MacD prefatorily coached Dakota on the rules for the Hollywood track: $40 for oral sex, $60 to $100 for intercourse, nothing less than $40. Because Dakota was white, she could charge what she wanted. MacD gave Dakota condoms and told her to use them; a condom was worth $40, one condom per service. If the client wanted to go longer or use another condom, Dakota was to charge more. (Pimps track the number of paying customers by the number of used condoms.) He also gave her a phone to let him know when to pick up the money. Dakota made between $300 to $900 a night on Sunset. MacD bought her clothes, but did not give her money. Dakota wasn't allowed to wear stilettos until she proved herself a real ho; her work clothes were "short outfits, flashy outfits," paid for by MacD, though, she later testified, "a lot of them were hand-me-downs from girls who would leave."

A few days after arriving in Hollywood, MacD told Dakota to "give your pimp some balls"; she went over to him, and he grabbed her hair and forced her head down on his penis, so it went "really far down" her throat. When Dakota tried to come up for air, MacD would push her back down, using both hands, telling her to continue. He ejaculated, saying, "Bitch, you better swallow that," and she did. Dakota said she didn't want to orally copulate MacD, but knew it would be out-of-pocket not to serve, and she did not want to be beaten and raped again.

Not long after that, Dakota was robbed by a trick. When she told MacD what happened, he became angry, punching and slapping her while saying that she should "rather die" than give up his money. The next night, two men in a truck tried to steal Dakota's purse. She fought back, was hit by the truck, and hospitalized for three days with a broken pelvis. Two weeks later, she was back to work.

On Halloween, MacD took Dakota and Tanya, another white ho, to a carnival, returning to the motel around 1:00 a.m. MacD unbuttoned his pants and told the women to undress. He told Dakota to get on the bed, telling Tanya, "This is how you give your pimp head. This is the right way to give your pimp some head." He grabbed Dakota and forced her head onto his penis and his penis down her throat. Dakota was gagging. MacD ejaculated, Dakota swallowed the ejaculate. She and Tanya had consensual sex, then Dakota fell asleep on the floor and MacD and Tanya fell asleep on the bed. At some point, Dakota woke, and got back on the bed; MacD grabbed her head again and pulled it onto his penis, she orally copulated him again and he went back to sleep.

The Good Loyal White Bitch

At trial, Dakota testified that she orally copulated MacD because she "knew the consequence of not pleasing him, [that] saying no to him wasn't an option, ever." Dakota said "it was a constant brainwash," as MacD alternated between being nice and mean, fun and abusive. Sometimes she wanted to be with him because she "became so lost in it, in him." MacD told Dakota he was the only one who cared about her, the only one who knew what was best for her and would take care of her. According to Dakota, "He was my world. He was my daddy." She believed he would give her the world. She was meant to be with him, she said, to be his "good loyal white bitch, I was a good bitch."

In contrast to his treatment of Rickie, MacD regularly let Dakota leave. When Dakota's mother had cancer, MacD dropped Dakota off so another friend could take her home. During her visit, Dakota told her parents that she had a pimp and "life was perfect and life was good and that he never beat me and that, you know, everything was fun and I was making lots of money, I was wearing nice clothes, and it was all good." Dakota testified she stayed at her parents' home for five months before returning to MacD. Her father even drove her back.

Once, MacD, Dakota, Tee, Tanya, and two other prostitutes drove to Washington DC with MacD's pimp friend, Preacher, and Preacher's ho, Peaches. Everyone shared the driving, alternating who sat in which brightly colored Cadillac. Sometimes the women drove one car and the pimps another. The women turned tricks in Arizona and Texas. In DC, MacD bought Dakota the stilettos he'd promised, but she got tired of his abuse and the East Coast snow and decided to leave. She confided in Tee, and the two decided to go together. Dakota's mother made flight arrangements for Dakota, who had saved $1,300 from her earnings. Dakota asked MacD if she could visit her sick mother, and MacD said she could, but when he found the money hidden in her vibrator, he said, "You know you're not going home, right?" Dakota answered, "Yes, Daddy." MacD then beat Dakota, and she stayed put thereafter. "Ho or die" was MacD's motto, and Dakota believed he meant it.

After Dakota was rearrested for prostitution, some detectives talked to her about testifying against MacD. At his trial, Dakota testified she wasn't promised anything in exchange for her testimony: it was just "the right thing to do." She said she decided to "stand up to" MacD after seeing fifteen-year-old prostitutes at the Children of the Night shelter in Hollywood. Jail was "the worse thing I've gone through in my life," she testified. "The sandwiches are horrible. The eggs taste like—you don't even want to know. I had everybody—like girls trying to take advantage of me—other women. I had to stand in line and be on somebody else's time, which was the guard. It was horrible."

Dakota explained that she decided to become a prostitute because "instead of working for $8 an hour at Starbucks, I could work for $300 an hour . . . providing a service." She was aware of the risks of disease, she knew the risk of being raped and robbed, knew she had to give all her money to her pimp, knew she had to please her pimp to move up in the world of prostitution. Dakota once told Tee she'd do "anything" to get closer to MacD.

The Defense: It's All in the Game

In defending MacD on the kidnapping charge, the defense's task was to show that Rickie and the other women had plenty of opportunities to run away, and that they chose to stay with MacD of their own free will, just as they chose to have sex with him.

The defense's principal witness was the woman named Tee. Tee has been a prostitute since she was sixteen, and has been arrested on the West Coast and in Washington DC. At the time of trial, Tee was twenty-four, working as a prostitute/stripper in San Francisco. Tee met MacD when she gave him a lap dance. After a couple of weeks, they began dating. Tee knew MacD as Genius; MacD did not prostitute Tee, though she did not have a pimp at the time. A month or so later, Tee came to Los Angeles with MacD in his Cadillac. Tee knew Rickie, and considered her a friend. They worked the streets together for about three weeks.

Directly contradicting Rickie's testimony about the swap meet, Tee said that MacD told Rickie to get in his car so he could get his things from her; she'd taken a CD player and some tapes. He opened the back door and went to the driver's side. Rickie walked around the car, got her purse from her friend, and got into MacD's back seat. MacD didn't slam Rickie against the car, hit her, or throw her into his car. Tee also testified that Rickie had several chances to run away that day, but didn't.

From the swap meet, for example, the three of them drove to Fashion 4 Less a couple of blocks down the street; everyone got out of the car, and Tee went into the store while MacD and Rickie stood outside, smoking. MacD then followed Tee into the store as Rickie stayed outside to finish her cigarette. Tee didn't see Rickie for fifteen to twenty minutes while she and MacD shopped. When they returned to the car, Rickie was sitting in the back seat.

Tee knew Dakota as "Ice." Dakota was already with MacD when Tee met him; she never saw MacD beat Dakota, and never saw Dakota bruised. When they were all in DC, MacD did get mad at Dakota: while she was packing to go to her parents' for Christmas, he began playing with her dildo, the dildo opened, and some money fell out. Dakota said she was taking money home, and not to get mad because "ho's steal money from the pimps." Tee knew Dakota was stashing cash because she'd seen her hiding it in pockets, shoes, and under the mattress. Hurt and angry, MacD said he'd planned to give Dakota $1,500 to get her parents "some stuff, some kids some stuff," then slammed out of the room. Tee went to buy a soda. When she returned, Dakota was crying on the bed, saying she did not want to make MacD mad. The room wasn't disheveled. MacD did not return for the next two days; when he did, he asked how they could treat him like this after all he'd done and all he'd bought for them.

Dakota would tell Tee that she made $1,300 in an evening when Tee would see her count out $800. She once told Tee that MacD had beaten her on a day when the two women had been together all day, and no beating had occurred. Tee testified that when she confronted Dakota, Dakota changed her story, saying MacD had only gotten angry at her, and that Dakota really just wanted to "suck his dick." Dakota told Tee, "I want to suck his dick so bad. I know, when I get the chance to finally suck his dick, it's going to be so great." Dakota and Tee drove back from Washington DC with MacD; the women drove the entire trip, and Tee never saw any welts or bruises on Dakota. Dakota never told Tee that MacD beat her in DC or that he took her money.

Tee testified that when you decide to become a prostitute, you take a chance of being raped, robbed, kidnapped, and/or killed. When you work for a pimp, your money becomes his money. A gorilla pimp will beat you for stealing fifty cents. Pimps will tell you what they think you want to hear to get you to stay; if you're smart, you know that "a pimp never loves a ho, never, and if he tells you he loves you, it's not true." A pimp's bottom bitch is the one who is first, who's been there the longest, who will stay no matter what. Tee has had seven pimps, including pimps who beat her. Those pimps did not start out using violence: a few months into the relationship, one pimp slapped her, then apologized, then beat her with a muffler a week later. She left him. If any pimp beat her, she would quit him, either getting another pimp or becoming a "renegade," pimpless, which she still is. According to Tee, whoring is "by choice, not by force. If I want to leave, I can leave. I don't have to stay." Leaving a pimp is not a sign of disrespect, but of unhappiness. Says Tee: "A pimp is never there to get in the car with you when you're doing a trick. He's not there to hold your trick's dick. He's not there while you're having sex with a trick. If you want to leave or whatever, leave."

Who Gets to Be an Expert?

As noted, MacD's conviction was driven in large part by the testimony of Lois Lee, court-appointed prostitution and pimping expert. At trial, the defense attacked Lee's credentials and objected to the admission of her testimony, but to no avail. The prosecution was able to get her qualified as an "expert," a title that carries substantial weight with most juries.

So who gets to be an expert, and how do courts treat their expertise?

In California, expert testimony is admissible only if the subject matter the expert is testifying to is, as the Evidence Code puts it, "sufficiently beyond common experience that the opinion of an expert would assist the trier of fact." Experts may testify to an opinion based on information, either personally perceived or made known to them, regardless of admissibility, that reasonably may be relied upon by an expert in forming an opinion on the subject of the testimony. Experts can rely on things like hearsay,[4] because the evidence they are supposed to present to the jury is their opinion—and that opinion may be based on whatever forms and informs it: studies in the field, news articles, experiments conducted by the expert, or information given the expert about the case at trial, which the expert may assume is true for purposes of generating an opinion.[5]

Like all things legal, this general rule of admissibility comes with a big fat caveat. A trial court must exclude from an expert's testimony any hearsay whose irrelevance, unreliability, or potential prejudice outweighs its probative value. The stuff the expert's testimony is made of must be in itself reliable, at least for purposes of giving a reliable opinion. As the California Supreme Court says, "Like a house built on sand, the expert's opinion is no better than the facts on which it is based."[6]

At MacD's trial, the prosecution used Lois Lee to testify that MacD had such a degree of control over his ho's that they were legally incapable of consenting to his demands, most notably for sex on demand.

Lee is the president of Children of the Night, a nonprofit child prostitute rescue organization based in Hollywood that she founded in 1979. Lee has a Ph.D. in sociology and anthropology; her unpublished dissertation, written in the early 1970s, is entitled "A Pimp and His Game," and identifies twenty-two strategies used by pimps to recruit and keep prostitutes. These same strategies were chronicled by Malcolm X and Iceberg Slim,[7] whom Lee calls "famous pimps in the 1930s through 1950s."

Lee testified that the techniques she describes are not all followed by all pimps: some pimps may only use a few of the gambits, though they are all "tried and true," and not much has changed since the early 1970s. These strategies also appear in movies and rap music, and on television. Some pimps use other pimps to inflict physical violence, some do it themselves; pimp violence has increased through the years, leading to the emergence of the "gorilla pimp." Pimp violence includes putting a prostitute on "punishment row," a track where there are a lot of beatings/rapes; forcibly sodomizing or raping a prostitute; making the prostitute perform oral sex on a circle of pimps; burning a woman between the legs with a curling iron or beating her with a coat hanger and putting alcohol on the wounds; and/or verbal abuse. The smooth-talking pimp will probably resort to violence from time to time, but will avoid hitting his ho in the face. Damaged goods.

According to Lee, a pimp will recruit a prostitute by first giving her "a quiz," asking her who she is, why she doesn't have nice shoes, where's her daddy. He finds out what she cares about most and uses that information to put himself in the "daddy role," fostering the woman's dependence by playing equally to her fears and needs. A set of social barriers is constructed, proscribing contact with those outside the prostitution world and other pimps. The woman can talk to other prostitutes, but never about her pimp. The pimp presents himself as omnipotent and omniscient, telling the woman that she is always being watched, and that even the police are on his payroll.

There are two types of recruits, said Lee: a "new turnout," someone who has never worked as a prostitute, who is recruited via wining and dining, and a working girl, who pays a "choosing fee," paying the new pimp in exchange for better security or other benefits. Prostitutes are sold between pimps or traded to a more sophisticated pimp. Pimps protect prostitutes from other pimps, not from police.

A pimp tries to keep an even number of women in his stable so they can work in teams. Opposite types are paired to ensure competition within the team and between teams. The women refer to one another as "stable sisters" or "sisters-in-law." A "bottom bitch," the pimp's main prostitute, may be allowed to drive, to handle money, or wear special clothes. Other women will vie for her spot, sometimes by accusing another of holding back money to prove fealty to the pimp, sometimes by orally copulating the pimp better or more often than the bottom bitch. Oral copulation is "part of the ritual" of pleasing the pimp.

Lee testified that MacD's use of the twenty-two "tried and true" pimping strategies not only lured Rickie and Dakota into his lair of degradation, but overbore their free will on all matters at all times. She claimed that the women couldn't consent to have sex with MacD because their consent was false, the product of a sort of temporary mental disability induced by the pimp by way of his professional techniques. More specifically, Lee essentially testified that Rickie did not, contrary to what she told MacD, agree to go back to the hotel with him, and Rickie and Dakota did not, contrary to their testimony, consent to sex with MacD because they were incapable of legal consent.

Rape Trauma and Related Syndromes

Though I take particular pains to dissect Lee's pimping expertise and pick apart her pimping theories, I am doing so purely in the context of her in-court testimony as an expert on pimping. I have no opinion as to Lee's credentials in any other arena, and her therapeutic work through Children of the Night can only be commended.

In her profile on the Children of the Night Web site, Lee states she "abandoned a promising career as a scholar and social policy expert" to devote herself to "rescuing America's children from the ravages of street prostitution." She describes her "single-minded" efforts to help child prostitutes by creating the children's drop-in center in Hollywood, the Children of the Night home; her other work as an instructor at the Los Angeles Police Academy, "training juvenile detectives [sic] in how to detect, treat, and rescue" child prostitutes; and her frequent service as "an expert witness for federal and state prosecutors enforcing laws against dangerous pimps." She writes that her unpublished dissertation is "relied upon by vice officers, district attorneys, and U.S. attorneys nationwide as a guide for their treatment of child prostitutes, for jury education, and for the prosecution of dangerous pimps."[8]

In MacD's case, Lee provided an expert opinion as to why Rickie and Dakota stayed with (and had sex with) MacD, despite his abuse. In giving her opinion, she analogized her theory of "pimping strategies" to battered wife syndrome (BWS), a clinical phenomenon in which women who are beaten by their partners remain with those partners until they kill them.[9] The first clinical syndrome used as a legal precept, at least under California law, was rape trauma syndrome. Rape trauma syndrome is an umbrella terminology used to refer to the various reactions a woman might experience after being raped, including denial, failure to report, self-blame, and/or destruction of evidence (showering, getting rid of clothes worn during the rape).

Originally documented in a 1974 *American Journal of Psychiatry* article,[10] rape trauma syndrome has been extensively documented in the relevant scientific literature over the past decades, and is recognized as a significant therapeutic tool for working with rape victims. However, expert evidence that a woman was suffering from rape trauma syndrome is not admissible to prove that a rape occurred. In *People v. Bledsoe*, the court wrote that rape trauma syndrome "was not devised to determine the 'truth' or 'accuracy' of a particular past event—i.e., whether, in fact, a rape in the legal sense occurred."[11]

Rape trauma syndrome is enormously useful in clinical therapy and victim advocacy because it helps a woman articulate her rape—the sex she experienced as nonconsensual. Rape trauma syndrome wasn't meant to, nor can it, "diagnose" whether a rape "really" occurred—"really" as recognized by the laws of the State of California, not "really" as in real life, as experienced by a real person. Because if a woman believes she was raped, she was.

The California Supreme Court compared rape trauma syndrome to battered child syndrome, which was composed of a very narrow set of criteria (certain types of injuries, for example) intended as a diagnostic tool to facilitate identification of potential child abuse.

Rape trauma syndrome evidence is admissible to explain facets of victim behavior—such as to rebut a suggestion that the woman's post-rape conduct was inconsistent with having been raped, or to dispel popular myths about rape. But there are no legitimate grounds for admission when the evidence is offered purely to corroborate the victim's allegation of rape—such as when the victim's post-incident trauma was entirely consistent with having been raped. If a crying woman calls the police and says she's been raped, there's no need for an expert to say that, in fact, many rape victims do call the police crying when they've been raped, and therefore, this woman's behavior is consistent with that of a rape victim. Lay jurors are as competent to judge the credibility of post-attack distress as experts. Under these conditions, the court in *Bledsoe* wrote that using the term "rape trauma syndrome" is "likely to mislead the jury into inferring that such a classification reflects a scientific judgment that the witness was, in fact, raped."[12] On the other hand, if a woman recants her rape accusation, evidence of rape trauma syndrome might be admissible that rape victims frequently disavow their allegations, particularly when the rapist is a husband or boyfriend.

Rape trauma evidence must be treated circumspectly in part because rape is a specific intent crime: as we know, a man's good-faith but mistaken belief in the woman's consent *legally* negates the rape. A woman who has equal good-faith belief that she did not consent would suffer the same *clinical* trauma as the victim of a legally cognizable rape. She may not have been raped in the eyes of the law, but that won't make any difference to her feeling of violation.

Similarly, Child Sexual Abuse Accommodation Syndrome (CSAAS) is a discrete set of post-trauma victim behaviors offered to explain why child victims don't disclose, or engage in delayed or partial disclosure of, their abuse. Like rape trauma syndrome, CSAAS was first developed as a therapeutic tool, and is predicated on the clinical assumption that the child was in fact molested. CSAAS testimony is also only admissible to refute a specific myth or misconception suggested by other evidence in the case. For example, children tend to reveal sexual abuse in stages, first divulging lesser contact, such as fondling, then later disclosing greater abuse, such as sodomy. Because adults tend to tell all or nothing, the child witness may appear to be embellishing, or lying, absent CSAAS testimony. However, if there is no myth/misconception at hand, the state's use of CSAAS improperly fashions a scientific lens through which a jury is invited to view the case.

There are thus two constants for proper consideration of a syndrome. First, its validity must rest on its scientific status. In each of the above illustrations, the attesting experts and reviewing courts cited a myriad of published sources documenting the existence or effect of each syndrome. Second, it must go against something we think we know. Experts testify about that which lies beyond the common ken; experts who testify about these syndromes testify about that which we think we know, but are mistaken. I know that I don't know how DNA amplification might affect the accuracy of a mixed-source-sample test. I don't know that I don't know that children who are raped tend not to tell simply because they are told not to, and that the ones raped most often are often the least likely to tell.

Expertise from a Bleacher Seat

Lee hasn't interviewed any modern-day pimps directly, she says, but has "seen their literature and their interviews on television." Her dissertation is used by shelter counselors to help children identify strategies used on them "in order to get them to be prostitutes and keep them in that role." Though not all pimps use all strategies, she says the strategies hold—"You can see it in the music and culture and the movies and the documentaries, the newspaper articles."

Look closely. Lee's testimony was legally irrelevant on any and all questions as a subject of expert opinion. There is no "Prostitute Syndrome" available or necessary to explain why an *adult* prostitute would not leave her pimp, and the pimping strategies Lee attested to—unlike CSAAS, BWS or RTS evidence—didn't tell anybody anything he or she didn't already know, and from the same source—the mass media. In *Kumho Tire*, the Supreme Court said: "[I]t will at times be useful to ask even of a witness whose expertise is based purely on experience, say, a perfume tester able to distinguish among 140 odors at a sniff, whether his preparation is of a kind that others in the field would recognize as acceptable."[13]

Under this standard, Lee's expertise stinks. There was plenty of lay evidence in MacD's case attesting to the pimp/prostitute relationship between him and his victims, and the terms of that relationship are easily understood. In a BET and MTV universe, where pimp rappers are Solid Gold, and major movie studios make *Hustle & Flow*, there's no privy we're not privy to.

Lee's "strategies," for all their *Playboy* documentation, are nothing more rigorous than, as Flannery O'Connor's neighbor once said, "how some folks *would* do." Lee's expert testimony—that pimps may sweet-talk a girl, or take her to dinner, or buy her clothes, or find out what she really likes, or threaten her with violence if she doesn't come across—simply iterates a spectrum of standard dating techniques, from the very good to the very bad, without adding anything by way of scientific research or third-party studies to support her conclusions. If a pimp beats a ho into submission, or physically forces her to have sex, then the pimp has raped the ho, and there is no need for an expert to explain this. However, absent an overt causal link between sex and violence, and given the sex-on-demand nature of the pimp–ho relationship, it is overreaching to posit all pimp–ho sex as nonconsensual. For all her laudable shelter work, Lee's expertise is a cottage industry, her testimony not the stuff of proper expertise, but an attempt to alchemize the anecdotal and inadmissible into proof of the truth.

Because the fact is that Lee is right: pimp culture is now firmly part of popular culture, as evidenced by the aforementioned mainstream movie and rapping examples plus the steady popularity of, inter alia, Ice-T, 1990s pimp promoter, then rap and now TV star; 50 Cent, former pimp turned reigning rap and movie star; old school rapper-Daddy revamper Snoop Dogg's haute pimp couture; television shows such as *Pimp My Ride,* and the advent of "pimp chic," street fashion that celebrated the "pimp & ho" look sported by celebs such as Andre 3000, Beyoncé, and Britney Spears. Pimps were elegantly documented in *American Pimp,* the Hughes brothers' 2000 film featuring interviews with all the players, detailing the game, as well as a consideration of pimp-as-historic-entrepreneur in the urban African-American community. The film included interviews with the legendary Iceberg Slim (Lee's source text) and Los Angeles's own Don Magic Juan, the pimp-turned-preacher I see picking up mail at our mutual post office.

Lee's testimony was also based on hearsay of the impermissible, unreliable variety—street-side statements of pimps and ho's, who may be bragging, or need three hots and a cot, or just want some sympathy, or maybe real therapy, or may simply be saying what they're saying because that's what the nice white lady wants them to say. If it is stating the obvious that people on the street lie, and if the veracity of prostitutes and pimps can be impeached by virtue of their vice,[14] then there is nothing but silt beneath Lee's expertise. It may be a perfectly reasonable basis for building a shelter and lending a hand, but it's got no place in criminal court.

The truth is, Lee's pimping strategies are CliffsNotes to better representations of pimping by pimps. Unlike Battered Women's Syndrome, Child Sexual Abuse Accommodation Syndrome, and rape trauma syndrome evidence, there are no confirming studies, no peer-reviewed journal articles—nothing to externally verify this self-acknowledged crusader's conclusions. Still, the world abounds with talking heads, and jurors should be able to ferret out the fallacious from the factual. But often they do not. Maybe it's the atmosphere of the courtroom, where everything sounds more settled, and

opinions lie heavy as litigants' hearts. Jurors are open-minded enough
not to pre-pick a side, at least not overtly, and close-minded enough
not to imagine that outright rejection of the system is an option. Jurors believe. They believe that the state is wholly represented by the
nice young woman in the neat navy suit, and that those resources
are matched by the young man in brown shoes sitting next to the
defendant. They believe, more frequently than you might suspect,
that police officers have no particular axe to grind and defendants'
neighborhoods are something like their own. They believe drug deal-
ers, upon seeing the police, immediately reach into their pockets and
throw their dope at the cops, just like the pink-eared officer testified.
They believe someone might actually buy a car that has to be started
with a screwdriver in the ignition, and someone else dissected his son
without premeditation. They believe DNA is a "test" rather than a
statistical conclusion, think paraphilia a diagnosis, and think there's
a Twenty-Two Point Plan for Pimping, which is as ludicrous on its
face as a three-point robbery rubric, where the first thing pointed is
the gun. Even if every robbery involves some version of "Hand it over,
bitch," that doesn't turn thuggery into choreography. But it is this
patina of authority that jurors grant expert testimony, even when that
expertise proves so much hot air. And why shouldn't they? The court
has admitted the testimony as "expert." A rose is, after all, a rose.

The Old Dominion Theory

More theoretically, Lee's take on the pimp and ho relationship is what
is called on the ivy-halled streets as "domination theory." This form of
feminism holds as its main tenet that women acting within a patriar-
chy have no free choice, so that voluntary sex workers are simply victims of false consciousness, the (unconscious) internalization by the
oppressed of the oppressor's ideology. Women who voluntarily engage
in prostitution have been involuntarily recruited by daily patriarchal
practices and institutional ideology: a woman whores because it's a
man's world.

The concept of false consciousness may be critiqued as suffering from the same authoritarianism as the dominant ideology it critiques: the only thing slightly less brute than the boot of the master is the savior's sandal. In the prostitution debate, domination theory is opposed by an alternative sociological construction that acknowledges the existence of a sex workers' rights movement. It maintains that not all sex work is forced or coerced, that many sex workers freely choose the occupation, and that it is a violation of civil rights not to be allowed to do sex work if one so chooses. Advocates agree with MacD's friend Tee that "because pimps respect free enterprise and competition, women are free to 'choose up' whenever they are dissatisfied with their current pimp . . . [I]t is in the pimp's best interest to keep his women happy."[15] Of course, the truth lies on both sides.

By and large, prostitution is a crap job, usually undertaken out of some degree of desperation (Rickie), *nostalgie de la boue* (Dakota), or the need for fast cash (Tee). I find the phenomenon of Ivy League coeds who dabble in sex work as Street Cred 101 to be another form of reactionary radicalism. This particular brand of idiocy compels would-be revolutionaries to behave entirely as the dominant ideology would have them behave, because they are busy reacting against a minority opinion that they mistake for the majority. I also know prostitution may be the best choice a woman might make for herself in a world of lousy choices: that, as Dakota noted, sucking it up can give a woman more economic freedom than serving it up. And in this, Lois Lee's testimony doesn't stack up.

Under Lee's tautology, pimps strategically override the will of prostitutes. MacD is a pimp; therefore, MacD overrode the will of Rickie and Dakota. MacD is guilty of kidnapping and forcible oral copulation because, like the intoxicated rape victim, his ho's cannot *legally* consent to sex with him because their ability to consent has been rendered moot by the inherently coercive pimp/ho relationship. Even though the ho may have consented to the relationship in the first instance, knowing the relationship involved sex on demand, and even though a ho might affirmatively want to have sex with the pimp—whether because she is staying in-pocket, or in love—these are the product of false consciousness. No free will, no voluntary consent, and thus, rape.

As a legal matter, there is a big difference between the role of the therapist and the role of the jury. A jury must determine what the defendant thought relative to the woman's consent relative to the actual event. It doesn't decide how the victim's *conscious* or *apparent* consent is belied by her *paradigmatic* oppression. Unlike the intoxicated rape victim, the ho is able to signal the withdrawal of her consent. Unlike the intoxicated rape victim whose consent is tendered only under the influence, but like the intoxicated rape victim whose consent predates the influence she's subsequently under, the ho steps into a sexual situation in which her consent should be counted for what it's worth—the act of a grown-up. Ill-advised, perhaps, but as presumptively legitimate a choice as many decisions that look darker in the bright light of the morning after. Women are adults. We don't need more professionals to create more ways in which women are absolved in advance or retrospect of the moral and legal effect of their actions. Ho's can be victims, true. They can also perpetrate. It is too naive to assume that a prostitute would not use her status as potential state witness to leverage some advantage for herself, or some revenge against her pimp.

In the prosecutor's closing argument in MacD's trial, the State summed up both its expert and its error: "[W]hen the defendant met each of these women, he did overcome their will. Each act of force or violence or threat that he made to them was an act in furtherance of the game. It was an act in furtherance of overcoming their will. Each act, whether it was violence, by physical force or words." But the harsher fact is that each act could equally be another move by another Player in the Game—that testifying for the government is a way to get a ticket out of town, shake off your own beef or probation violation, or ditch the gorilla pimp. Although there may be a visceral difference between the contractual bout of oral sex given by a prostitute to her pimp and the hair-pulling sodomy described by Dakota, I'm not sure that difference is recognized in the Game. And if you are going to play the Game, you play by its rules.

In this sense, the big winner in MacD's case was Dakota. Rickie got a one-way ticket out of town, the prosecution equivalent of a hearty handshake. But Dakota got to reinvent herself and her story, going from rebel girl sex worker to rejuvenated rape victim, getting, in the process, a fair amount of help and immeasurable sympathy. Rickie went to the police. The police came to Dakota. It's too easy, but also true, that the white girl was treated that much better as having fallen that much farther than the black girl, who, after all, came saddled with a ho's past and no future. But Dakota rose, purified by the ordeal into pure victim. By pure, I mean both absolute and born-again virginal: the criminal process washed away not only the social sin of paid sex, but the (maybe greater) sin of a broken contract. What was a cold and unenviable business arrangement became, by lore of pimp and whore, revised into the story of a brainwashing, a softer, stickier saga of male dominance and female passivity. What ho?

CHAPTER 9
FEMMES AND FEMINISMS

ESCALUS: How would you live, Pompey? By being a bawd? What
do you think of the trade, Pompey? Is it a lawful trade?
POMPEY: If the law would allow it, sir.

Measure for Measure 2.1

A S AMERICANS, we have a bad tendency to always ask how we can
fix every sticky situation. That's an approach I don't always agree
with. In the chapter on offender registration, for example, I was care-
ful not to take sides. But let's say we want to think prescriptively about
prostitution. If so, it may help to take a longer view. To balance what
happened with MacD and his ho's in Los Angeles, let's step back and
look at some different models of prostitution and the different ways it
has been perceived in the Western Anglo cultural context. We will
also consider the role of feminism and social reform in addressing
the issue of sex for sale. And in all this, let's bear in mind how social
reform in general, and feminisim in particular, have shaped contemporary rape laws and rape culture—and, by extension, our current
cultural concepts of guilt itself.

Feminism and prostitution, those twin administrations of women's
bodies, each claiming province of their hearts and minds, have been
conjoined since the Victorian era. The early and middle Victorian
ages were notoriously tolerant of prostitution. Visitors to London were
confounded by the sheer number of working girls, from half-dressed
street whores in the alleys to the "pretty horse-breakers" in Hyde Park
(so-called because of their fine horses and carriages). One girl in sixteen became a whore, and sixteen was about the average age of initiation. In 1793, London's population was 750,000, of whom about

50,000 were prostitutes. Though William Blake warned "The Harlot's cry from Street to Street Shall weave Old England's winding Sheet," that warning was prefaced with the admission that "The Whore and Gambler, by the State Licenc'd, build that Nation's Fate."[1]

The cause of the Fall was pinned on the fallen themselves, for sin was the simple source of sexual depravity, the shared sin of the human condition. Or, more precisely, shared sin as it translated to women naturally tempting men who then naturally tempted women to sin. (Well put in that anonymous bit of coupleted wit: "Hogamus, higamus, men are polygamous. / Higamus hogamus, women, monogamous.") A conceit that fueled the Victorian image of the soiled dove as much as it fuels today's image of sex worker as service worker among service workers—as pervasive a product of human nature as a quarter-pounder with cheese.

Before, During, and After the Fall

The English Victorians, who viewed prostitutes as "unfortunate" or "fallen" women, were morally split between reformers and condemners, and split further over time, and over motivation. In the Victorian mind, "fallenness" called up both the original Fall and a more individual tumble—from pure maidenhood to impure maid, virginal angel to common dollymop, the milliner's or dressmaker's girl who augmented her wages by occasional (and seasonal) whoring. As chronicled in Judith Walkowitz's foundational 1980 book, *Prostitution and Victorian Society*, these falls were mostly temporary stumbles in the life of a working girl.[2]

Casual or part-time prostitution was usually done for just a few years, usually with members of the woman's same socioeconomic class (usually the lower), and usually ended when she found a better job or married one of her best customers. Still, a woman's downward spiral was the stuff novels, or at least cautionary tales, were made of. Charles Dickens managed a home for fallen women for ten years[3] and frequently used the story of the fallen woman—though only as sidebar, never as the main story, which tended to concern the triumph of the natured-good individual over the despotic English class system. Dickens reaffirmed the general cast of that system, however, giving his humble hero a leg up in his inevitable ascent by furnishing him with an upper-class (though initially unknown) birth.

The fallen woman can't rise, however. The "free and agreeable" Nancy of *Oliver Twist* dies at the hands of her lover/pimp, so it's a good thing she doesn't have a similarly elite pedigree. Nancy, by the way, is that book's only morally ambiguous character. In a world of good and evil, she is the gold-hearted whore who is killed while making sure Oliver is reunited with his family (and his family's fortune). Nancy synthesizes Woman Good and Woman Bad, Pure and Impure. When some readers complained about the presence of whores and cutpurses in their monthly paper, Dickens responded in his preface to the 1858 Library Edition of *Oliver Twist*: "I saw no reason, when I wrote this book, why the very dregs of life, so long as their speech did not offend the ear, should not serve the purpose of a moral, at least as well as its froth and cream." That moral? The causes of sin may be socially parsed, but their consequence is individual and total, at least on this earth.[4]

The United Kingdom: Sociology and Medicine

This conclusion was also reached in a series of social surveys during the 1840s, beginning with A. J. B. Parent-Duchâtlet's *De la prostitution dans la ville de Paris*, a demographic study of 12,000 Parisian prostitutes.[5] It gave the first statistical proof that prostitutes were unexceptional members of an unexceptional class, poor women who turned pro in their early twenties, then later left the life, if not the class. The study led to similar British projects, including William Tait's 1840 survey of Edinburgh prostitutes, *Magdalenism*.[6]

However, as Walkowitz notes in *Prostitution and Victorian Society*, consideration of prostitution's social causes led to its rounder social condemnation. Any critique of the social structures that spawned whoredom, she writes, "was undermined by a compulsive need to build defenses" of those structures. The demands of bourgeois capitalism may have fostered the flesh market, but because there was no getting rid of bourgeois capitalism, the flesh market would have to go. So that in 1840, Tait advocated banning prostitutes from public gatherings, because prostitutes had "abandoned the prerogatives of civil liberty."[7]

The reformers began to have their way mid-century, passing the Contagious Diseases Acts of 1864, 1866, and 1869, which officially recognized the existence of prostitution in certain military towns, and allowed police to detain and medically inspect any woman suspected of venereal disease. This meant any woman they wanted to detain and inspect, which meant women of the lower class. If a woman was found to be infected, she would be held in a "lock hospital" for up to nine months. If a woman refused to comply with the inspection, she could be held for trial, at which time she had to prove her virtue. But again, prostitution was mostly a part-time activity, used to supplement non-living wages, or as transient employment for the unemployed: there was a porous relationship between the poor and the criminal. As more and more poor and laboring women were rounded up, the sin began to be seen as primarily social, the cause, economic, the amorality, alcoholic.

The unintended consequence of the Contagious Diseases Acts was to fuel the first wave of British feminism, as Florence Nightingale, the Rescue Society, and the Ladies' Associations for the Care of Friendless Girls all stepped in to save and reform the fallen women. This set off other, grander expectations of female political power, particularly that flexed in various reform movements, such as temperance, which dovetailed nicely with the female role of moral guardian. Josephine Butler went from prostitute rescue work to become the leader of the anti–Contagious Acts movement, protesting women's loss of legal safeguards "hitherto enjoyed in common with men,"[8] unfettered police authority over women, the official facilitation of the debauchery of England's sons, and the punishment of vice's victims and the failure to punish its perpetrators.

The Acts were eventually repealed, but the bad taste stayed behind.[9] In her 1993 book, *Tainted Souls and Painted Faces*, Amanda Anderson detailed how the prostitute's fate and fortune became reversed in the public imagination.[10] Whereas social rot had been seen as *leading* to prostitution, the constant association of prostitution with social rot ultimately meant prostitution began to be seen as *causing* social rot: the bad apple blights the tree. As the Bible says in Proverbs 29:3, "Whoso loves wisdom rejoiceth his father, but he that keepeth company with harlots spendeth his substance."

Moral reform took on white slavery and child prostitution as its raison d'être, leading to passage of the Industrial Schools Amendment Act of 1880 and the Criminal Law Amendment Act in 1885 ("An Act to make further provision for the Protection of Women and Girls, the suppression of brothels, and other purposes"). These surpassed the Contagious Diseases Acts in their draconian effect on poor women and children. Brothels, many of them family owned, were raided, the children removed and the madams prosecuted, homosexuality was outlawed, and the age of consent was raised.

The anti-brothel provisions meant that if a family rented a room to a working girl, their children could be taken and put into industrial schools. These were state-run institutions to which children from seven to fourteen could be sentenced for vagrancy (homelessness), begging, lawlessness, or being in the company of thieves. All irony aside, there were reports from several of these schools of severe corporal discipline (such as caning) by administrators, and sexual abuse among children. And a series of local clean-up campaigns restructured prostitution from a brothel-based, part-time neighborhood economy to a constant criminal occupation.

The shift from prostitution to child prostitution and white slavery, solely defined as forced prostitution, shifted the moral onus. If child prostitution was the real problem, then chastity was the only way to assure childhood purity and disease-free maidens. If white slavery was the greater danger, it was criminals who were the cause, not the bourgeoisie. If homosexuality's the rot within, blame the foppish aristocrat, cum Oscar Wilde. The cultural upshot: feminism on the march, a feminism based on woman's victimization, sexual repudiation, and class reform. Enter the pimp, the lone whore's muscle and beard, avatar of this newer underworld.

The United States: Rum and Reform

In the United States, reformers cut straight to the jug: the twin roots of fallenness were the presence of the bottle and the absence of the Bible. The "Cult of True Womanhood" celebrated in early nineteenth-century popular culture required that an American woman embody the four cardinal virtues of piety, purity, submissiveness, and domesticity,[11] private virtues that, with the possible exception of submissiveness, did not contemplate public vice. According to Barbara Welter's classic essay on the cult of domesticity, a fallen woman was a "fallen angel," unworthy of the celestial company of her sex.[12] To contemplate such loss of purity brought tears; to be guilty of such an offense, said all the popular women's magazines, brought madness or death.[13]

Revivalism was part of reform, and the New York Female Moral Reform Society would shelter street girls if they repented, and lobbied for the shared shame of sin—newspapers started publishing names of johns, and laws were passed to punish them as well as their service providers.[14] The Temperance Movement, which had wrestled with an abolitionist agenda that kept it from gaining national traction, became a juggernaut social force with the debut of the saloon-busting Women's Christian Temperance Union in 1874. Female reform addressed all manner of inequity, including suffrage (Susan B. Anthony started as a temperance worker), labor laws involving women and children, and sex.

The unfortunate woman was now unfortunate by virtue not so much of her lack of virtue, but by her lack of social and economic power. In our corner of the Western world, women are in theory employable at what is in theory a living wage, and the female bourgeois enjoy choices beyond marriage or the street. MacD's ho Dakota said that she could have worked at Starbucks. Or she could have stayed in college. Or she could have decided that being a pimp's bitch is no more independent than living off your parents, and left the patriarchal bosom of both. These notions give the lie to Dakota's tale of herself as born-again victim, whose modern sin was a lapse in self-esteem. In the too-liberal imagination, each of the Seven Deadly Sins is attributed to a mutilated Me: the glutton is only starved for affection, the violent lashes out to reach out, and the murderous just doesn't get the rest of us. Though the conservative thinker has got no corner on truth, ascribing the sins of many to the sins of his liberal brother, decrying the lax moral environment that breeds breeding (by the unwedded or the unworking), or worse, nonbreeding (through abortion, homosexuality, or condoms), as if the cure for the curse of us is more of us to curse.

All these things are true in their way, and all should be (but aren't) beside the legal point. If the job of the law is to paternalistically protect, then, like the good father, it must also know when to let go. Or at least acknowledge its incestuous ambivalence. The myth of Dakota's rebirth is all the more remarkable as it occurs within a culture that can't get enough of that funky stuff.

The Sexy Web We Weave

Supreme and sexual license has become celebrated, in song and online. Alongside the greater acceptance of "pay to play" is a greater rejection of sexuality as a human desire with human consequences, that is, if you play, you ought to pay. At this point, it seems the only payment that sex demands is cash money. Sex is sold everywhere, and is everywhere free. Every pimp I've represented has a finger in the Internet pie, some Web site where one can go to access in-house ladies who work outside as well. There are estimates that Americans spend more than $40 million a day on prostitution, that our indigenous porn industry grosses more annually than our music and movie businesses combined, that more is spent yearly on going to strip clubs than on attending opera, theater, ballet, and classical and jazz concerts combined. Via their holdings in DirecTV, Rupert Murdoch's News Corporation and General Motors Investment Corporation, a General Motors subsidiary, sold more porn videos than *Hustler's* Larry Flynt.

There's a river of gold in store-bought cooch, and no one seems particularly interested in stopping the flow. Moreover, there's a false and collusive divide between legit and illegit sex work, which illogically holds that strip clubs are fine, and so are pictures of split beavers, but the latter can't be displayed in the former, and it's all right to get a hand job, as long as it's over the phone, because it's your hand, even though it's her mouth at the end of the line. You can be paid for pumping onscreen, but not off. Whores come from somewhere, however, and anyone who's done the exotic dance down by the airport has whored at least part-time, and phone sex operators and porn stars are getting money for providing sexual services same as the ho.

Most people who engage in prostitution are women. In the United States, the average starting age for prostitution is around fourteen. If we wanted to keep women and children from turning to whoring, we would outlaw all porn, including the live porn of strip shows and the canned porn of the DVD and online variety. We would curb all prostitution, including phone sex and escort services and massage parlors that promise only clean Asian women. We would have to, because this is where whores are born. Alternatively, if we wanted to protect women and children from being harmed by whoring, we would legalize adult prostitution, with very strict government regulation, such as in the Netherlands, where brothel prostitution was decriminalized in 2000. The prostitutes pay taxes, may be unionized, and are required to have a European Union passport; they work in rooms monitored by closed-circuit security, and cooperate with police.[15] Sweden decriminalized the prostitute while criminalizing the john and increasing the punishment for pimps and traffickers as part of its 1999 law prohibiting "the gross violation of a woman's integrity."

The dissonance between the way we see ourselves and the way others see us grows greater just as we have greater access to those things, such as the XXX-Internet, that might wreak havoc on our self-image.

But the ability of a forty-year-old man to cast himself as a teenage girl or simply to become unmarried as he logs on, denies the divide. With the easy shucking of the shell of self comes the erosion of self itself. This contradiction of a contradictory self mirrors a similar schism within the young and transgressive, those who see themselves in equal parts as sexual outlaws/entrepreneurs, commanding a certain kind of cultural cachet, and as sexual victims, commanding cultural pity.

Rickie and Dakota may have been victims, but they weren't just victims of MacD; they were victims of a host of forces that facilitate people putting themselves on the block, and other people playing pitchman or priest. We want it all. We want to sing songs of innocence and experience. For as preachers and politicians know, to be born again is better than birth because you can reap and sow your worldly experience, then parade the refreshed purity of your soul.

Prostitution and Modern Porn

The debate around prostitution and pornography used to be a face-off between those who would outlaw commercial sex and those who would be outlaws. The abolitionists were traditionally represented by such theorists as law professor Catharine MacKinnon and the late activist Andrea Dworkin.

MacKinnon's essay "Equality and Speech," which appears in her 1993 book *Only Words*, famously argued that First Amendment protection of pornography should yield to constitutional guarantees of equality.[16] Her argument: Because pornography, as an expression of anti-woman sentiment (or group defamation/degradation) leads to sexual violence, it neither deserves constitutional protection, nor enjoys privileged status among constitutional interests. Given that equality is an affirmative constitutional value (i.e., one the State has an interest in furthering), the State may and should abolish pornography as a way of promoting sexual equality.

Dworkin joined forces with MacKinnon in the early 1980s to author a draft ordinance, passed by the City of Indianapolis in 1984, enabling "anyone hurt through pornography to prove its role in their abuse, to recover for the deprivation of their civil rights, and to stop it from continuing." The ordinance was quickly struck down as a violation of the First Amendment.[17] In *Only Words*, MacKinnon called the court's decision at best a wrongheaded application of a constitutional guarantee meant to protect political dissent, and at worst a crabbed collusion between male judges and male pornographers. Canada, she points out, came to an entirely different, and more civilized, conclusion in upholding an obscenity law that proscribed, among other things, "undue exploitation of sex."

The affirmationists have been represented by a farrago of feminists, from Margo St. James, who founded the prostitutes' union COYOTE (Call Off Your Old Tired Ethics) in 1973, to the National Task Force on Prostitution (NTFP) and the International Committee for Prostitutes' Rights (ICPR). But these groups are by no means monolithic.

Affirmationists contend that voluntary sex work is like any other skilled service work, that sex workers ought have the same protections and consideration as any skilled service worker, with additional considerations, such as police protection from violent clients or state-funded gynecological medical care, as needed.[18] Marxist feminists, who mostly affirm affirmationism, warn that there may be a fundamental problem with seeing one's sexual self as property that one then alienates as product (at least when one is a woman and the seeing is done within a patriarchal system). Liberal contractarians see constraints on prostitution as "purityrannical" interference with women's essential autonomy and humans' need for sex.[19]

Critics of the contractarians point out that only *some* humans seem to need commercially available sex, and they tend to be men. And how mutual are arrangements when one party has a historic and economic upper hand? There are also abolition-affirmation hybridists who would proscribe certain kinds of whoring, such as child and street prostitution, and permit others, such as brothel prostitution, escort services, and pornography. Still other thinkers eschew the term "prostitutes" for "prostituted women," putting the whoring (and its onus) outside the woman herself.

All of these theoretical perspectives are equally satisfying and dissatisfying by turn. The absolute affirmationists' stance that sex work is just work falls apart under its own terms: if sex work is just work, then child prostitution is merely a violation of child labor laws, and on some visceral level, that just can't be true. On the abolitionist side, if pornography should be outlawed because it causes sexual violence, then photos of lynchings should be outlawed as well, and those pictures are First Amendment–protected political speech on a platter. If adult pornography is protected, then street prostitution should be protected, for there is no appreciable (legal) difference between someone fucking someone for cash in front of a camera crew and doing it offstage.

But the problem with all these theoretical perspectives is that they try to forge a cohesive response to an inchoate argument. Basically, they're all premised on the idea that the world is the world, and the world of the bourgeoisie is the same world as the world of the whore. But it's not. Just as a young woman in Victorian England might not consider part-time prostitution any more soiling than work in a textile factory, a college student who chooses to play bottom bitch for a while may view it as an educational semester abroad. A call girl might think an afternoon porn shoot—early call, camera crew, bored co-star, and multiple takes—less lucrative and more unpleasant than her regular day job. A "strawberry" (will do sex work for drugs) may think she's getting the best of a bum bargain. A brothel whore may feel the track worker is better able to up and quit, because nobody knows how many tricks the street sister has turned, so skimming money is that much easier. And pimps come in many guises—strip club owner, adult-video producer, macdaddy. One thing Lois Lee failed to testify to is that the pimp is as iconic in one urban community as the padrone is in another.

Worlds Apart

Prosecutors always argue that no one would falsely accuse someone of rape, especially someone she didn't know, and therefore had no motive to malign. Besides, trials are inconvenient, and cross-examination unpleasant. But this reasoning does not hold in the underworld, where it may be entirely realistic to accuse someone else of rape to avoid having your own probation violated. Or where you're in court anyway, on your own beef, and why not at least try to get a bit of a break by cooperating with the authorities. Or, alternatively, where you understand that violence is part of some gigs, and sexual violence is part of the sexual gig.

These aren't great choices. But neither was the choice between the shirtwaist factory and the lock hospital. In a world where it's considered natural for women to shake their moneymakers, choice is just another grade of meat. The game involves a wider reckoning of morality and guilt, of lives that compete in inconsequence, and we refuse to see it. We want to believe victims because they are victims, even though, like the pimp's prostitute, what they are victims of may not be exclusively the defendant's fault. There are assumptions about which player has more power in a game that starts on the street and ends in the court, and which may be, in fact, played among equals. In many quarters, feminism has come to mean drawing room manners, thickly spread. The term manages to signal a sort of simultaneously sensible-shoed sourpussishness and a too-precious worldview, and is dismissed by many as an overly restrictive label rather than a potentially liberating philosophy. I consider myself a feminist of the street variety: I'm not very interested in furthering legal or social structures that protect women by way of bubble and shrink wrap. Or those that preserve the status quo by merely visually expanding the pool of who gets to become a corporate attorney, or run a corporation. What I want is not reform, but real change. The goal should not be how can we pass more laws to shelter more women or treat more women like most men, but how the law can work to create the freedom and support for everyone to contribute freely to the social whole of work and family. The young American women who believe they are postgender and postgender politics, still can't walk across campus at night, and still don't see that the ability to hire other women to tend to their children is not the apogee of gender equality. What neither current law nor feminism is willing to recognize, let alone upend, is the impolite reality that we are presently people and chattel. The pimp and prostitute relationship is a relationship that clumsily recognizes this brute fact.

This is not a Camille Paglia or Katie Roiphe–type bid for tossing rape's responsibility back on the victim. It's an acknowledgment that, as Simone de Beauvoir wrote, "man, like woman, is flesh, therefore passive, the plaything of his hormones and of the species, the restless prey of his desires."[20] And all flesh is the plaything of the restless and consumptive culture in which it plays and preys. Playthings are trivial. Playthings are disposable; they break, you get another. Pimp and ho culture, however haute, mocks the disposable lives of disposable people. Why do we expect one plaything to treat another with any more respect than the society grants either? We have pimps because we want whores. Just as, sometimes, we make victims because we want perpetrators.

CHAPTER 10
DATELINE: TO CATCH A PREDATOR

A man is walking through the forest with a little girl in the dead
of night. The girl begins to cry.
MAN: "What are you crying for?"
GIRL: "It's dark and I'm scared."
MAN: "*You're* scared? I've got to walk back on my own!"

M Y FAVORITE PART of Iceberg Slim's autobiographical novel
Pimp is the preface, which reads:

In this book I will take you the reader with me into the secret inner
world of the pimp. I will lay bare my life and thoughts as a pimp.
The account of my brutality and cunning as a pimp will fill many of
you with revulsion, however if one intelligent valuable young man or
woman can be saved from the destructive slime then the displeasure
I have given will have been outweighed by that individual's use of his
potential in a socially constructive manner . . . Perhaps my remorse for
my ghastly life will diminish to the degree that within this one book I
have been allowed to purge myself. Perhaps one day I can win respect
as a constructive human being. Most of all I wish to become a decent
example for my children and for that wonderful woman in the grave,
my mother.[1]

There is much that is funny about this gob of earnestness, including
not the least its uncanny resemblance to Daniel Defoe's preface to
Moll Flanders. Though Slim's version is even more hilarious, given
that the "wonderful woman in the grave," his sainted mother, turns
out to be, if not a pro, a gifted amateur, who dumps Slim's kindly
stepfather in favor of a series of no-accounts. Slim does thank her,

however, for not leaving him in a dumpster at birth. As he points out in another book: "I am convinced that most pimps require the secretly buried fuel of Mother hatred to stoke their fiery vendetta of cruelty and merciless exploitation against whores primarily and ultimately all women."[2]

"Archbishop" Don "Magic" Juan, a 1970s pimp turned 1980s preacher and author of *From the Pimp Stick to the Pulpit*,[3] has said we live in a new "mackallennium." Though he was referring to the faddish embrace of pimp and ho culture by pop culture, pimping has itself become a way of achieving a certain kind of social/sexual respectability. For example, Snoop Dogg's persona makeover from tight-bellied, thugg4life cornrow-sporting, wifebeater-wearing, cop-killer gangsta rapper to an Afro'd and platform-shoed, tight-trousered, fuzzy-coated, sweet-talkin' macdaddy was a redemptive move from nihilist terrorist to a man with a plan, a man that's got cash in pocket and cocha on hand. In a July 15, 2004 *Salon* article, author Baz Dresinger argued that the Snoop transition, along with the ascension of other pimp-stars, signaled a shift from hip-hop as the articulation of real urban threat to hip-hop as mall culture: parents who worried about their sons and daughters valorizing hope-to-die, hardcore rappers don't care (and/or don't believe) that the pimp-rapper is "actually out on the street, overseeing a gaggle of girls." Real gangstas became fake pimps. Moreover, this faux pimping helped recast gangsta rap itself as feigned, to the everlasting comfort of the pale, pampered consumer.

The nouvelle rap scene parallels the World Wide Wrestling Federation: an abundance of testosterone slapping up against itself, an exaggerated display of super-slick macho that both covers and shows the po'boy version of a fashion show—all hairstyle and shiny, clingy clothes—the WWF's bubbled butts and buffalo pecs in red, white, & blue spandex, or Dre's stable of rippling six-packs 'n' arm cannons, sweaty and shirtless. Because the disposable income majority wants its nightmares to be "like" nightmares, like horror movies, something safely experienced, something about which it can be said: "It's only a nightmare," "It's only a movie," "It's only Snoopy." It's not much of a stretch to point out that culture as a whole is far more comfortable with an abstract victimization of women/whores/black women than it is with the hypothetical popping of police, or those pesky toddlers who seem drawn, moth-like, to gangbanger crossfire. And even less of a stretch when calculating the inevitable mercantile potential, for the honey-colored pimp dream is a lot easier on the eyes, and can itself be peddled and pimped in far more ways than the real *cauchemar* of brown folks blowing each other up.

But now that pimps and ho's have become supafly Barbies and Ken, the communal sex stress has fallen on an easier target. Like the Victorians before us, we as a society have bailed on the larger, more culturally complex problem of prostitution in favor of the easier problem of child sexual abuse. There are no pros in child molestation, in any sense of the term, and it provides a nice bandwagon we can all jump onto. No niggling notion of potential redemption or reformation muddies the waters. Once you've bathed in the river of sin, you're sunk, mister, for now and forever after, amen. The hyperbole is essential, as is the attendant hysteria. Which brings me to the recent phenomenon of *Dateline: To Catch a Predator*, and the question it poses: Are monsters born, or handmade?

An Introduction to Perv TV

For those who haven't seen the show, here is a précis:

Dateline: To Catch a Predator is a very successful network news-ish show; as indicated by the title, it is a special edition of NBC's weekly news magazine, *Dateline*. As of 2008, there had been twelve stings, each taking place in a different U.S. city, all hosted by Chris Hansen, author of *To Catch a Predator: Protecting Your Kids from Online Enemies Already in Your Home*.[4] The show, like the book, like the Web site, is structured around the sting: a town is targeted, and local law enforcement and sting volunteers go online, pretending to be minors looking for friends. They respond to men who respond to them, and who respond to them sexually. After a man solicits the decoy online, an in-person meeting is arranged at the sting house. The men are recorded by hidden cameras arriving at the sting house to have sex with the faux minor who stalls them.[5] They are then confronted by Hansen, who questions them along general lines of "What *were* you thinking?" and are arrested when they leave the house. There is a tag at the end of each episode, indicating what has happened to the men post-arrest (who pled guilty, who is "fighting the charges"), and perhaps a side discussion of weighty matters writ lite, such as the decreasing availability of offender treatment programs or the rate of offender recidivism.

Online decoys are primarily provided by Perverted Justice, a volunteer-based organization described by Hansen as "PJ," an Internet-vigilante-cum-"computer watchdog" group.[6] Founded by the pseudonymous Xavier Von Erck, Perverted Justice (it prefers "PeeJ") just calls itself vigilante; one PeeJ T-shirt reads: "Attention Please! I Have Been 100% Certified as An Anonymous Vigilante! Approach With Caution!" PeeJ's founder's former blogsite was Evilvigilante. com. At first, PeeJ volunteered its *Dateline* services but is now a paid consultant to the show (a reported $70,000 to $150,000/sting, though $100,000 is usually cited). In his book, Hansen defends the practice of paying PeeJ against charges of "checkbook journalism" on grounds that the show needs the group's expertise, and "After all, I was getting paid, my producer and crew were getting paid." Reasoning that, like the show, blurs the line between community service and commercial enterprise, though PR-wise, it's probably better to subsidize a "watchdog" than a "vigilante."

The *Predator* phenomenon raises questions involving two legal concepts. The first is the general law of entrapment. The entrapment defense is designed to deter government abuse of police power: the government can facilitate a crime, but can't unfairly lure people into becoming criminals. Similarly, the government can't sanction and encourage entrapment by private citizens, then benefit from that abuse because the fundamental evil—the state crossing the line—remains the same. The second is laws that allow evidence of prior offenses to be used to prove character or disposition. In other words, statutes that codify the common-sense principle that if you did it before, chances are pretty good you did it this time because you're the sort of person who would do something like this sort of thing.

Entrapment is said to be a defense "collateral" to a defendant's guilt—he's guilty, but his guilt is not the point. The point is that the cops cheated. There are two distinct approaches to entrapment, subjective and objective. The federal judicial system uses the first, California and a number of other states use the second.

The "Subjective" Entrapment Test

The subjective entrapment test focuses on the defendant's intent—if the defendant was predisposed or otherwise inclined to commit the crime, any police inducement to do so is fine. Therefore, the federal entrapment defense has two components: (a) government inducement, and (b) the defendant's lack of criminal predisposition.[7] Predisposition is the main element, involving a determination by the jury of whether the accused is an "unwary innocent" or an "unwary criminal."[8] In other words, the prosecution must prove that the defendant was a criminal waiting to happen, not just a sucker for a line. Usually this is done by showing some instigation or alacrity on the defendant's part to commit what's called the "target offense."

The leading Supreme Court decision on entrapment is the 1992 case of *Jacobson v. United States*.[9] I'm going to lay out the facts at length, because the setup of the case is such a classic of the genre.

Jacobson, "a fifty-six-year-old veteran-turned-farmer," was convicted of receiving child pornography in the mail. He ordered magazines featuring nude teen/preteen boys from an adult bookstore; after he placed his order, the laws changed, outlawing such material. The government took Jacobson's name from the bookstore's mailing list and targeted him for a sting operation—and began authoring a very long criminal scenario.

First, a U.S. postal inspector sent a letter from a fictitious society advocating First Amendment-ish freedoms relative to pornography. Jacobson responded to the letter by returning its "sexual attitude questionnaire," which asked him to rank his sexual preferences on a scale from 1 to 4. Jacobson put preteen sex down as a 2, but said he disapproved of pedophilia. About a year later, Jacobson got another letter from another fictitious entity, a consumer research company asking about his interest in sex involving those of the "neophite" [sic] age. "Neophite" was not further defined; Jacobson sent back his reply, indicating he was affirmatively interested in teenage sexuality, and in receiving more information. A third entity, a fake lobbying organization dedicated to the protection and promotion of sexual freedom and choice, sent Jacobson another letter and survey, and Jacobson ranked his interest in preteen sex as above average, not high. Jacobson also wrote his own defense of First Amendment freedom, including freedom of the press, agreeing that it must be kept safe against encroachment by fundamentalist Christians.

The fake lobbying organization answered, stating that its pro-sex lobbying efforts (repeal of statutes regulating nonviolent sexual activity) were funded via its catalog sales. The catalog was forthcoming; a government pen pal came sooner. Using "mirroring," whereby the agent reflects the target's interests, the agent said he too was primarily interested in male-male items, and wondered if Jacobson was satisfied with the quality of professional videos. Jacobson said he liked "good-looking young guys (in their late teens and early 20s) doing their thing together." Jacobson stopped corresponding with the agent after a couple of letters; by that time, the U.S. Postal Service had spent thirty-four months investigating him.

Enter the Customs Service, with its own sting operation. Jacobson was now sent a brochure from a fake Canadian company advertising photographs of young boys having sex. Jacobson placed an order, but the order was not filled. The Postal Service then sent Jacobson another letter from a fake company from the "Far East," taking the federal government to task for spending good tax dollars promoting censorship versus suppressing drugs and crime, and referencing media "hysteria" around so-called pornography. The letter promised that any material sent from the company would sail through customs, and invited Jacobson's response — but only after requiring Jacobson to sign an affirmation stating he was not a government agent. Jacobson signed away, got a catalog, ordered the magazine, *Boys Who Love Boys*, and was arrested.

At his trial, Jacobson said, "Well, the statement was made [in the letter] of all the trouble and the hysteria over pornography and I wanted to see what the material was."

The U.S. Supreme Court reversed his conviction, finding the government had not proved Jacobson's independent predisposition to commit a criminal act. Jacobson had been the target of two and a half years of sting contacts that began with him placing an order for lawful pornography, and ended with his being hectored into defying government censorship. Before the government got into it, Jacobson's "personal inclinations" were just that, personal. By emphasizing individual freedoms and government censorship, wrote the Court, the Postal and Customs Services "not only excited petitioner's interest in sexually explicit materials banned by law but also exerted substantial pressure on petitioner to obtain and read such material as part of a fight against censorship and the infringement of individual rights." The State had predisposed Jacobson to commit a crime that the State then facilitated in order to convict him of committing it—a crime tailor made to government specifications.

The "Objective" Entrapment Test

The other approach, used by a minority of jurisdictions, is an *objective* test. As explained by the California Supreme Court in 1970, this concept of entrapment "is not based on the defendant's innocence. The courts have created the defense as a control on illegal police conduct out of regard for [the court's] own dignity, and in the exercise of its power and the performance of its duty to formulate and apply proper standards for judicial enforcement of the criminal law."[10] "Such defenses are collateral to the defendant's guilt or innocence *because they are collateral to any element of the crime in question.* Thus, the defense of entrapment does not bear on the defendant's conduct in any way, but solely on the conduct of the police."[11] The defense of entrapment is established when a defendant can affirmatively prove that, but for the government's actions, he would not have done the deed.

In the words of the standard California jury instruction, "the conduct of the law enforcement agents or officers . . . would likely induce a normally law-abiding person to commit the crime." The instruction advises that police can provide an opportunity for the commission of a crime, including "reasonable, though restrained, steps to gain the confidence of suspects." But, the instruction cautions, police may not "induce" crimes by "overbearing conduct such as badgering, coaxing or cajoling, importuning, or other affirmative acts likely to induce a normally law-abiding person to commit the crime." Predisposition, as such, is not part of it: the key is whether the ordinary citizen would have succumbed to temptation, given what's been put out as bait. For example, if I offer you a million dollars to have sex with me, that may well be a proposition a reasonable person would find hard to refuse. You agree, and I can't then arrest you for engaging in an act of prostitution. But if I offer you twenty bucks for a date on the track, I can bust you like a nut, even if you testify that you would have done it for fun and for free.

Entrapment issues include whether the defense of entrapment applies if the person instigating the crime is not a government agent, or acting as a government decoy. The police don't usually use third parties as decoys, but the issue remains the same: did the State bring its resources to bear unfairly on the will of the accused? Generally speaking, if a third party is not acting on behalf of the government, there is no entrapment defense because the evil of police overreaching is not implicated by the actions of purely private citizens. But if the purely private citizen strong-arms the defendant on behalf of the government, the defense applies. This is true whether or not the purely private citizen is aware of his decoy status, for the point is that the government's hand was involved. This will be relevant in our *Predator* discussion.

In federal court, a defendant can also raise the defense of "outrageous police conduct." Under this doctrine, even if the defendant has a predisposition to commit the crime, law enforcement can't do something so outrageous that due process bars the government from using the judicial system to get a conviction. The standard for what constitutes outrageousness is very high: the conduct must "shock the conscience" or offend one's "universal sense of justice."[12] This issue comes up most frequently in what is called "sentencing entrapment," in which the cops convince the defendant to commit a much greater crime than the one he was predisposed to commit in order to jack up his sentence. But for the outrageous police conduct—they plopped a half-pound baggie of cocaine on the table in front of him when all he asked for was an eighth of an ounce—the defendant wouldn't have bought so much cocaine.

Evidence of Your Disposition

In California, as in the federal system, there is a statute that permits juries to consider evidence of prior sex offenses to prove the defendant has a criminal disposition: that is, a propensity to commit sex crimes.[13] The logic of this law—a law that runs directly counter to three centuries of English jurisprudence—is that because it is entirely unusual to be accused of a sex offense, someone who has been accused more than once of such a crime has essentially shown a proclivity toward sex offending, and this can be taken into account by a jury deciding whether new charges are true. Too much smoke, *got* to be fire.

On the surface, this reasoning makes sense. We decide whom to hire and what stocks to buy based on prior performance. But what makes good common sense falls apart at the touch of logic, and the law. For the law swears itself to be, like an aging suitor, favorably myopic. Throughout the history of common law jurisprudence, a criminal trial is about conduct, not character. You stand accused of *doing* something, not *being* something. Weighing the worth of a man's nature is better left to Almighty God and surviving blood relatives. In terms of logic, the problem is that prior convictions are already admissible to prove a number of very specific facts. For example, priors can be used to establish a modus operandi. If the defendant has been previously convicted of coming through the bedroom window wearing a ski mask, that makes it more likely he is guilty in the current case of coming through a bedroom window wearing a ski mask. Or to establish intent: if the defendant has been found guilty of molesting those other children, then he probably touched this child with the requisite lewd intent. Or knowledge: if he was guilty of receiving stolen property before, he probably knew he was buying a hot TV. Prior convictions have the added attraction of being convictions; the defendant either pled guilty or was found guilty of the charges in the previous·case, so courts and jurors can comfortably rely upon their veracity in the current case.

The California Supreme Court initially upheld the law permitting disposition evidence in part because the court saw little harm in confronting a man with a prior sex-offense conviction. After all, the accused had an opportunity to defend against the charge before, and lost, so he can't really complain that it's unfair to bring in the same evidence in another trial. But to be admissible, there is no statutory requirement that the prior sex offense resulted in a prior conviction, or, for that matter, a prior criminal charge or even a prior arrest. This also means that stuff can and does come up that the defendant has never confronted before. As long as someone is willing to get on the stand and say that the defendant previously offended, this can be used as evidence that the man has a predisposition to commit sex offenses, and is therefore probably guilty of the current offense.

The problem, of course, is that if you are being accused now of doing something way back when, you probably won't be able to present much by way of a defense now, except for a blanket denial. I've had cases where family members have alleged abuse twenty or thirty years before the present charges, including cases where the conduct took place between then-children (the defendant was eleven, the victim was five; he asked her to suck his penis, she said no, and she told on him), and where there had never been any prior talk of impropriety—no one had ever accused the guy before of anything. There's also the common situation in which a victim corroborates her own story by saying that it happened before. The topsy-turvy legal logic being that because the victim said he did it before, that shows he's the sort of guy who does those sorts of things, and does those sorts of things to her, so the jury should believe her when she says that he did, in fact, exactly that sort of thing to her *again*. In many of these situations, no alibi can be presently produced, no witnesses are available beyond accuser and accused, and very little can be done in cross-examination. The defendant may barely remember being twelve, or that particular visit to grandma's house at fourteen, though he'll explain that everyone knows that cousin is crazy—an explanation to which juries are resoundingly impervious.

Even if the defendant was found not guilty of the prior charge, that may not be enough. Having thought he'd put all that to rest, he now has to re-defend, with the same practical difficulties. In addition, the prosecutor will argue to the new jury that the earlier acquittal doesn't mean that the defendant didn't do the earlier crime, just that the state couldn't prove it beyond a reasonable doubt. For the defendant, this is a major distraction. All of this is a side show to the main show, taking place in a current trial on current offenses, where the defense and its resources need to focus on the current charges, because that's what he's going to go to prison for.

Logically, there is no reason to elevate the accusation of a prior impropriety above any other accusation: you were accused, no more, no less. But an accusation, without more, is less—the diminishment of a person's character and of the presumption of innocence. Legally, there is nothing to be gained by allowing disposition testimony other than to show that the defendant may be a very bad man. The subtext here is our hysteria, in which allegations become the same as proof, and sex offenders are a different breed to whom different rules apply. The poet Paul Valéry said, "The true character of history is to play a part in history itself." It's true: the man who seems to have been guilty in the past will be found guilty in the future. The lead bottom of this looking glass is that as convictions are brought about more easily, the ultimate price—the bleeding and warping of civil rights and moral right—costs us our hope, alongside our integrity.

Sex Crime as Entertainment

As the Supreme Court famously said, your inclinations and fantasies are your "own and beyond the reach of government."[14] But not beyond the reach of popular entertainment. And this is where *Dateline: To Catch a Predator* makes accomplices of us all.

In his online *Predator* accounts, host Chris Hansen favors use of the second-person conspiratorial: "You won't believe what he admits to me," "You won't believe what we found out about him," "What do you suppose was in the bag when he arrives?" "And you'll never guess what this man does for a living," and, "You know what happens next." Web advertisements run toward lifestyle products such as State Farm auto insurance, PerfectMatch dating services, *Entrepreneur* magazine, Nutrisystem, and the Hair Club for Men. There is usually a link to the National Center for Missing & Exploited Children. Hansen's book first appeared "above the scroll," so you had to page down for things like the "Online Safety Kit: What You Need to Know."

On its Web site, PeeJ tends toward the soft-boiled prose noir of Marvel Comics: "Slamming wannabe pedophiles with a little Perverted Justice." "Examples? Hell, we have too many of them." "Welcome to Convictiontown!" The site is crowded with PeeJ Opinions, Random Convictions, Top 10 Most Slimy, Guys Like These (a slideshow), Conviction Counter, Faces of PeeJ, and PeeJ Store. PeeJware includes hats, cups, and clothing, marketed like Pabst Blue Ribbon.[15]

In each *Dateline: To Catch a Predator* episode, the overwhelming majority of men stung are first-time offenders, or at least it's their first arrest. Most say they've never done anything like this before. This is usually patently untrue in terms of soliciting a minor online, but perhaps true in terms of showing up in the flesh. On camera, Hansen rejects out of hand any claim of innocence or novice status, or of an intent to "save" the wayward adolescent. This is tempered slightly in the book, as one of the experts states that some of the men could be feeling very ambivalent about actually going through with the encounter, and could be telling themselves some sort of do-gooder story to help them make the long drive to the short stuff.[16]

Those stung who have sex-offense priors elicit additional *Predator* outrage, though it's a curious reaction, and a curiously rare phenomenon on the show, given what the producers are trawling for. But it does provide Hansen a platform to fan the flames. When one registered sex offender showed up at the California sting, Hansen immediately started pluralizing his pronouns: "They're supposed to be known to law enforcement. But despite their history they're free to come and go, and one of them walked into our house." But the fact is, "they" *are* known to law enforcement; registration does not mean restriction. Registration is what you do after you serve your sentence. After you serve your sentence, you are supposed to be free to come and go, subject to those residency requirements.[17] Note that one of the police experts in Hansen's book thoughtfully points out that residency requirements don't deter anyone from committing any offense, but simply make it more difficult for registered sex offenders to find a job and a place to live. And taking away basic forms of power and control is a bad thing to do to someone who commits crimes as demonstrations of power and control. The freedom to come and go, like the freedom to choose where one works and lives, includes the freedom to sashay into a revival meeting or *Predator* damnation. Hansen says he is disturbed by the nonsexual criminal histories of some of his targets, though this would obviously correspond to the high rate of antisocial personality disorder among all offenders. Following this general pattern of novice, pervert, and scumbum, Hansen divides up the stung: one-third predators, one-third opportunists, one-third first-timers.

Is It Entrapment?

Before we address the ramifications of this accounting issue, some legal problems: on the *Dateline: to Catch a Predator* Web site, there's a "frequent viewer question" section, a variation of the FAQ sheet.[18] Question number 2 is "Is it entrapment?" The answer—"No"—is provided by two commentators, Ken Lynch, otherwise unidentified, and Mike Burns of the Darke County (Ohio) Sheriff's Department. (Burns and Lynch are not pseudonyms, merely apt.) Lynch cites the "otherwise-law-abiding" standard of entrapment, warning that in "our situation, first of all, there was no police conduct. So, there is no entrapment."

Burns is more expansive:

> How can it be entrapment when you set up a profile, you present it with illicit things about it, strictly innocent, and they contact you? And they are the ones that begin talking about wanting to have sexual encounters with you. They initiate it. Because they get caught once they've initiated it is not an entrapment issue.

Burns is on thinner ice here. In Ohio, PeeJ members were deputized, making their actions official police conduct. As this so obviously highlights the entrapment issue, their deputization did not initially make sense to me. Hansen's book simply says there was a "quirk" in local law so that deputization would permit the filing of more serious charges. My research indicated that the Ohio law that makes it a felony to solicit a minor online requires that the solicited person either be in fact thirteen years old, *or be a member of law enforcement*. In other words, if a man just comes onto another adult online who is posing as a child and who is not a cop, there's no crime.[19] Later, I realized that without deputization, PeeJ volunteers could be considered aiders and abettors in any subsequent charge of attempted sexual conduct with a minor. Or at least that's how I'd argue it if I were in Ohio.

Given the funding/consulting relationship between *Predator* and PeeJ, it could be as easily argued that *Predator* was also a para-police entity in the Ohio sting. Hansen acknowledges this in his book by saying that deputization led to criticism in journalism circles that "we were too cozy with law enforcement." ("We," apparently referring to the single working unit of *Predator* and PeeJ.) More broadly, any state would have a hard time maintaining there was "no" police conduct, because the cops are so fully in cahoots with the sting, escorting the new arrestees from the threshold of the sting house to the Big House based on evidence provided by *Predator* and PeeJ. *Predator* and PeeJ make much of the fact that police officers aren't physically in the sting house during the confrontation, and Hansen (and PeeJ) have called the police work a "parallel" investigation. But the only way in which it's parallel is Euclidean. PeeJ, now subsidized by *Predator*, sets up some potential stings, and *Predator* decides which ones it wants in on. According to PeeJ, the hardest thing about coordinating the on-air stings is keeping the cops and the crew "in different dwellings." As any first-year law student knows, the test isn't so much the spatial relationship between parties (think paid informants), but the symbiotic one. *Dateline* provides the trough from which the government feeds.

Again, Is It Entrapment?

Assuming there is sufficient police conduct, the question becomes whether the conduct is entrapment. In *Jacobson*, the Supreme Court put the standard point blank: the government can't do that which leads to the "apprehension of an otherwise law-abiding citizen who, if left to his own devices, likely would have never run afoul of the law."[20] Again, this is the federal test, and again, the California standard, for example, is different, as it does not require the defendant to be as the undriven snow. Either way. You can't cast real cops and real arrestees in your production of *Law & Order*, then pretend you're not part of the play. Similarly, the question can no longer be whether the third party is acting "under the government's control," for when everyone's playing a coequal part, the arm of the state is thereby if not elongated, multiplied.

While Ohio Sheriff Burns's argument is a little garbled ("you present it with illicit things about it, strictly innocent, and they contact you"), it would appear that if these things are illicit in themselves, such as a sexually compliant thirteen-year-old, then the government is furnishing both the initial opportunity and the means for completing the crime. After all, there's no law prohibiting grown men from contacting thirteen-year-olds online (though there is a social rule, and children should be taught to immediately leave any area, real or otherwise, in which this happens), and although this does not automatically translate to entrapment, it does start to chip away at the premise that the government's hands are sufficiently clean in all cases. Moreover, there's no way to tell in the abstract whether the decoy went beyond cracking the proverbial door into improperly egging on entry. As chronicled on its Web site, *Predator* chat logs can be as long as two hundred sheets; according to Hansen's book, sting chats can go on for ten minutes, three days, or four weeks. PeeJ volunteers have publicly acknowledged encouraging contacts to meet, and that, in order to get a meeting, a decoy will not only express increasing willingness for increasingly explicit conversation, but increasing willingness (and desire) for real sex.

From thousands of chat hours logged, the PeeJ Web site tabs 306 convictions from June 2004 to January 2009. Though these numbers are not in themselves particularly large, they demonstrate the police-type force of *Predator's* participation. *Predator* does not partner in all PeeJ stings, but *Predator* money fuels other PeeJ operations. PeeJ's solo activities led to just forty convictions from June 2004 to the end of 2005. PeeJ began partnering with *Dateline* in 2006, and more than doubled their total conviction rate before the year was out.[21] All this, even though a high-profile Internet-safety task force, created by forty-nine state attorneys general, has found that online sexual solicitation of children is actually not a significant social problem.[22]

In cost/benefit terms, the Predator/PeeJ operation compares poorly to a similar law enforcement–only sting. In April 2007, Polk County, Florida officials conducted a week-long operation involving fifty officers from various jurisdictions communicating with 250 individuals, resulting in twenty-eight arrests made at the decoy house. The press, it should be noted, was relegated to the role of witness. So the cops' sting was over a shorter period of time, which at least on the surface suggests less cajoling, and netted about a 12 percent arrest rate for, at minimum, the higher offense of attempted sexual contact. The regular fisherman may be less prone to cast the wider net, or improperly jailbait the hook.

During the *Predator* stings themselves, a number of men drive to the sting house, then drive on. One man says in his online chat that he's afraid the meeting is a setup, and circles the area without stopping; he is later arrested for online solicitation. Another man circles the house a few times, then goes home to pick up his children as promised. He is pulled over, and arrested for online solicitation; his children are returned to their mother by a police officer. Other men walk back and forth outside the sting house, deciding. They too are subject to arrest. The question in each of these men's trials will be whether they would have done as much as they did had the decoy not encouraged them to do so. The question I have is why most of these men are only charged with online solicitation. If they are the hope-to-die pervs PeeJ purports them to be, I would expect their computers or CDs to be teeming with kiddie porn or proof of other "pedo" pursuits. But, assuming law enforcement is doing its follow-up job, executing warrants on the men's homes and offices to search for and seize the weapon used to commit the crime and to determine if other like crimes have been committed, there should be proof of other offenses. (Particularly if we assume that these offenses are habitual.) But the stats are too low. Not only are most of the men charged only with solicitation, the sentences tend to be misdemeanor terms—a little jail time, or probation. There are a few stiffer ones, usually either involving the attempt to molest or a criminal history that provides its own problems (probation/parole violation, the elevation of a crime because it's a subsequent offense, for example). As I recall, however, the longest sentence thus far was about six years for a married rabbi who sent the decoy boy pics of himself orally copulating a man. He charged toward Hansen during the sting, and Hansen loves to drag him out as trophy and bogeyman. In my opinion, Hansen's references to the incident start to smell a little anti-Semitic after a while, due to his persistent identification of the man as "the rabbi," but you take your perpetrators, like your victims, as you find them.

In one *Predator* episode, the decoy stuck her head out the door and called several times for a reluctant man to come inside. In another, a man approached the door, then retreated, then stood, then paced a few steps parallel to it, then approached, then retreated, then paced, all while Hansen's voice-over chastised him for being "too afraid" to go in. This was, to me, the greater obscenity—remembering that to that man, there was a thirteen-year-old inside he'd come to take. Was it fear that made him hesitate, or conscience? Do we care? We don't require moral purity—we can't. We require behavioral conformity. It doesn't matter if that man abandons his act because he's horrified by the actual prospect of bedding someone wearing braces or because he suspects a setup, or because he decides he'd rather just go get a pizza. He has done no harm. For Hansen to present this man's failure to go into the house as cowardice—even if he is only doing this to pander to his audience—is to put the carnivorous dictates of his show, and the presumed appetites of his viewers, above any basic concern with criminality or humanity. I guess the script rewrites and overwrites real decency, yet we're still supposed to buy the soft soap it shoves down our throats.

So Where Do We Go From Here?

All this flame fanning sets up *Dateline: To Catch a Predator* for that great docudrama coda: *Now, folks, what are we gonna do about all this?* To which the producers' response is divided into the soprano and bass of vics and perps: protect the first and pop the brother. Protection consists of sound advice to tell your children: Put privacy settings on high and don't put any identifying information online. If you have a MySpace or Facebook site, no real first names, no photos, no telephone numbers, addresses or partial addresses, no softball teams, no favorite malls—nothing, in short, that a reasonably enterprising person could use to track you down. Don't let anyone you don't know into your virtual space. If you go into a chat room, don't tell anyone anything that might help identify/find you; if someone says something sexually inappropriate, quit the chat and tell your parents. Like your room, let your parents into your site after you clean it up. Don't ever give out your phone number (cell or home) to someone you've met online.

On the perpetrator side, there has been some public consideration of treatment options, including physical or chemical castration. More effective appears to be long-term therapy, particularly group therapy.[23] In a group setting, and with group support, a man can begin to accept responsibility for his conduct and begin to make behavioral changes to reduce the level of sexual temptation and the likelihood that he will sexually relapse or act out. The analogy is to alcoholism: don't keep a keg next to your bed, stay away from taverns, and don't take the odd nip now and again to see if you still like the taste. Unfortunately, no state is willing to spend money on preventative treatment, though, as has been noted, some treatment will be available for those found to be sexually violent predators. A case of too little, far too late. These discussions, however, nowhere near rival the air time given the sting. I know that's not the point of the show, but perhaps that's the point of the point. If the service *Predator* primarily provides is ringside seats for a perp walk, they might as well have their camera crews stand drinks at the corner bar and film the patrons' crackups on the drive home.

The first chapter of Hansen's book details the 2002 murder of a thirteen-year-old girl targeted online by a forty-seven-year-old man pretending to be seventeen. The girl lived in a small Arkansas town where her father was a police officer; she met her killer in a Christian chat room. He spent the next year chatting online and on the phone with the girl and her friends. The girl was smart, and never planned to meet him. He was smart, too, and never said anything sexually inappropriate. He drove cross-country from San Diego to abduct her. The account is wrenching in its inevitability: the girl ended up naked and raped, chained to the floor of a rented minivan and shot through the head. The perpetrator killed himself as the police approached the van.

It's a terrible story, and it's true. The predator will prey. The man who hunted down the thirteen-year-old girl in Hansen's first chapter is a genuine predator. He would have found some child to rape and murder — he had to. The only difference the Internet made was that the child he found was half a country away, instead of next door. I represent some of these men. They do not see us as any more human than the chair we sit in or the chicken we choose for dinner. And like any cruelty in human form, they will relish our execution. But there's little policy point in weeping over that girl's murder unless we are prepared to offer some sort of way to belay the perpetrator. Predators begin as potential predators. One of the men profiled in the *Predator* series described the "drumbeat in his head" that pushed him toward child molestation. How does turning up the volume silence that?

During *Predator's* 2006 sting in Murphy, Texas, one of the men who solicited a decoy also shot himself in the head as the police came to arrest him. He was an assistant district attorney, and he'd pretended to be a nineteen-year-old college student when he hit on the pretend thirteen-year-old. Their online chat went on (and off) for two weeks; at some point, the decoy talked to the prosecutor on the telephone, and eventually, they discussed meeting. The man never showed up. But there was that online solicitation. Other news agencies have criticized *Predator* for this incident, most notably ABC's *20/20*, which explored allegations that Hansen pushed for the prosecutor's arrest. In a 2007 Web entry, "Setting the Record Straight," the *Predator* Web site said that it has exposed 250 predators in three years, leading to 120 convictions. *Predator* then bullet-pointed some of their competitors' allegations, the sum effect of which is that it did no more in the Murphy sting than in any other. My point is not that the Murphy sting was special. My point is that the Murphy sting, like the other stings, was entrapment as entertainment. The only difference is the Murphy sting had a body count.[24]

In the January/February 2007 issue of the *Columbia Journalism Review*, editor Douglas McCollam calls *Dateline: To Catch a Predator* enterprise journalism that has devolved into tabloid entertainment. When McCollam asked Hansen how he felt about the Texas prosecutor's suicide, Hansen said his first reaction was "as a newsman who had to cover the story for his network." Hansen did not feel in any way responsible for the man's death, adding, "I sleep well at night." He must sleep the sleep of the dead.

Are the people *Predator* catches really predators? Legally, they are. Morally, they may or may not be, because online is virtual reality, and virtual reality is partial fantasy. We understand this to the marrow of our cultural bones. Online, there's game playing, and there's risk taking that seems more like a game and less like a risk than anything done face to face. The Internet has proved a most efficient dispenser of information and pornography, though the pornography may be more hardcore than the information, and the porn will search for you. (The *Dateline* Web site has an advertisement link to a book about the addictive allure of cybersex.) That drumbeat must get pretty loud playing alongside a constant stream of pink-cheeked tweens and spreads of cherry pie.

Even the subtitle of Hansen's book—*Protecting Your Kids from On-line Enemies Already in Your Home*—plays into the Internet reality of things being as they appear to be. The enemy may be online, but he is not really in your home. The computer is in your home. The enemy is somewhere out there, like the obscene phone callers of my youth, dialing up or broadbanding like crazy, trying to find some innocent to jag off to. Or not some innocent at all, but just some other adult with a pulse who gets a kick out of playing a pube online. The other gross secret is that everyone I've ever known who is involved in prosecuting or defending sex crimes has some Pavlovian response at some point to the data fed into the head, some titillation provoked merely by the thought of friction. Porn is porn, and in this manner we are born, and no one—not PeeJ, not the cops, not Hansen, not you, and not me—can stay completely clean, at least not on the inside.

After the fact, the citizens of Murphy, Texas, objected to the use of their community as a trap, arguing that authorities ought not have exposed their neighborhoods to four days of roving sexual predators, even those en route to a date. Perverted Justice responded to the criticism: ·

> Which are worse—the predators out there trying to rape children they befriend on-line, or ignorant elitists who enable their attempts by trying to stop law enforcement from dealing with this issue? Our vote? Damn them both equally.

Besides the idiocy of rebuking a community for insisting on having a voice in its own policing, and the stupidity of equating free speech to pedophilic rape, the vigilantes' response is a breathtakingly current, and particularly American, riposte. Accuse the critic of real-world ignorance plus rarefied elitism, the combination of which aids and abets the forces of darkness. I guess I'm supposed to keep my mouth shut except to boo the pussyfooting perv. I guess I'm supposed to be disappointed when a man won't pounce as scripted. I guess I'm supposed to cheer on cue as *Dateline* puts out figlets to tempt the tenderloving palate, and I guess I'm not supposed to notice, not really, that we in the home audience dance equally to the drumbeat of risk-free Internet sex and the bang-bang of cops and robbers.[25]

Is *Dateline: To Catch a Predator* trivial? In some senses, of course. It is a popular entertainment among popular entertainments, the bastard child of *Cops* and *America's Most Wanted*—the gluttonous bastard child that won't wait until a perp's perped, but greases the skids to the shuddering delight of the box populi.

In a larger sense, however, *Predator* isn't trivial at all. Like the Internet and the Internet predator, it comes into your home, dissolving the line between inside and outside, between safe and unsafe sides. The physical person of the predator marks the divide between the virtual reality of the computer and the visual reality of geography, and, at the same time, indicates that this divide can be crossed in an instant. It is emblematic that the emblematic story that opens Hansen's book involved a man who traveled across the country to kill his thirteen-year-old victim: the threat wouldn't seem half as real if he'd lived next door. In order to be an incalculable and therefore supreme danger, the Internet predator must be seen as unconfined to any location beyond the computer screen—it doesn't matter where you live, says Hansen, for they are *already in your home*. The identity of geography is dissolved along with geographic security—these are the real terrorists, because they've already infiltrated your innermost sanctum, and you invited them in. In this, the online predator shares the television producer's talent, for the only difference between the predator and the predator's predator is the language of their story: the predator frames his invited entry as seduction, however louche; the predator's predator frames his as salvation, however lay.

And this is where *Dateline: To Catch a Predator* is genius: it too comes into your home with the same titillating temptations, as it offers an immediate absolution from sin. We'll get off on this, then we'll get him. "In America sex is an obsession. In other parts of the world, it is a fact," as Marlene Dietrich once said. *Predator* gives you obsession bacon-wrapped with fact. For the happy *Dateline* punchline is that no matter how damn sexy your kids are,[26] the bad guys have been intercepted, the borders are secure, and—best of all—you can watch it all, in the privacy and comfort of your own home. *Predator* is reality's end game—it's pervs and pedos and pubes on parade, it's man, bone-free, and everywhere in chains. There's no longer any significant difference between *CSI* and *Predator* because it's all show and all showstopper, on different channels and at the same time. The public, or more precisely, the consumer, can be entertained by the spectacle of *Law & Order*, which reaffirms the *Predator* spectacle of law and order—for in the land of vics, perps, pops, and cops, we're all wannabe deputies.

GUILT & POLITICS

CHAPTER 11

THE TALLY OF GUILT: THE THOUSAND-YEAR SENTENCE

Am I to be thought the only criminal when all human kind
sinned against me?

— MARY SHELLEY, *Frankenstein*

THIS IS THE FINAL STOP. The hell-terminus, where it all adds up.
There's no exiting here, no wondering whether guilt lies, or
ought to lie, or whether under a more considered culture, mercy
would interplead with justice for more righteous results. These are
the damned. The ones you lock up without blinking, and the ones
you wish you'd never seen.

And still, there are questions.

This chapter is about hard time, the very longest sentences the law
will allow, a number of years that appears to be infinite. A thicket of
legal justification surrounds these extreme sentences, but we are still
dealing with men. Men who are among the very worst criminals, perhaps, but men in human flesh nonetheless. The question is: Given the
constraints of mortality, what is the point of a thousand-year sentence?

I discuss two defendants' cases in this section: a man who for several months tortured his family, and a serial rapist of mostly elderly
women. The amount of testimony at trial was huge, and I debated
how much detail to recount here. I worry that too much might seem
gratuitous, a kind of pointless victim-porn. My clients' stories are neither cocktail-party anecdotes nor numbing tales of terror turned matter of course. The torturer risks the first sin; the serial rapist risks the
second. But this chapter is about maximum guilt and maximum sentences, and it would be cheating to minimize the crimes. Too much
editing or condensing would unfairly sanitize what my clients did, or

unfairly explain their doing it. So I will give a brief summary of the of-fenses and their resulting sentences here. The full details—exhaustive and sometimes gruesome—can be found in the book's appendixes.

One of the problems with both cases is that the prosecution facts are so extreme, and the defense facts so few. Which is how the cases came to me on appeal. Rocky the torturer's defense wasn't that he didn't do it but that he may not have done it as many times or to the degree alleged. Mark the rapist's defense was simply "some other dude did it," some other dude who happened to have the same or a strikingly similar genetic profile. Neither argument prevailed below, or on appeal; both convictions and sentences were upheld.

Case #1: The Torturer

In 2003, Rocky and his wife "Michelle" were in their mid-thirties, had been together seven years, married five, had three young children and a tract house in a middle-class Los Angeles suburb. Michelle also had two older children from her first marriage, Jennifer, fifteen, and Jake, twelve. During the first few years of their relationship, Rocky had not been physically violent with Michelle: he would throw or break things when they argued, but never hit her. But when he learned that his wife had had an affair, things changed.

Over the next months Rocky repeatedly kicked and punched Michelle, whipped her with a belt, cut her with a knife, threatened her with a gun, raped her with a flashlight, shocked her many times with a stun gun, assaulted her son, raped her daughter, and shot the girl in the knee. When the police arrested Rocky for spousal abuse, they found an arsenal of weapons in the house, including a sawed-off shotgun, revolvers, eight rifles, two homemade cannons, and a set of handcuffs.

Rocky was found guilty of a dizzying array of charges: making crim-inal threats, assault with a deadly weapon, use of a destructive device and explosive to injure/destroy, possession of a destructive device near a private habitation and other public place, spouse abuse, aggravated mayhem, discharging a firearm with gross negligence, spousal rape, assault with a semiautomatic firearm, false imprisonment by violence, assault with a stun gun or Taser, sexual penetration by foreign object, attempted torture, child molestation, rape, ex-felon in possession of a firearm/two priors, possession of a deadly weapon, possession of an assault weapon, possession of a destructive device, illegal possession of ammunition, witness intimidation, and stalking. His two prior convictions for assault with a deadly weapon and robbery were found to be true, as were various multiple victim and weapon-use allegations. Rocky was sentenced to a total of 1,002 years in state prison, plus thirty-nine life terms.

Case #2: The Serial Rapist

Mark was convicted of raping many mostly elderly women in and around Long Beach, California. The evidence of his factual guilt was substantial, and conflicting. Some of the DNA evidence was single source (came from one person), and matched his genetic profile. Some of the DNA evidence was mixed source, and didn't necessarily match Mark's DNA. The physical descriptions of the rapist(s) varied wildly. In some of the victims' testimony, the rapist was described as thin, white, and hairless. Mark was dark, stocky, and hirsute. Mark confessed, but his confession seemed fed to him by the detectives, or at least the small portion of it that was audiotaped.

Mark was charged with fifteen counts of residential burglary, ten counts of forcible oral copulation, twenty-nine counts of rape, five counts of assault with intent to commit a sex offense, one count of forcible sodomy, and two counts of sexual penetration by foreign object. Sentence enhancements for committing a sex offense during burglary, for burglary committed with intent to commit sex offense, and of having multiple victims were alleged as to all counts, which would allow full-term consecutive sentences. One prior strike allegation and two five-year prior allegations were also made as to all counts. (One prior strike doubles the sentence, two priors gets you twenty-five to life. A "five year prior" adds five years for every prior violent or serious felony conviction.)

Mark was found guilty as charged on all but three counts. Receiving what the Los Angeles District Attorney's Office then called "the longest sentence ever imposed in California," he was sentenced to a total of 1,040 years, plus ten life terms.

Mark's millennial sentence was calculated using a combination of sex-crimes sentencing rules and three-strikes provisions, as he had one prior offense, which automatically doubled each term. The California appellate court, while finding that the 1,040-year sentence was "unseemly and at the far end of discretion," also found it wasn't disproportionately cruel and unusual, and upheld both sentence and conviction.

In my appellate brief, the first paragraph of my cruel and unusual punishment argument read:

> Medieval justice included putting a man in a hanging cage, keeping him there till he died, and, after birds of prey picked clean the skeleton, keeping the skeleton on as warning to other miscreants: perhaps this is something like what the trial court had in mind in sentencing the defendant to 1,040 years in state prison, in addition to ten life terms. A sentence of 1,040 years plus ten lives is barbaric on its face, and constitutes cruel and unusual punishment in contravention of the Eighth and Fourteenth Amendments and article I, section 17 of the California Constitution.

The Law: Thicket and Thorn

Sex-offense sentencing laws are arcane sets of rules that easily lead to extraordinarily long sentences. In California, each separate sex offense may be separately punished. An act is considered a separate offense if the perpetrator had an "opportunity to reflect" on what he was doing, and continued to offend, that is, he could have changed his mind, but didn't. As applied, every time a penis slips from a vagina and is reinserted, it becomes a separate rape, which may be separately punished. Separately punished means the defendant can receive separate, full-term consecutive sentences.

By way of comparison, in the usual course of non-sex offenses, if you commit a series of acts that are part and parcel of one ongoing offense, you're punished for the offense as a whole. So the sentence on whatever is the lesser offense will be subsumed in the sentence for the greater crime. The key question is whether the various offenses shared a single objective and intent. So if I rob the 7-Eleven, and take money from both the cash register and charity jar, I'll be charged for only one robbery. Even if I commit a series of discrete offenses against the same victim (I first carjack your car and then take your wallet), the sentencing rules usually set one-third the midterm on secondary offenses, and allow for concurrent sentencing. As a rule, there are separate sentences for separate victims of violent crime (if I rob three people at the same time, I will be sentenced for three separate robberies), and separate sentences for separate acts of violence (if I rape and beat you, I can be sentenced for rape and also for assault by means of force likely to cause great bodily injury).

A Sentence of Infinite Duration

The Eighth Amendment of the Constitution guarantees against overtly cruel and unusual punishments. In a series of decisions between 1972 and 1982, the Supreme Court held that a punishment is constitutionally noxious if it is "grossly out of proportion to the severity of the crime," disproportionate to a defendant's "personal responsibility and moral guilt," or "so disproportionate to the crime for which it is inflicted that it shocks the conscience and offends the fundamental notions of human dignity."[1] Although legislatures have broad discretion in enacting penal statutes and specifying sentences, the final call as to whether a punishment exceeds constitutional limits is judicial. And although Eighth Amendment jurisprudence has been most recently focused on affixing the perimeters of proportion, the mark remains fixed: punishment "must not be so severe as to be degrading to the dignity of human beings."[2]

Over the last thirty years, however, Supreme Court decisions on the Eighth Amendment have generally been unfavorable to defendants. This reveals the changing sentiments of the Court, and the civics lesson that what is popularly considered "the law" is neither

monolithic nor monovocal, but rather the sausage-product of com-
promise or a grudging consent to the least problematic point of view.
These decisions are largely due to the current textualism of Justices
Scalia and Thomas, and, to a lesser degree, Justice Alito and Chief
Justice Roberts.

Commonly referred to as "strict constructionism," this view is a
text- and origin-based interpretation of the Constitution that limits
application of constitutional rights to those that existed at the time the
Bill of Rights was adopted. If it wasn't cruel and unusual in 1791, it
isn't cruel and unusual today. (Justice Scalia says he's not a strict con-
structionalist, but rather a diviner of original intent: if our Founding
Fathers didn't recognize a woman's right to a first trimester abortion,
he argues, neither should we.)

Strict constructionism isn't a term favored in legal theory, but persists in the larger culture as a politically charged bulwark against so-
called judicial activism. Judicial activism implies judicial interference,
and has gotten a bad rap, but it's simply another way of characterizing
instrumentalism. That's the view that the Constitution is a normative
standard rather than an itemized or prescriptive list. Besides, judicial
activism is whatever you say it is. Upholding Jim Crow laws as constitutionally approved may be deemed activist, just as striking them
down could be considered judicial interference.

A more accurate distinction would be between the broader concept
of legal *formalism*, which maintains that the law is the Law, a set of rules
that can be known beforehand and applied in a predictable fashion to
particular facts, and legal *instrumentalism*, which holds that laws should
be interpreted so as to achieve their purpose. The problem with formalism is rigidity and a willful ignorance of political ideology. The problem
with instrumentalism is unpredictability and a shifting-sands sense of
moral or ethical legitimacy.[3] The inclinations of any given set of Justices
dictate which way the Court is leaning at any given time.[4]

In 1980, the Court upheld a life sentence for a nonviolent third-
time felony offender in *Rummel v. Estelle*, finding the Texas recidivist
statute tough but not constitutionally untoward.[5] But only three years
later, in *Solem v. Helm*, the Court reversed a sentence of life with-

out the possibility of parole for a nonviolent, seven-time felon as "significantly disproportionate to his crime."[6] In 1991, seven years after *Solem*, Justice Kennedy's concurring opinion in *Harmelin v. Michigan* sought to harmonize the two prior cases by suggesting that "the Eighth Amendment does not require strict proportionality between crime and sentence. Rather, it forbids only extreme sentences that are 'grossly disproportionate' to the crime."[7]

With the advent of three-strikes laws, the Court revisited the proportionality debate in 2003 in *Ewing v. California*,[8] ultimately finding that the Eighth Amendment contains a "narrow proportionality principle" when applied to noncapital sentences. Under this analysis, only "extreme sentences that are 'grossly disproportionate' to the crime" are proscribed. There's no constitutional requirement for courts to conduct either inter- or intra-jurisdictional comparisons between offenses and punishments. The fact that a defendant may have gotten a far shorter sentence for the same offense in another state, or a lesser or equal sentence for a greater crime in the same state, is irrelevant. The Court concluded that because the Eighth Amendment does not prohibit California from exercising its authority to incapacitate repeat offenders, a defendant with two serious prior convictions getting a sentence of twenty-five years to life for stealing $1,200 worth of merchandise wasn't grossly disproportionate, given the government's interest in punishing recidivists.[9]

In *People v. Deloza*, the late California Supreme Court Justice Stanley Mosk strongly objected to the defendant's sentence of 111 years plus four life terms. He also put it in a larger context:

> Regrettably, multi-century sentences are becoming commonplace and generally remain unchallenged. Certainly there is understandable revulsion directed towards a defendant who has committed numerous counts of illegal conduct. Not infrequently the charges are sexual in nature; that conduct appears to draw the monstrous sentences.[10]

Mosk then referenced *State v. Robinson*, an unpublished 1996 Oklahoma decision in which a sentence of 30,000 years was upheld without comment.[11] The dissent in the *Robinson* case had called the sentence "shocking and absurd," and called for appellate courts to implement "an honest system of imprisonment. If we don't, sentence 'inflation' will make a mockery of us all."[12] For his part, Justice Mosk felt that the absolute maximum sentence ought to be life imprisonment—a term, he said, that "a defendant is able to serve." In egregious cases where there are "exceptionally numerous victims" the maximum might become life without possibility of parole.

The California jurist's opinion echoed that of U.S. Supreme Court Justice Stephen Field a century earlier:

> The State may, indeed, make the drinking of one drop of liquor an offence to be punished by imprisonment, but it would be an unheard-of cruelty if it should count the drops in a single glass and make thereby a thousand offences, and thus extend the punishment for drinking the single glass of liquor to an imprisonment of almost infinite duration.[13]

The Odd Logic Behind Millennial Sentences

I have quoted from so many cases because the question of whether a sentence is grossly disproportionate isn't confined to lengthy sentences for relatively minor offenses,[14] nor is it circumscribed by the Supreme Court's current proportionality standard. For the overarching principle articulated by the Court half a century ago in *Trop v. Dulles* still holds:

> The basic concept underlying the Eighth Amendment is nothing less than the dignity of man. While the State has the power to punish, the Amendment stands to assure that this power be exercised within the limits of civilized standards.[15]

By *this* standard, a sentence that exceeds the bounds of humanity—that the defendant must be locked away for a millennium—mocks the dignity of humanity. Still, defendants have been sentenced to millennial terms, though the cases are few and the justifications illogical.

In one California case, a defendant appealed his sentence of 559 years to life. Citing an earlier decision affirming a sentence of 428 years to life plus 53 years, the appellate court said it was "immaterial" that the defendant could not serve the sentence, for "in practical effect, he is in no different position than a defendant who has received a sentence of life without possibility of parole." Given that life without possibility of parole isn't cruel and unusual punishment, the court opined, neither is multicentury sentencing. Such a sentence "serves valid penalogical purposes: it unmistakably reflects society's condemnation of defendant's conduct and it provides a strong psychological deterrent to those who would consider engaging in that sort of conduct in the future."[16]

In *Callins v. State*, another Oklahoma case, a defendant was convicted of first-degree rape in 1972. Under the indeterminate sentencing scheme then in place (five-year minimum, no maximum), the jury sentenced the defendant to 1,500 years in jail.[17] The appellate court upheld the sentence, citing the imposition of a 1,000-year term for rape in an earlier 1972 state case, *Fields v. Phillips*. The majority rejected an Eighth Amendment challenge, stating "the practicalities of life compel us to observe that a sentence of 1,000 years is, for all intents and purposes, a life sentence." Furthermore, "it could be argued that a jury panel could assess a term of 25,000 or a million years, if they choose to do so."[18]

A Texas court took the same tack, writing that the actual effect of a thousand- or million-year sentence was abstract because the defendant was still eligible for parole after he had served either twenty years or one-third of his sentence, whichever was less.[19] That was the rule in Texas. In California, you must serve half your sentence before being eligible for parole. (For Mark, that would be 751 years.)

One Oklahoma justice who had concurred in *Fields* wrote in his dissent in *Callins* that he didn't see the "relevancy" of affirming a thousand-year sentence. If the practicalities of life mean that a thousand-year sentence is just a life sentence, he wrote, then "this Court should act within its wisdom and cause the sentence to reflect 'life imprisonment.'"[20] Though the judge agreed that the facts of the case would make anyone want the defendant permanently removed from society, he also thought it was the courts' duty to apply the law rationally, not to be guided—like the jury—by emotions. The justice then wrote:

> [W]hen trial courts permit and accept jury verdicts of excessive punish-
> ment . . . it makes a mockery of the jury system . . . and, further, when
> appellate courts approve such ridiculous verdicts they only magnify
> that mockery and perpetuate the travesty of justice. *It should be re-
> membered, a just society isn't judged by how it treats its best citizens, but
> instead, how it treats its worst citizens.* In the instant case there is no
> possible way for the sentence to be satisfied, unless upon defendant's
> death his embalmed body is placed upon the cell bunk for the balance
> of the 1,500 years.[21]

Is Sex Worse than Murder?

In most cruel-and-unusual-punishment arguments the defense compares the defendant's sentence to a standard twenty-five-years-to-life
sentence for first degree murder. But this yardstick seems to have lost
whatever cachet it once had, so it may be more useful to consider the
minimizing effect of millennial sentencing.

What Justice Mosk presaged has come to pass: as sentences of hundreds of years become commonplace, the thousand-year sentence is
born. And as the thousand-year sentence makes its advent, the twenty-
five-to-life term, once considered a serious penalty reserved for the
worst offenders, becomes an average sentence, an existential midterm—despite the fact that the underlying crime has stayed the same.
Legislatures can do what they want, and what they want can be the
People's will. Yet the whole point of our constitutional system is to
enable courts to step in when the majority oversteps.[22] The State's
legitimate penological purpose of wanting to put away recidivists does
not automatically legitimize a thousand-year sentence or moot the
question of whether that sentence is cruel and unusual. Because the
grossly inflated sentences given to Rocky and Mark cannot be recon-
ciled with any concept of real time or real humanity, theirs are the
"exceptional sentences." And they are absurd.

If, for all practical purposes, a millennial sentence is life imprisonment, then it's no more incapacitating than life imprisonment. If, for all practical purposes, a millennial sentence "unmistakably reflects society's condemnation" of the conduct punished, then it is no greater condemnation than life imprisonment. If, for all practical purposes, millennial sentencing provides a "strong psychological deterrent" to those who would commit similar offenses, it can provide no more or less a deterrent than life imprisonment. There can be no parole,[23] and there will be no pardon.[24] What reviewing courts fail to grasp is that millennial sentencing is also *not* a life sentence—to sentence someone to life in prison is the most the law can exact from a person without taking his life. To sentence someone to hundreds or thousands of years in prison makes the ordinary life term meaningless. To sentence someone to a thousand years makes a joke of a life and of its waste. Millennium sentencing also elevates sex crimes above all others, including murder, adding to the illusion that just as his crime is no ordinary offense, the sex offender is no ordinary human. He is a monster, and needs a sentence commensurate with his monstrosity. But as much as we make monsters, we become monsters.

The Supreme Court once took a more metaphysical approach to sentencing, in *Furman v. Georgia* in 1972, when it wrote: "The primary principle is that a punishment must not be so severe as to be degrading to the dignity of human beings." In other words, no drawing and quartering in the public square, no "particular apparatus" in our penal colonies. According to the Court, a punishment's extreme severity "may reflect the attitude that the person punished isn't entitled to recognition as a fellow human being," such as found in torture, wherein the man is refused human status, or in criminalizing disease, where the man is treated as "a diseased thing rather than as a sick human being."[25]

The Court in *Trop* wrote that a punishment may also be impermissibly degrading simply because of its enormity, such as expatriation, "a punishment more primitive than torture, for it necessarily involves denial by society of the individual's existence as a member of the human community."[26]

While sentencing Mark the rapist, the trial court used the words "inhuman" and "monster." But however measured, Mark is human. He will die, as we all will die, more or less shy of some double-digit birthday. Just as you can only kill a man once, you can only imprison him for life: to imprison any man for the ages is grossly disproportionate to any offense and grossly disproportionate to any civilized sense of human worth.

The Visibility of Power

Almost all my clients are serving life-plus terms. Most are doing somewhere between one hundred and two hundred years in addition to life. I've had a number of five-hundred-year sentences, several eight-hundred-plus stretches, and two millennial terms. When I told one of my clients, who had been sentenced to 250 years for pimping, about Rocky's 1,002-year-plus sentence, he said, "I know this is stupid, but it makes me feel better." It shouldn't. He's serving the same sentence for pimping as the other man is for serial rape: the one that ends when you are taken out of prison horizontally. Is a Hollywood pimp indistinguishable from a man who tortures and rapes his wife and stepdaughter? Are all bad crimes bad in the same way? Is my serial rapist the equivalent of my strike-three junkie?

These are big questions, attached to bigger questions about the purpose of criminal justice, and justice itself.

In her 2007 book, *Inventing Human Rights*, historian Lynn Hunt writes that "human rights require three interlocking qualities: rights must be natural (inherent in human beings), equal (the same for everyone), and universal (applicable everywhere)."[27] Hunt date-stamps the Western Anglo-European concept of human rights at the Enlightenment, and thinks the rise of the novel, and its insistence on the reader's empathetic imagination, facilitated rights development. It's a nice and worthy thought.

Of course, offenses have always been tied to offenders, which was why the body of the offender has traditionally been used to demonstrate the corpus of the crime. Michel Foucault's book *Discipline and Punish* chronicled the move in Western penology from putting the bad man on grinding public display—the guillotine, the hanging-tree, the whipping-post—to isolating the miscreant, shunting him off into penitentiaries that move farther and farther from the town square, and from the eye of the populace. By 1975, the time of the book's first publication, rehabilitation had became the end point of discipline, and Foucault elegantly demonstrated how the King's use of the criminal's body to enact the power of the King was gradually replaced by a system wherein the condemned became the property of society, "the object of a collective and useful appropriation." In the modern world, "each punishment should be a fable," an object with an object lesson; the perfect means to transmit discipline would thus be "a single gaze," the unitary and unifying eye that would see all and be seen by all.[28]

The visibility of royal power gradually became the invisibility of power's power—who runs the prisons?—and the invisibility of divisibility—a man becomes not a name but a number, a "case," one among any other numbers and cases. Foucault understood that the penal system needs perpetuity: the King wanted to destroy the body of his enemy, to prove the permanency of the King. The State wants to keep its offenders to prove the permanency of the administrative state. Foucault concentrated on the rehabilitative model's creation of prisoners constantly in need of reformation while denied the means to reform, and leading to a "carceral system" that alternatively medicalizes and stigmatizes, dooming one set of offenders to perpetual criminality by way of psychology and another via culture. The sociopath and the delinquent are assured ongoing official attention, with all its perpetual apparati. But they do not live in a rehabilitative model. They live in a packaging plant.

Efficacy First, Verdict Afterward

In the 1980s, when I was in law school at Boston University, it was still possible to speak of rehabilitation as one of the top four reasons for imprisonment. The other three, according to my criminal law and criminal procedure professor, were protection of society through incapacitation of the offender, deterrence of crime through threat of incarceration, and revenge against the offender. We're now down to two permissible prompts, incapacitation and revenge, and the greater the one is observed, the more both are considered served.

The State legally packages incapacitation and revenge into the person of the offender, who is then repackaged to the public by the State as a demonstration of official efficacy. Gross sentences serve the propaganda function once performed by the public corpse. The guillotined crown head lifted toward the crowd, the lynched uppity Negro, the dead varmint propped outside the saloon each illustrated who held power: the Jacobite, the Grand Dragon, the Sheriff. Still, the question remains: Is the State truly served by a surplus of lifers? By 2030, California will have about 33,000 geriatric prisoners, each of whom will cost the State twice as much to house as their younger counterparts. In most prisons, there's now an old-timers section, men shrunk by time to wheelchairs and walkers. Alzheimer's is becoming a penalogical issue, and razor wire seems like wishful thinking as prison geriatric wards require more nurses than guards.[29]

When society has forgotten the criminal, the criminal can't remember his crime, the victim is long gone, and the victim's family has moved on, who profits from endless incarceration?

The question is weighted with lead sinkers and strung to the question of whether man has a soul, and whether that matters. In the Anglo-Saxon metaphysical world, there used to be a lingering sense that a man should be regarded as essentially Man, that is, made by God. And because God made Man in His Image and in His Name, man's humanity could not be denied without denying the existence of God. The man not only *could* be separated from the crime, but *had* to be—sometimes, as with witches, forcibly—so that there could be the possibility of repentance and rehabilitation, based on the belief that kernelled in the rottenest of us was some pip of purity. And now, though we've stopped believing in the universal Fall from which we may all hope to rise, don't we still want to believe, even now and even a little, in the precious snowflake gift of each of us?

But let's say we don't believe in that. Let's say that we Americans choose one of two sides: secular humanism, with its moral relativism, and Calvinist-like fundamentalism with its rigid moral condemnation. Neither camp allows for salvation except for the few, who, as it happens, are exactly like us. Let's say we're happy as clams in this present state, being a sort of hybrid of self-regard and self-righteousness. After all, we love to see ourselves reflected in our better judgments. And though we ourselves may not last, our superior opinions will. In this sense, a thousand-year sentence is a grand testimonial to the Duracell Self, the man who just keeps on going—our immortal virtue proved by virtue of the immortally immoral, the monster-man. The problem is that as each monster is raised before the public eye and razed in the penitentiary, a void is left that the public must fill by creating another fiend, another kiddy snatcher or granny whacker, another bogeyman whom we can then master, because good will out over evil and we insist on our own goodness.

Studying Human Evil

Stanford professor Philip Zimbardo has spent a lifetime studying the human facility for evil. In 1971 he devised the famous Stanford Prison Experiment (SPE), in which a mock prison was set up on campus and male volunteers were randomly divided into prisoners and guards. SPE participants were to play their respective parts for two weeks; the only restriction on the guards was not to use physical violence, and the only weapons they had were billy clubs and mirrored sunglasses. The first day, the mock guards were ordering the mock prisoners to stop giggling during orientation. The second day, the prisoners rebelled. Between the rebellion and the fifth day, the guards went from ordering push-ups and attendance counts as disciplinary tools to ordering the prisoners to leapfrog over one another, exposing their genitalia; to having the prisoners simulate sodomy; to putting bags over their charges' heads, chaining their legs, and marching them around; to denying them food, water, and sleep; to insisting that those on hunger strikes eat; to shooting them with fire extinguishers; to stripping them naked; to dragging them through the yard. In only five days, a college experiment had become real prisoner abuse, and Zimbardo stopped it only after one student pointed out that _he_, the professor, was responsible for the students' cruelty.

Fast-forward three decades. In 2004, Zimbardo testified on behalf of Staff Sergeant Ivan Frederick, one of the seven MPs charged with abusing detainees at Abu Ghraib prison in Baghdad. Frederick pled guilty to conspiracy involving a nonverbal agreement to maltreat prisoners; dereliction of duty (the duty to treat prisoners with dignity and respect); assault and battery (punching a prisoner in the chest); maltreatment of detainees—this was the hooded prisoner forced to stand in a stress position, on a box, his arms extended, electrodes taped to his fingers, who was told if he fell off the box he would be electrocuted—as well as pyramiding nude detainees, and putting "Shitboy," a detainee who covered himself in excrement between two mèdical litters (as instructed by medical personnel), then sitting on him for a photo; indecent acts with another—forcing detainees to masturbate in front of other soldiers and other detainees—and taking pictures "for personal reasons."[30] Sergeant Frederick told Zimbardo that he understood that what he'd done in the prison was wrong, but didn't understand why he did it.

In a 2007 _Harper's_ interview, Zimbardo tried to explain: "The situation totally corrupted him. When his reserve unit was first assigned to guard Abu Ghraib, Frederick was exactly like one of our nice young men in the SPE. Three months later, he was exactly like one of our worst guards."[31] Orders from higher-ups to soften up detainees for interrogation "created an environment that gave guards permission to become abusive—plus one that gave them plausible deniability." Zimbardo's testimony in mitigation didn't convince the military judge, who sentenced Frederick to eight years in the stockade.

In his 2007 book, _The Lucifer Effect_, Zimbardo argues that anonymity, conformity, and boredom are the unholy trinity that turns good apples bad.[32] Put a mask on a man, and he'll do all sorts of things he wouldn't face up to, which is why the Klan cottons to hoods. Conformity is served by the mask as well, though any uniform promotes the sense of sameness that allows one to act not as one but as a member of the many. Street gangs famously normalize things like putting a bullet in a passerby's brain, just for the sake of hearing it go *pop!* And every rapist I've ever represented felt that what he did was no worse than anything anyone else had done, as if that made it any better. This underscores the effect of conformity, of going along with the group no matter what it is the group is willing to do—and groups are usually willing to do much more harm than isolated individuals, and give much less help.[33] In this sense, illegality is another form of order, of complying with rules that are, for all practical purposes, the laws in that situation.

Every time I hear someone in authority say that the aggregate "we" needs to toe more lines, I think that a certain anarchic lawlessness isn't really the result of individuality gone crazy but just another group mentality. It can be a street gang, a frat house, soldiers guarding suspected terrorists, or guards terrorizing soldjas. History's greater problem hasn't been anarchy; it's been marching in lockstep, promoting the twin towers of strength and unity.

Boredom Run Amok

But boredom, that's a real bear, particularly as we've gotten out of the habit of personal engagement and effort, at least in the off hours. Our entertainments are spooned into us in episodic doses, and interactivity is considered a selling point, a bit of bells and tin whistles that proves the thing's nowness. We're a bored nation. We're bored with politics, bored with books, bored with TV, even reality. We like voting, if it's for *American Idol* or our *America's Next Top Model*, because that vote seems to count. We don't dance, don't make music, don't play at poetry—none of the ways those with a little leisure used to amuse themselves. When we're not working two jobs, or two jobs' worth of hours, we immerse ourselves in things to consume that promise to consume us.

Does it all make you wonder, as it did me, whether the surge in Internet porn and the titillation of *Dateline: To Catch a Predator* are

boredom run amok? Certainly, all of Zimbardo's corrupting factors
are at play for the men who get caught in the sting: lives spent sitting
in front of a computer, or yet another screen. Screens are masks; no
one knows who's really on the end of a high-speed line. The screen's
a game: we make up names and sidle next to each other, half wishing
it were real, half hoping it's not. Do you honestly want to know if the
hunky guy you're "friending" has a sagging belly and a wife at home?
Do you truly want to find out if she's truly thirteen? Does it matter?
Not really. It's not real. Except, as noted, for the Show. That's definitely not boring. Except, as noted, it bores through the soul.

The killing ground we've created is made of all our degradation.
We've choked out the individual, the person alone who thinks and
thinks subtly, who questions science on science's terms, who believes
that expertise is just information that can be gathered; who considers
responsibility, personal and social, to be the duty of being human;
who knows that a disposable culture is one built on detritus, that there
is a terrible cost in favoring the momentary over the monumental,
and that justice can't and shouldn't be captured like on live TV. The
public square is now the many one-in-many screens, and in these
screens are framed the bodies of men who are not men, but bits of
programming, and the public has the right of absolute execution—
turn the channel, turn it off.

Millennium sentences are medieval. Not simply because it's barbaric to sentence a human being to a thousand years in prison, but
because there is a cruel metaphysic behind such a sentence. The medieval punished someone past death based on a belief that there was
a hereafter and that the individual lived, and could suffer, into that
eternity. So the hanging cage and the denial of the skeleton's burial
was a refusal to provide a terminus for the body, officially denying
the possibility of resurrection, and literalizing the metaphor of eternal
damnation. It is barbaric, but there is a grace note under the barba-
rism: that, as given to man by God, the individual life has at least
talismanic importance. By demonstrating the fate that awaits he who
dishonors the Divine gift, one condemned man may yet save another
man from damnation.

By comparison, today's millennium sentence evidences no belief but the belief in the irrelevancy of life. There is something desperate at work here, something that betrays a need to punish and dehumanize for the sake of punishment and dehumanization, something darker and deeper in our nature than even the fact of rape itself. The excremental pit that spews horror with a human face will always exist. Brains are not made the same, and individual criminals are a given. But the ability of a culture to act both vindictively and anonymously guarantees that people will undo their children with the same cool disregard as society shuns the poor. We don't even feed our hungry. Why are we surprised when they feed on us?

CONCLUSION
"THEATRES OF PUNISHMENT"

What is really important is that the criminal is at the
very heart of the law.
It's obvious: the law could not exist without the criminal.

—ANDRÉ BRETON

I'VE SPENT A GOOD PART of my life stocking a horror show in my
head, images and transcriptions of so many rapes and molestations
that they have to be subdivided into things like "good" rapes and bad,
gang rapes and first-date rapes, teacher rapes and preacher rapes and
bad daddies who, like good ones, treat all their children the same,
and the burglar who raped the mother three weeks after he raped
her daughter—they never did fix that back door. I unwillingly curate
a bright red, white, and blue gallery of autopsy snapshots and kiddie
porn money shots. I've memorized the look in the eye of a five-year-
old with a missing barrette and crusted mouth. I also hear, daily, the
voices of the men who do all this, the ones, like the serial rapist, who
live in two worlds at once. In the one where we meet, he is soft-spoken
and quite sweet. Or the pimps, who do know how to talk to a lady, or
the sexually violent predator who screams obscenities at me because
he can't take no for an answer.

People ask how I can do what I do, and then ask, more pointedly,
how can I defend those who are guilty, knowing that the guy did it,
and that it was very bad, how and why am I on his side? Every great
question deserves a facile answer, especially at parties. And every facile answer hides a profound response. This is the nature of grief.

My answer is that I pray that all my clients are guilty, because it's
too easy if they're innocent. Which, of course, is absolutely untrue. I

pray that all my clients are guilty because if they're innocent, something went hideously wrong at trial, and that something is almost always impossible to undo.

I once represented a man convicted of molesting his niece. He was a man of unimpeachable character, not in the way of a child molester, but in the genuine way of someone who'd spent fifty-odd years doing the humble work of good citizenry. The niece, on the other hand, had been bounced into the home of her aunt and uncle because she'd claimed her mother and stepfather had sexually abused her, but the authorities in that state couldn't find anything to back it up. The uncle, my client, eventually asked the niece to leave his home after she broke the front door lock with a pair of scissors. After she left my client's house, she accused her grandmother's friend of abusing her, but the authorities in that state couldn't find anything to back that up either, and she said someone else did something as well, but there was nothing to make that allegation any more believable than the others. Two years after she left my client's home, she alleged that he had fondled her while she was living with him.

In what is called a "pretext call," the victim phones the accused and confronts him with his abuse, trying to get a confession by way of apology; the cops listen in. During the call in this case, the uncle kept not quite understanding what his niece was getting at. But he did apologize for sometimes losing his temper, and that statement helped convict him. The jury seemed to believe that if he admitted he was guilty of something, he might well be guilty of everything.

The Court of Appeal said that although it may have reached a different result, it was not going to override the jury's verdict. That man is now in a gallery of another sort of horror, one where systemic madness is suited in dull logic and there's nothing that will alter its operations, no matter how rotten the results. Under the civics I was taught, the equation is innocent = free, and better ten guilty men go free than one innocent man be found guilty. Under the civics I've come to know, there's plenty of fodder for the good people of the Innocence Project, and the public prefers preemptive incarceration and deference to the State, and best tolerates others who are most like us.

Our Expanded Present

We've become a nation that insists on innocence. Unlike other countries, we've been able to dodge a lot of blame based on our lack of collective history. Though the United States started as a colony, and presented itself as history in the making, we no longer see ourselves as temporally contiguous with our undeniable past. We are solely a nation of immigrants and underlings, the children of go-getters and get-aheads, slate-clean of the sins of our forefathers, for they were not our fathers. We came later, and better. Our history was simply a matter of geography—events that took place where we now happen to be. But even our geography facilitates our absolution. Those of us who live in the Wild West easily unstick the wrongs wrought by the East, and the very settling of a frontier is usually someone else's story, someone who came from Pennsylvania, shooting Red Indians along the way, not someone like me, who hopped a red-eye from Boston to Los Angeles and shipped my stuff by UPS. Similarly, the North absolves itself from the slave narrative, shunting its rotten Southern artery, and Texas believes it has its own history that's got nothing to do with nobody else.

So unless our very own paw is dripping, we've got no blood on our hands; we're a Teflon people who like to elect unscented presidents, we're eager to abjure our political history in favor of a pleasing blend of mass media and niche marketing, with a little product placement thrown in. Like a big dog, we're happy just to be. We don't see ourselves on TV, no matter how much it mirrors what we want to see, or note that the Internet drips with what we shoot into it, or even acknowledge that we bear any particular responsibility for our part in the symbiosis between the U.S. and us.

According to social psychologists, deindividualized people exist in an "expanded-present" moment in which emotion trumps thought and action beats reflection, and the cognitive dissonance necessary to maintain truly contrary sets of beliefs and behaviors increases as the rationale for the behavior decreases. In other words, the less genuine justification someone has for what he's doing, the harder he'll work internally to create a plausible rationale, whether it's the guy who shows up at the sting house with condoms and says he's there to mentor the errant teen, or the serial rapist who lectures his victims on the need to stay safe from serial rapists. Or then there's me, here, explaining innocence as a conceit and pointing out how much guilt there is to go around.

It was once the height of science and law to prick women's bodies for signs that they had made a pact with the devil. With the passage of the Witchcraft Act of 1604, witchery became a serious offense in England. People with a particular expertise in the scientific investigation and detection of witches were in high demand. Matthew Hopkins, famed "Witchfinder General," got twenty shillings a day for divining witches at a time when the average man's daily pay was two and a half pence. Hopkins, whose motto was Exodus 22:18 ("Thou shalt not suffer a witch to live") did his job mostly by use of a retractable needle: the telltale "devil's mark" was a spot that could be scratched but not wounded—a three-inch spike in a spring-loaded handle provided the appearance of being scratched without causing any injury. Other methods of detection, such as the "swimming test," cut more quickly to the chase.[1] Confession was key, and whereas torture per se was illegal, starvation, sleep deprivation, solitary confinement, cross-legged binding, and constant waking and walking of the prisoner, coupled with random greetings of "Good morning" and "Good afternoon," regardless of time of day, inexorably led to disorientation and then capitulation. More than three hundred women were hanged on the basis of Hopkins's expert findings, with nineteen strung up in a single day. Officially, the crime of witchery was the crime of *maleficium*—an evil act toward the victim, done by the power of Satan.

There is an ongoing discussion in the psychiatric community over the propriety of forensic psychiatrists testifying about evil. New York University's Michael Welner has developed a "Depravity Scale," identifying twenty-six features of depraved intent.[2] These include the intent to maximize damage, emotionally traumatize/permanently disfigure, prolong suffering, cause unrelenting emotional or physical harm with no regard for the victim or taking satisfaction in the victimization, and the tendency to project responsibility for the victimization onto the victim. According to its creator, the Depravity Scale addresses the lack of a "standardized definition" for evil, focusing on elements of the offense, rather than the offender, in determining which are the worst of the worst, and the "degree of a specific crime's depravity." On Welner's Web site, he expresses the hope that this will eliminate bias and enhance fairness in sentencing. All factors on the Depravity Scale correlate to legal precepts, such as intent and premeditation, and all correlate to diagnostic categories, such as sadism, narcissism, and antisocial personality disorder.

I don't know. A fair number of those accused of being witches may well have been. As I've said, I'm no expert on innocence. And it seems to me that if you live in a world that believes in witchery, that world would be well stocked with witches. And if you live in a world where evil is another diagnosis, or can be quantified by another standardized test, then that world will be riddled with clinical cases. The creator of the Depravity Scale sees things forensically. He is, after all, a forensic expert. But evil is not case bound. Eichmann was evil. Stalin was evil. My client who used, in between sodomies, a claw hammer and ice pick on his wife—she who smelled like a mortuary by the time they got her to the emergency room—was evil. How do you standardize inhumanity without becoming inhuman? The fact remains that a system that reveres expert pronouncement over hard sense is a system that coolly pricks the flesh of real people and damns them to real death.

Accusations and a Confession

This book has presented the four facets of guilt: factual, legal, ethical, and moral. The factual was a turn of the screw, to show how DNA evidence and psychiatric diagnoses are still essentially human calls, and that by acting as if they exist in a more certain world than the world of the essentially human is to engage in another quintessential human activity—belief in a power greater than oneself. The legal was to suggest that the parameters of guilt aren't well defined, and largely depend on infrastructures, formal and informal, deliberate and coincidentally convenient. The ethical wonders what the collective us is doing when we willingly shunt large populations into prison, or when we encourage the emasculation of women, or when, in the name of empowerment, we only enrich the State. The moral is hot and murky, circling the question of what makes us human. Moral guilt is the hardest to divine, and the easiest to spot. One of my clients—the one who raped a woman three weeks after raping her daughter—was positively identified on the scene by the daughter: She walked to the patrol car, saw him inside, and vomited. That was an immediate and conclusive nonscientific verdict of moral guilt.

I don't know if this book is meant to be redemptive. Maybe the best wish is for rehabilitation. My accusations against the law are also my confession. Just as the mirrored sunglasses worn by the Stanford student guards reflected back to the prisoners the image of themselves as prisoners, this book should mirror the state of us. There's no getting out from under the calloused communal thumb, because in today's Western world, even artists abrogate their artistic identity, and authors their authority, and it's all big business, or big business writ small, for even indie's corporate-lite, and where there once was a thirst for culture, now there's not much left but a gag effect. We are people playing at being people, watching other people play at being people, and people who are as playthings are playthings. Playthings entertain. Playthings also underscore the role of role playing, how pretending can become its own realization. The child who plays teacher will teach, the set of blocks results in building, and I grew up in a world full of small white dolls and televisions that still showed cowboys and Indians.

For the *Dateline: To Catch a Predator* predator, the idea of the crime is the crime for which he will be publicly punished. Foucault posited that in "analogical punishment," punishment that is derived literally from the nature of the crime (theft punished by confiscation, arson by the stake), "the power that punishes is hidden." In the "punitive city," there will be "hundreds of tiny theatres of punishment."[3] What Foucault didn't foresee is that this hidden power would become the hidden camera, the hundreds of tiny theaters could be TiVo'd, and the single perfect eye would be reflected in, and the reflection of, all our little eyes. The man who preys via a screen will be punished via a screen, sentenced to be our evening's plaything. The offender can be rerun, and eventually put into syndication. The fable that Foucault identified as the product of modern penology has been supplanted by the fable of the production of the fable. There is more money to be had from the body of the criminal than ever before, whether as a locus for hard science or the learned art of psychology, as a cellblock of publicly owned flesh to be farmed out to publicly held private corporations, or as the made-for-TV product of our cognitive dissonance. Whatever we play with, we are. Recreational drugs affect the mind no less than those taken for a medical purpose. If we watch the seduction of pedophiles and support justice perverted, if we believe that people are diagnostic entities, that guilt comes in blocks like cement, that evil is just another form of guilt, and your guilt's got nothing to do with me, we're creating the situation and the system of ultimate immorality.

In 2007, the *New York Times* reported that sex offenders, having registered in their communities, strained the faith of those communities. Suddenly faced with known sin, congregations were being forced to decide between their desire to protect themselves and their belief in the redemptive power of belief. According to one minister, "I think what we have here is a loss of innocence."[4] All crime is loss of innocence. We imagine crime as filter, a mesh between us and them. But guilt is a lens, a rhetorical point of view. To use an overused example, killing is killing. Killing on the battlefield is forgiven as, in part, an acceptably extreme rhetorical device: I kill the enemy because I am called a soldier. Killing in the home is forgiven as a justifiable exercise of property rights: I kill the intruder to safeguard my house. Did I say killing in the home? That was unacceptably lax; I meant killing a stranger in the home, one not invited in. For killing in the home is also an unacceptable rhetorical device: I kill my wife because the bitch deserved it. The offense is not what the evildoer did, but why it was done. Because why it was done violated current social convention.

This is a simple concept, but hard to remember. It was once acceptable to stuff children into chimneys, so long as they were put there to
sweep. It was once permissible to marry fourteen-year-olds, and good
luck to you both. It was once entirely okay to sell your children into
indentured servitude and to barter darker people's babies. And now it
is all right to download chicklet porn and snuff other people's futures,
to decry the intolerances of the few while maintaining the hate of the
many, to use the scrim of individual guilt to cover our collective sins.
Individual crimes no longer exist, not really. We see enactments of
them on TV, and reports come in now and again of particularly hei-
nous events, and we read some statistics provided periodically by the
FBI, but there's no sense of the porousness of criminal offense—that
the line between innocent and guilty is, well, not fine, because that
implies a razory divide, but more like a swath of smoke.

The Victorian poor would do a little whoring on the side, as need
be, and it wasn't until the law intervened that these women turned
pro, that is, criminal. What's intervening now is the State and/as Corporation, and although I admit it's an old and creaky idea, there it
is—applicable as a sales tax—intervening by way of those deemed
guilty. How many of us indulge in a little online jerk, who hasn't had
a round of forgotten or forgettable sex, or did you ever take yes for an
answer when the answer was more likely no? We can't stand to be
guilty, and so guilt can no longer be that of individual culpability for
an individual crime, but of crime itself.

And crime is committed against innocence itself. The real object
of today's crime is not the victim, not the state, but the idea of safety
and inviolability, of pure heart and best intentions. That's why virginal
thirteen-year-olds are easy to rally around; the defense of virginity is
at stake. That's why DNA analyses must provide proof of innocence
beyond a reasonable doubt, why we have no qualms about civil commitment of sexual predators, why it doesn't seem insane to measure
depravity on scaled tests, why we have to lock 'em up and throw away
the key, why we believe some men are monsters, for only a monster
could be so very, very guilty. Guilt is what separates our monsters and
men, but we don't understand that we are them. We are the system in

which they live, we are the situation in which they were bred, or were brought into being.

We live engulfed in images, and there is no transcendence. Not even for the religious, who just have to wait for the rest of us to be god-damned. And in this absence of transcendence in which we all live, there is nothing more or less than the expanded present. No past, no future, just an endless now, to be buttered and made more palatable. Responsibility flows out systemically, from the decider to the decided, from the divine to the undivided. We live in the end of time, and we're all in it together. There's no milky human kindness coming from me, no promise of salvation. I work for the guilty. I am guilty. My guilt affords me a kind of grace, I suppose, or at least that's the consolation prize: I have been privileged to witness and revere the muck-filled fact of real humanity, and the feeling of raw fraternity. As the Roman poet Terence said more than twenty centuries ago: "I am human. Let nothing human be alien to me."

We are not containers of innocence and guilt, or subjects to be tested and studied, but individuals who must constantly reassert our individuality in the only way we can, through the steady and studied regard for the scuffed elbows and dirty toes of the worst of us. Even the pornography of sin and salvation, production and consumption, whispers some perverse sense of the man behind the digital mask, peeping tremulously out at—himself.

ACKNOWLEDGMENTS

The author would like to thank and excuse the following for their support, critiques, and kind attentions: The lawyers and staff of the California Appellate Project/Los Angeles, in particular Kathleen C. Caverly, Richard B. Lennon, and Susan H. Heir; Bicka Barlow; Jennifer Calkins; Susan C. Wolfe; Robin Miller; Margaret Wertheim; Christine Wertheim; Maggie Nelson; Matias Viegener; Kim Rosenfield; Toni Rabinowitz; Judith Freeman; William Rodarmor, my fine editor; and, always above all, Judith Gurewich and Teresa Carmody.

APPENDIX A
THE TORTURER

In November 2003, Rocky and his wife, "Michelle," were in their mid-thirties, had been together seven years, married five, had three young children and a tract house in a middle-class Los Angeles suburb. Michelle had two older children from her first marriage, "Jennifer," fifteen, and "Jake," twelve. During the first few years of their relationship, Rocky had not been physically violent with Michelle: he would throw or break things when they argued, but never hit her. Rocky also got upset if Michelle, whose first language was Spanish, didn't use the right words or disagreed with him. He would tell her she was stupid, didn't know how to speak, and should take English classes. Michelle once took the children out of the house for a couple of hours because Rocky was breaking things; Rocky told Michelle that if she left again, he would kill her and have a "shoot-out" with police. She believed him: Rocky and Michelle frequently went hunting, and he had a lot of guns.

In late October, Rocky taped Michelle and a coworker talking on the telephone, and accused her of having an affair with the man. She denied the accusation, though the two had had a year-long sexual relationship which had ended a few weeks earlier. Rocky told Michelle that she had to either quit her job or he'd divorce her. Michelle quit, but returned to work to finish an assignment. Rocky became upset. From then on, Michelle wasn't allowed to leave the house unless accompanied by Rocky or his mother.

In early November, Michelle and Rocky went on a weekend hunting trip; while they were gone, some of Michelle's things from work were delivered, including a get-well card from the coworker. Rocky spent the next several days questioning Michelle, telling her he knew she had an affair and she might as well tell him the truth. Finally, Michelle confessed. Upset, Rocky called his godparents, told them Michelle cheated on him, and asked them to talk to her.

Michelle got on the phone; Rocky went outside, returned, said he wanted to die, and shot his .357 revolver into the ceiling. He lowered the gun, and Michelle took the weapon away from him and removed the bullets while Rocky was talking to his godfather. Afterward, he started to walk out of the garage, saying, "You should be thankful that I got these godfathers that can talk me out of things." As Rocky walked by Michelle, he kicked her in the leg with his boots, leaving a laceration and large bruise on the back of her leg.

That night, after the children were in bed, Rocky called Michelle into the living room and said that he wanted her to feel what he felt about her infidelity. He took a folding knife, pinched the skin of her arm and put the knife through the folded skin. She tried to grab the knife, cutting her fingers; he told her not to worry, she wouldn't bleed to death because there were no major veins in that area. He put a sock on the cut, then got a first aid kit and dressed the wound. The next day, Rocky began punching Michelle in the arm and calling her a whore.

Several days later, as Michelle was cleaning the house, Rocky asked her if she was ready for a whipping. He took her to a back bedroom, where he said she was dirty, a whore, and deserved whipping. Rocky hit her on the back with a folded leather belt, asking if it hurt. She said it did and asked him to stop; he refused. After being struck in various places, Michelle fell at the edge of the bed; Rocky said, "Get up, bitch, get up!" and hit her again.

The next day, Rocky took Michelle to the back bedroom and told her to undress. She did, and he hit her with a brown leather belt on her legs and back. She cried and tried to block the blows. Rocky then folded a black leather belt and hit her on the back, lower legs, and butt. Next, Rocky pushed Michelle onto the bed and had intercourse with her, saying, "Hold me, bitch. Act like you like it." Michelle lay there, crying and shivering. After Rocky ejaculated, he told Michelle he was going to whip her more, and hit her four or five times on her lower legs and back. One of the belts broke, and Rocky yelled at Michelle for ruining his new belt. Michelle was very bruised from the whipping. At the time of trial six months later, she still had a belt mark on her upper left thigh.

Over the next several days, Rocky constantly questioned Michelle about the affair, calling her a whore and a bitch and punching her arm, leaving more bruises.

About ten days after Michelle first confessed her infidelity, Rocky wanted to know which motel she and her lover had gone to. She drove him to a motel. Rocky wanted to know which room they had used, and Michelle told him. Rocky became upset, called her a bitch and backhanded her in the chest. She lost her breath and fell forward, crying. He said he didn't care if it hurt, then punched her arm, causing bruises to the arm in addition to those on her chest.

For the next two weeks, Rocky hit Michelle in the upper arm once or twice every day except Sunday, when they went to church. When she complained of the injuries to her arms, he began hitting her in the face, bruising her cheeks and lips. Three days after the motel visit, Rocky came home drunk, took a 9-millimeter gun out of the gun safe under the bed, and said, "You bitch. I want you to die. I want to kill you," and shot, once at the mattress and once at Michelle, whom he missed. After emptying the chamber, Rocky grabbed Michelle, said she was dirty and a whore and he felt like throwing up. He dragged her to the bathroom, where he vomited, then grabbed her neck, pinned her against the mirror, and choked her. She was coughing, gasping for breath. He said he wanted to kill her, then let her go.

For the next four days, Rocky told Michelle she should report her coworker to the police for rape. She refused. On the fifth day, Rocky told Michelle that her coworker had molested fifteen-year-old Jennifer when Michelle took her daughter to work. Michelle was shocked; Rocky wanted to report the man, and told Michelle to report him for raping her as well. He said that if it went to trial, the jury would believe Jennifer because of Michelle's report. Rocky and Michelle took Jennifer to the local sheriff's department, where she and Michelle gave statements to the officers. When Michelle asked Jennifer about the purported molestation, Jennifer didn't answer.

A week or so later, Rocky asked Michelle if she'd had oral sex with her coworker, then punched her in the chest, bruising her; she fell back and began crying. He said to get up, he didn't care if it hurt because she was worth nothing, a whore, dirt, a bitch. Rocky asked Michelle why she didn't commit suicide, and handed her his open folding knife, saying, "Make sure that you do it right." Michelle didn't understand; Rocky said that she was so stupid she wouldn't kill herself correctly, and walked out. Michelle became emotional, and went to the back bathroom, where her daughters were. Jennifer, the oldest, asked what was wrong. Michelle, crying, said there was nothing wrong and left the room. She returned a little later, and was talking to her daughter when Rocky came in and said that Michelle was a bad mother and a whore, that he was going to send her to a Christian home for a year, and that Jennifer would become his wife. Neither Michelle nor Jennifer believed what Rocky was saying; Rocky told his stepdaughter it would be okay, then took Michelle to the bedroom and told her she had better tell Jennifer to do what he wanted or he would kill Michelle.

Rocky brought Jennifer into the bedroom to talk; he said she had to kiss him in front of Michelle to show that she also agreed to the arrangement. When they came out of the bedroom, Rocky again told Michelle that she'd better tell Jennifer it was okay. Michelle said if Jennifer didn't kiss Rocky, the agreement would be broken and Jennifer would separate the family. This scared the girl, who then agreed. Rocky added, "See, your mommy isn't going to get mad," and kissed Jennifer, putting his tongue inside her mouth.

That night, after the children were asleep, Rocky had Michelle sit on the living room couch as he repeatedly punched her in the stomach. After Michelle tried to block the blows, Rocky handcuffed her arms behind her back, then continued punching her stomach.

The next day, Rocky babysat while Michelle and Jennifer went to the mall to buy lingerie. At the mall, Michelle told Jennifer that she should sleep with Rocky to keep the family together, even though "it wasn't right." Michelle didn't try to get help because she was afraid Rocky would hurt the other children. That evening, Rocky had Michelle and Jennifer model lingerie as he sat on the bed with the toddler, giving the child to Jennifer as he caressed Michelle, then having Michelle take the baby as Rocky touched Jennifer's breasts and said he wanted to sleep with her.

After the children were asleep, Rocky told Michelle that Jennifer was to be "a full wife," and he would have intercourse with her. Rocky hit Michelle in the stomach, and said, "Oh, I know what I'm going to use." He went to the garage, returned with a stun gun, and used it on Michelle. Her legs jerked, he asked if it hurt, and she said yes. Rocky shocked Michelle six to ten times on each leg, leaving burn marks; at some point, he gave her a blanket to bite on, stopping the shocks when Michelle said she was urinating on herself. Rocky then had Michelle remove her pants and underwear, and inserted a mag flashlight twice into her vagina. After the first insertion, Michelle complained of pain; Rocky said he didn't care. She yelled during the second insertion. That night Michelle slept with the rest of the children, and Rocky slept with Jennifer.

He came to the bed, removed his shirt and boxers, and told his stepdaughter to take off her top. When she didn't he got mad, saying she wasn't cooperating. She removed the top, lying on her side and covering herself with the blanket. Rocky hugged Jennifer from behind, and she felt his penis and pubic hair on her butt. He rubbed her breast and kissed her back. Jennifer fell asleep. At school the next day, Jennifer didn't tell anyone what happened.

The next morning Rocky told Michelle that he didn't love her anymore because she was a cheater, a whore, and dirt. He backhanded her across the face, and she huddled on the floor in a fetal position, crying. He said, "Get up, bitch," she said she was hurt, he said he didn't care, kicked her in the tailbone, and picked her up by her hair. Looking at Michelle's face, Rocky noted that she was going to get a nice bruise from the hit. He took Michelle into the living room, where he asked her where she wanted to go with their relationship. They discussed divorce; Rocky told her to "Get the fuck out of here." When she began packing, he asked her what she thought she was doing, and said she wasn't going anywhere. He had her kneel in front of him, saying, "You're going to do everything I tell you to do. You're nothing. You're dirt." He told her to bark like a dog; she did. He said, no, act like a cat. She did. He said no, not like that, to use her hands like a cat; she did. He kicked her in the chest, she fell back and refused to get up. He said she was an object, like dirt, and he was going to sweep the floor with her, and did. He asked her why she was crying, she said her body hurt, she had a headache, he gave her some Advil. He told her to sit down, asked what she wanted to do; she said watch television. At some point, Michelle's niece called, and Michelle asked to borrow money for the mortgage, and arranged to meet her at a bank that afternoon.

After Michelle left, Rocky told Jennifer that he wanted to have sex with her. Rocky told Jennifer's brothers to stay in the living room and watch a movie, and told Jennifer to go to the back room and undress. Jennifer thought Rocky would hit her if she didn't comply; she went back and took off her pants and shirt. Rocky came in and got mad, saying she had to remove all her clothes. Jennifer said she had her period, Rocky said that was okay, it would be easier for his penis to go in because blood was a natural lubricant. Jennifer said she would leak on the bed; Rocky put a towel on the bed. Jennifer removed her underwear; Rocky climbed on top of her and put his penis in her vagina. Jennifer began crying, told Rocky it hurt, and repeatedly asked him to stop. Rocky said wait because he wasn't finished. Five to ten minutes later, Rocky took his penis out of Jennifer's vagina and wiped her with a couple of baby wipes. As Jennifer got her clothes, Rocky "smirked," and said, "We just moved on a step." Rocky told his stepdaughter not to worry about getting pregnant because he "tied his tubes." Afterward, Jennifer's legs hurt, she couldn't walk straight, and it burned when she went to the bathroom. Shortly thereafter, Rocky took Jennifer into his office, unzipped his pants, took out his penis, grabbed Jennifer's hand and made her hold his penis and testicles. Rocky told Jennifer it was all right because "it" was clean.

Michelle met her niece at the bank and told her what had been happening. The niece bought a disposable camera, and photographed Michelle's injuries. Medical personnel later testified that Michelle had bruises "all over her body," "bruises on top of bruises": bruises on her left arm and forearm, bruises on her right arm, bruises on her legs and back, and defensive bruises as a result of blocking blows. Michelle had belt cuts that were scars by the time of trial, injuries from being kicked and tasered, head injuries, an eye injury, and "busted lips." Michelle could not move her left arm for two to three weeks after her husband's arrest; her leg wound took three weeks to heal, though the area was still "hard" at the time of trial, some six months later. After Michelle left, her niece had the photographs developed at a drugstore and took them to their police station. Around 11:15 p.m., the telephone rang. Rocky answered; Michelle peeked outside and saw a police car. Rocky was arrested for spouse abuse and taken into custody. At trial months later, Michelle testified she was angry with her husband, but still loved him.

About a year before, Rocky accused his stepson Jake of taking money from his wallet. Jake told Rocky that he hadn't stolen the money; after repeated accusations/denials, Jake said maybe Jennifer had done it. Rocky told Jake to put a shirt under his shirt, saying, "When I shoot you, I want you to pretend to cry. And then she will say that she did it." Jennifer came by, and Rocky asked her if she'd taken his money; she said she hadn't, but that another brother had. Rocky had Jake take off both shirts and sit on the sofa with Jennifer. Jake said he'd taken some quarters from a change jar, but that was all. Rocky brought out a B.B. gun, pumped it once, and asked Jake again if he'd taken money from his wallet. Jake said no; Rocky shot Jake six or seven times in the stomach. At the time of trial, six months later, Jake still had scars from the shooting. Rocky also shot Jennifer two or three times in the knee. After the shooting, Rocky sprayed a Q-tip with mace and put it under Jake's eyelid.

Rocky was convicted of threatening Michelle's coworker, and of assaulting his mother's boyfriend, who had been taking money from Rocky's wallet. One day, when the boyfriend opened the wallet, it exploded "like when you burn a little firecracker." The man wasn't hurt; Rocky told Michelle that he'd booby-trapped the wallet to find out who was stealing his money.

After Rocky's arrest for spouse abuse, Michelle helped police locate weapons in the house and garage. Police found a stun gun in the living room, a 9-millimeter gun in a fanny pack next to Rocky's bed, a Marlin rifle, a Remington shotgun, a Bushmaster XM15-E25 assault rifle, a Carbine Ruger rifle, and two SKS Russian rifles from a gun safe in the back bedroom closet. A sawed-off shotgun and a .357 magnum revolver were recovered from a file cabinet in the house, and there was a Mossberg shotgun in the back bedroom under the bed. A Raven Arms semiautomatic handgun and two Smith & Wesson semiautomatic handguns were taken from the living room, and bullets, live rounds, weapons paraphernalia, gunpowder, and eight additional rifles were recovered throughout the house. A shotgun barrel, a Garand M-1 rifle, a JC Higgins rifle, a Remington shotgun, a German .98 rifle, a Spain Fabricade Arma rifle, and two homemade cannons, along with cannon ammunition, propellant, powder, and fuses, were recovered from the garage. A set of handcuffs, a broken belt, a wallet with electrical wiring, and rifle ammunition were also found, along with a book called *How to Own a Gun and Stay Out of Jail*.

Rocky's day planner contained a list of questions about Michelle's relationship with her coworker, and calendar pages from the charged period were annotated: "Planted my cassette recorder on phone"; the following day states, "Hell begins." Three weeks later: "Beat Michelle"; four days later: "Beat Michelle"; the entry for the next day is a circled "B" and Michelle's name. Two weeks later, "Made agreement with Jennifer" is marked with an asterisk and a heart. The next day: "Nite, nite."

Rocky's defense was basically that things were not as bad as Michelle made out, and that there was no sexual abuse involved: whatever injuries Michelle sustained were the result of a single bout of rage triggered by Rocky's discovery of his wife's infidelity.

Rocky's mother testified that for the three weeks before Rocky's arrest, she babysat for the family almost every day from 7:30 a.m. to 7:00 p.m. and never saw Rocky hit or kick his wife. She said her son and his wife did argue, especially after Rocky found out about Michelle's affair. During this same period, Michelle was no prisoner, she said. She left the house twice a week to pick the children up from school and went to the store every day. Twice, Rocky's mother saw Michelle holding a gun, implying that Michelle had access to the weapons as well. Michelle never said anything to Rocky's mother about Rocky beating her.

APPENDIX B
THE SERIAL RAPIST

Long Beach is a seaside city of five hundred thousand just south of Los Angeles. Home to both the aged yet elegant *Queen Mary* and commercial trawlers, Long Beach is likewise a motley of the working-class and the well-heeled. I am most familiar with its criminal courts building, and though neighboring Compton's Superior Court gets the hardcore prize, Long Beach sweeps the creep category. The Compton courthouse juts up from nothing, a block of Big Brother slapped in the middle of a low-slung, low-prospects neighborhood featuring clapboard liquor stores, taco and rib joints, single-home day cares, and storefront Pentecostal churches. All that's missing are a couple of tumbleweeds and the dry crackle of gunfire. Meanwhile, on the other side of the city line, the Long Beach courthouse sits near sleek corporate quarters and the beautiful blue-gray sea, where palms stereotypically tickle the firmament, and office folk walk against oncoming traffic as their unfortuned fellows shuffle through the court's metal detectors. Thumb-squat and squalid, reeking of moldy Eisenhower chic, the place has the nastiness of a pigeon dumped into a plate of squab.

Mark was charged with, and convicted of, numerous counts of rape involving mostly elderly victims. Because of the number of victims, I am simply going to refer to them by number; though this feels improperly inhuman, it also seems impossible to keep track of that many names (pseudonyms) in such a short account.

Counts 1, 2, 3, and 4: Jane Doe #1
On January 17, 1997, Jane Doe #1 was living alone in a modest seaside neighborhood; she went into her bedroom between 11:00 p.m. and midnight. As she was preparing for bed, a man came up from behind,

grabbed her arms, and told her to cooperate and she wouldn't get hurt. The man, wearing a navy blue ski mask, forced her onto her bed, removed her underwear and orally copulated her, stopping periodically to talk. If Doe #1 began crying, the man would threaten her again; at some point, he put his mouth on Doe #1's breasts and neck, and asked her to orally copulate him. A minute later, he turned her over and put his penis in her vagina, ejaculating outside the vagina five minutes later.

The man retrieved his underwear, wiped Doe #1's back, and told her he had broken in earlier that evening, and waited while she left the house to return a video. The man said he walked through her home while she was gone, looking at her things; he asked Doe #1 if she had a boyfriend. She said she did; she also told him she went to church. He mentioned things he'd noticed in the house, like a light that needed repair, asked her when she was to get up the next morning, and if she'd set the alarm. The man didn't say anything about himself. After twenty minutes, he dressed and left. Before leaving, the man told Doe #1 not to do anything for twenty minutes; after he was gone, Doe #1 called the rape hotline, then the police. The man was in Doe #1's home for at least two hours. Doe #1 described her assailant as five foot six or less, 140 to 150 pounds, and Hispanic. Doe #1 identified the same Hispanic man in two photographic lineups[1] as possibly being her assailant.

Counts 5, 6, 7, 8, and 9: Jane Doe #2:

A year later, on May 13, 1998, Doe #2 was fifty-eight years old, and lived alone in the same general area as Doe #1. By about 10:30 that night, Doe #2 had fallen asleep in bed watching TV; she woke to feel a hand over her mouth. A man whispered, "I don't want to hurt you." He had Doe #2 roll onto her stomach. When she said she had a bad back, he had her roll onto her back, and pulled her nightgown over her head. She felt the man against her, and thought he was naked. The man kept saying things like, "I don't want to hurt you; I just want to make love to you." Doe #2 thought she'd try to cry, but the man's voice got harsh, and he told her to stop it. She decided it was best to "get it over with as soon as possible."

At trial, Doe #2 said that the man touched her breasts with his hands and mouth, then put his penis in her vagina. She couldn't tell if he ejaculated before he withdrew, but he put his penis in her vagina a second time, and orally copulated her. Throughout, the man told Doe #2 that he only wanted to make love to her. After, the man said he was going to leave and to count to fifty. As Doe #2 heard the man leave, she asked him to close the door so her cats wouldn't get out; she heard him go through the kitchen and close the sliding glass door. Doe #2 then called police.

As a result of the attack, there were multiple bruises on Doe #2's leg; she had genital tears and a hematoma on her genitalia, indicative of sexual assault. Doe #2 described her rapist as white, in his twenties, with no body hair. At trial, she could not identify Mark, the defendant.

Counts 10, 11, 12, and 14: Jane Doe #3:

Doe #3 was in her sixties, and lived alone in the same neighborhood as Doe #1 and Doe #2. On July 31, 1998, she returned home from a trip to the supermarket around 2:00 a.m., and noticed her cats were under the bed and her back door was open. She closed and locked the door, took a shower, and went to sleep at 2:30, waking at 3:15 because someone's hand was around her throat. The person took Doe #3's glasses and told her if she screamed, he'd snap her neck. Doe #3 said she wouldn't scream, the man pulled her nightgown over her head and told her to open her legs, she did, and he put his penis in her vagina. The man then took his penis out of Doe #3, lifted her leg and reinserted his penis. Next, the man turned Doe #3 over and put his penis in her vagina a third time while pulling her hair back. Doe #3 was bleeding; the man got a towel from the bathroom, wiped her, lay on the bed, and told Doe #3 to get on top of him. She did, and he penetrated her.

Afterward, the man lay next to Doe #3; he told her that "it was a date" and to think of him as a lover. The man said he had chosen her because she was a little overweight and "looked like Suzie Homemaker." He said he liked her breasts, and bit and licked them. Doe #3 said her back hurt, and the man rubbed her back. He told her again she was a little bit overweight; he said he knew she had a bicycle because he had stood outside her door where she kept her bicycle: he told her he'd meet her on the bike path. The man said he "wanted to come," climbed on Doe #3 again, and reinserted his penis in her vagina. Doe #3 thought he may have ejaculated. She told him he was hurting her, that she'd had enough. He said he would leave, but lay back down again, asked what her name was and where she worked and if she wanted him to come back and see her again. Doe #3 said no. The man said he would send her a guardian angel to watch over her, and said he liked the angel tattooed on her ankle. He asked if she already had a guardian angel watching over her, and she said she didn't think so. "You didn't die tonight," he pointed out. He asked again if she wanted him to return, she said no, and he said he wouldn't be back. He said he knew she was going to call the police, but to wait twenty minutes after he left; he also told her to take a self-defense class "so this wouldn't happen again."

The man left; Doe #3 immediately locked her door and called the police. Doe #3 had bruises on her arms and legs, multiple tears to her vaginal walls and outside the vaginal area, and tears outside her anal area. At the time of her attack, Doe #3 was a virgin. She described her assailant as between five foot nine and six feet tall, with hazel eyes and dark hair "like little dreads or curls, but more like dreads." She said he was thin, but had well-defined arms. The man had a thin moustache, a lot of freckles, including on his shoulders, and wore fingerless bicycle gloves on his hands. He was naked during the assault, and was well tanned, white, possibly Greek or Puerto Rican. He said his name was "Tino."

At trial, Doe #3 believed she would recognize her attacker's voice: the judge instructed Mark to speak. When Mark repeated, "Don't scream. I'll snap your neck," Doe #3 identified Mark as the man who had raped her. Doe #3 said she had "not really" followed Mark's story in the newspapers, though she had read some articles about the case and the evidence against him, including reports that DNA evidence "conclusively proved" Mark was the rapist. Doe #3 said she wanted to see him convicted.

Counts 15 and 16: Jane Doe #4:

On September 18, 1998, Doe #4 was fifty-four years old, living with her adult daughter and eleven-month-old grandson; that evening, her daughter wasn't home. Doe #4 went to bed around 10:00 p.m., her grandson was asleep in another room. Around 11:00 p.m., Doe #4 woke to find a man standing beside her bed with his hand over her mouth. The man was wearing a glove that exposed his fingers, and had something covering his face. There was a struggle as the man turned Doe #4 facedown into her pillow, telling her, "Stop screaming. Don't make me hurt you." He asked her name, Doe #4 didn't respond, he asked again, she didn't respond. When he asked a third time, she told him her name, and he repeated his admonition, calling her by name. Doe #4 stopped struggling; the man touched her bare breast and put his penis in her anus. After withdrawing his penis, the man pushed Doe #4 down, covered her with a blanket, and left.

Doe #4 told police she thought her assailant was white or Hispanic, had a slight ethnic accent, and was short and of average build.

Counts 17, 18, 19, 20, 21, 22, and 23: Jane Doe #5:

On November 21, 1998, Doe #5 was thirty-two years old, living alone in a duplex in Long Beach; that night, she came home at 10:00 p.m., and was in bed by 10:30. About 2:00 a.m., Doe #5's cat made a sound that woke her; she got up to look for the cat, turned on the light, and found a man in the bedroom doorway, wearing pants, gloves, and a white-hooded pullover jacket with stripes on the chest. Doe #5 could not see his face clearly because she was half asleep and wasn't wearing her glasses.

Doe #5 screamed; the man put his hands over her mouth; they struggled and fell to the floor. The man was on top of Doe #5, holding her down; he asked why she bit him and said if she hadn't bitten him, he wouldn't have had to hurt her and that she shouldn't have "done that." Doe #5 didn't recall biting the man. He had her sit in a director's chair in the living room, he said he wanted to give her an orgasm, and moved her legs apart. The chair was unstable, so the man took Doe #5 to her bedroom and orally copulated her for ten to fifteen minutes, then cuddled her and asked if she was married, what her sex life was like, what her name was, if she had children, and where she was from. At some point, Doe #5 said she was thirsty, and he went to the kitchen, returning with a cup of Pepsi. He said he wanted to "make love" to her. She tried to dissuade him by saying she had Hepatitis B and C and was afraid to take the HIV test because her "fictional ex-husband lover" had tested positive. She asked the man to use a condom, and gave him a box she'd received as a gag gift from a friend.

There was another struggle, which Doe #5 again lost. After putting on two condoms, the man put his penis in her vagina while she lay on her back, begging him not to do so. About five minutes later, the top condom broke; the man withdrew, replaced the condoms, and reinserted his penis. Another five minutes later, the man withdrew again, put Doe #5 on her hands and knees, and entered her from behind. He then repositioned Doe #5 on her side, again entering her from behind, then put her on her back, her hands over her head. During these repositionings, the top condom kept breaking; the man would replace the condom, then resume penetration. The man also kissed, fondled, and sucked Doe #5's breasts.

The sexual activity ended when Doe #5, who was "torn up badly," could no longer stifle her cries of pain. He cuddled Doe #5 for a few hours, telling her that he had never "done it" before, was sorry, wanted her to forgive him, and wanted her address so he could send her flowers. Doe #5 asked the man's name; he said "Max." During their conversation, the man spoke in a deliberate whisper and appeared drowsy, but not enough to drop his head. Doe #5 lied, saying she was from Puget Sound; he seemed familiar with the Washington and Oregon area, particularly the waterfront. The man said he would leave before dawn, and did; he told Doe #5 to wait ten minutes before doing anything, and the next time this happened, she should kick the person, fight him off.

The encounter lasted about three hours, leaving Doe #5 with multiple abrasions and lacerations in her labia. Doe #5 thought the man was five foot eight or five foot nine, based on a comparison with her own height, and described him to police as "mocha" colored, possibly a light-skinned Hispanic, with a wiry, muscular build, about 160 pounds, and small braids or dreadlocks.

Counts 27, 28, 29, and 30: Jane Doe #6:[2]

On August 21, 1999, eighty-one-year-old Doe #6 had fallen asleep in her chair in the front room and was awakened by a hand on top of her head. She said, "Not you again!" The man answered, but Doe #6 wasn't sure what he said, or if he remembered the previous incident because he didn't know what her colostomy bag was.[3] Doe #6 asked the man how he'd gotten inside, he said he'd climbed through a window. The man told Doe #6 to shut up, took her to a divan, pushed her down, then moved her to a wider window seat, covering her face with a pair of her shorts. The man digitally penetrated Doe #6's vagina, then put his penis in her vagina. His penis slipped in and out of Doe #6's vagina, though she could not recall how many times. The man referred to himself as a "hot cock" and said, "Relax and you'll enjoy it." Doe #6 thought he ejaculated. Afterward, the man put a pillow over Doe #6's face and told her not to move for ten minutes.

Doe #6 only saw the man's right hand and three or four inches of arm above his wrist. According to Doe #6, she told the police that either the man was white or "wasn't black." According to one of the officers at the scene, Doe #6 identified her attacker as white.

Counts 31, 32, 33, 34, 35, 36, 37, and 38 : Jane Doe #7:

By 6:00 or 7:00 p.m. on April 2, 2000, Doe #7 had showered and gone to sleep. As was her habit, the eighty-year-old woman had locked all her doors, and had set sticks behind each door and on all windows except the bathroom window, which she kept partially open for ventilation. Doe #7 woke to find the hall light on. Someone then "pounced" on her, she said. A gloved hand was put over her face, a finger into her mouth; Doe #7 bit down hard. A man rolled up Doe #7's nightgown and used it to cover her eyes and ears, tying it in the back, and putting her hands behind her. He said, "Do as I say and I won't hurt you." She said she would, and asked him please not to hurt her. He asked what her name was, and if she was alone; Doe #7 told him her name, and said—falsely—that she had a friend who occasionally came in after midnight to sleep at the house.

The man asked how long it had been since Doe #7 had been sexually active. She said "many years." The man put his penis in her vagina, removed his penis, and told her to put his penis in her mouth. As she did, she noticed a "metal ring" around his penis. The man then took his penis from her mouth and put it back into her vagina; periodically, he had her change positions from back to side, withdrawing to do so. Doe #7 said she didn't remember how many times this happened, though it was more than twice. The man told Doe #7 to lie facedown; Doe #7 became worried he would anally penetrate her, and asked him not to, because she had hemorrhoids. He didn't, but had her orally copulate him two or three times. Doe #7 was in a lot of pain throughout as the attack happened shortly before she had hip replacement surgery; she told the man about her discomfort, and he put a pillow on the night stand to support her leg.

After a while, Doe #7 said that she was in a great deal of pain; the man asked her for five more minutes, and after five minutes, left, telling her not to move for twenty minutes. She didn't hear him, and he repeated the instruction. About ten minutes later, Doe #7 called the emergency number. As a result of the rape, Doe #7 had bruises on her body, one breast was reddened, and she had "pinpoint" bruises and multiple tears around her labia and outside her genitalia.

Doe #7 periodically caught "glimpses" of her assailant's face during the assault. The man's hair was dark blond or light brown, with "loose curls" on top and short on the sides. She thought his eyes slanted a little on the outside, and noted he had "quite a bit" of body hair, but not dark or black body hair, and a medium to slender build. She described him to police as white.

Counts 39, 40, 41, 42, 43, 44, 45, 46, and 47: Jane Doe # 8:

On June 11, 2000, Doe #8 was sixty-one, living alone in a mobile-home park about a half hour drive from Long Beach. That night, Doe #8 went to bed at 8:00 or 9:00 p.m. At 1:10 a.m., she woke and saw a naked man standing between her bed and the bedroom door; the television was on, lighting the room. The man covered Doe #8's eyes with his hands, putting her on the bed, saying if she did what he said, she wouldn't be hurt. Doe #8 thought she began screaming. Keeping her eyes covered, the man led Doe #8 around the room, looking for something to blindfold her with. He finally tied her shirt around her head, and led her back to bed. He asked Doe #8 her name, she told him, he said she wouldn't be hurt, just to do what was asked. The man had Doe #8 lubricate herself with her fingers, and put his fingers in her vagina, then his penis, then had her orally copulate him, then reinserted his penis in her vagina. Doe #8 thought the man may have orally copulated her, and that he put his penis in her vagina "at least four" times. Doe #8 told the man she was hurting "a little."

The encounter took thirty to forty-five minutes. The man talked to Doe #8 throughout: she said that he was "nice." He told her nicely what to do, and asked how many children she had, and if she would like a drink of water; Doe #8 said yes, and he gave her a drink from the water by the side of her bed. When he was finished, the man tucked Doe #8 in and told her to stay there for five or fifteen minutes, then left, still naked. Doe #8 tried to call the emergency number, but discovered that her telephone had been disconnected. She dressed, went to a neighbor's house, and the police were called.

Doe #8 described her vagina as "really ripped." According to the forensic nurse, she had a large tear along the side of the urethra, two tears above the urethra, two hymeneal tears, a red mass inside her cervix, and a periurethral edema (a swelling around the urethra).

Counts 48, 49, 50, and 51: Jane Doe #9:

On May 11, 2002, Doe #9 was seventy-one, also living alone in a mobile-home park about thirty miles from Long Beach. Sometime after 12:30 a.m., she said she was awakened by a gloved hand over her mouth, choking her and yanking back her head, repeating, "Don't scream. I don't want to hurt you." The man took off her pajama bottoms and poured something cold down her back and into the buttocks area. He then entered her vagina. Doe #9 told the man that he was killing her, that she needed water. She reached for a bottle of water on the night stand, took a drink, and dropped the bottle on the floor. She couldn't catch her breath; she repeated that the man was killing her and that she needed more water; he got up and took her to the kitchen. After Doe #9 drank a glass of water, the man took her and her water back to the bedroom, set down the glass, then brought her to the bathroom.

In the bathroom, the man stood Doe #9 on one leg while stretching the other on the counter; he covered the nightlight with a washcloth, then entered her vagina, withdrew, and took her back to bed. There, the man piled pillows behind Doe #9 and put his penis into her vagina a third time as he sucked on her breast. She testified she kept whining, "You're killing me," and asked how long he was going to stay. The man led her back to the bathroom and told her to give him ten minutes. When Doe #9 left the bathroom, she called the police.

Doe #9 was taken to the hospital: she was bleeding down her legs, had multiple bruises on her chest, abrasions over her face, and what appeared to be dried blood in her hair; there was redness, swelling, and tears to the genitals. She suffered congestive heart failure and was kept in the hospital for three days.

Doe #9 only saw her assailant in the dark. He was wearing white gloves, and his skin was dark. His hair was curly, like "a bird's nest," she said, parted in the middle, with bangs across the forehead from the sides, and very short on the sides. Doe #9 could not tell how tall the man was; she described him to police as clean shaven, five foot six to five foot seven, 160 to 170 pounds, in his twenties, not hairy, a "thin, wiry" white man.

Counts 52 and 53: Jane Doe #10:

Doe #10, sixty-eight, lived alone in the same trailer park as Doe #9, though the two women didn't know one another. The same night Doe #9 was attacked, Doe #10 had fallen asleep on her couch. She woke to find gloved hands covering her nose and mouth, making it hard for her to breathe. Doe #10 screamed and struggled, a man told her to shut up and put a small sofa pillow over her face. He took her down the hallway. She asked where they were going, and he said he was taking her to the bathroom because he thought she was going to call the police. At the bedroom door, the man punched Doe #10 on the right cheek with his fist and threw her facedown on the bathroom floor. He removed her pants, but then stopped. After some time, Doe #10 realized the man had left, and called police.

Doe #10 had abrasions on both sides of her face and back and bruises on her body. She could not identify her assailant, but thought he was a small person. His forearms were hairless.

Counts 54, 55, 56, 57, and 58: Jane Doe # 11:

On June 26, 2002, Doe #11, sixty-one, was living in the same Long Beach area as most of the other victims; that night, she went to bed around midnight. At 2:35 a.m., Doe #11 woke to the sound of the dining room floor creaking. She sat up, turned on the lights to find her glasses, picked up the phone, and started to dial 911. A man jumped into the doorway, naked except for socks on his hands and feet, and a T-shirt over his head. He flew at Doe #11, hit her in the jaw, knocked the telephone across the room, and jumped on top of her. Doe #11 began screaming, he turned off the overhead light, she started struggling, he told her to be quiet. The man orally copulated her, keeping one hand over her face as he did so; she bit his hand through the sock, and he jerked his hand back, dislocating her jaw, and telling her not to fight.

After orally copulating Doe #11 a couple of times, the man put his penis in her vagina. She continued to struggle and he pushed her across the bed and against the wall, shoving her head to one side. His penis slipped from her vagina; he pushed against her until she complained that he was breaking her neck or hurting her. Doe #11 believed the man reinserted his penis at some point. Doe #11 told the man that he must have hated his mother or his grandmother, then began reciting the Lord's Prayer. She thought he started to hesitate. When she reached the line "Deliver us from evil," he backed off, withdrew his penis from her vagina, and tried to turn her over. Thinking he was going to anally attack her, Doe #11 said, "No, not this. Please, not this," and grabbed his penis. The man told Doe #11 to turn over, she said "no more," and he stopped, rolling her over and putting her sheet over her. He rubbed her back and said everything would be "fine." The man told Doe #11 to give him ten minutes before calling the police. She said the assault lasted between twenty and sixty minutes.

Doe #11 had multiple contusions and abrasions on her face, and fresh abrasions to the posterior of her vagina; she complained that her face hurt. Doe #11 told police that she didn't feel any body hair, but that the man had straight hair on his head and was either white or Hispanic. Later she said he was olive-complected, about five foot seven or five foot eight, heavy, but not defined or muscular. He had a goatee.

At trial, Doe #11 didn't recognize Mark as her attacker. She had seen his photo in the newspaper and believed he was guilty based on those reports and what she'd been told by the prosecution.

Counts 59 and 60: Jane Doe #12:

On August 13, 2002, Doe #12 was seventy-four, living in a large house in Huntington Beach with her grandson. That evening, she was home alone and in bed at 11:30 p.m., crocheting and watching a baseball game. She heard a noise, got up, and went down the hall, turning on all the lights along the way. Seeing nothing amiss, she returned to her crocheting and began watching the news. She heard a thud, thought she had a prowler, and called 911. As she dialed, she was grabbed from behind, sending her glasses and the telephone "flying," she said. Doe #12 yelled, "He's in my house and he's attacking me," turned, and saw a naked man with a towel over his head. She tried to attack his eyes and tried to remove the towel, but couldn't. The man knocked her arm away, she grabbed his penis, finding what she thought was mesh underwear. The man pushed Doe #12 to the floor and got on her back; the phone rang and the man ran down the hall. He was naked except for the towel and a black G-string. Doe #12 thought the man was wearing something like a gardener's glove on the hand he had pressed against her face; she had some temporary red marks on the left side of her face.

Doe #12 told police her assailant had "very smooth," hairless buttocks, and a "fairly light olive" complexion: he wasn't white or black. She didn't identify Mark.

Counts 61 and 62: Jane Doe #13

On August 15, 2002, Doe #13, a thirty-four-year-old Latina, was living in a guest house behind her landlord's house. The night before, she had gone out with her parents, coming home about 1:00 a.m.; she collected her mail, got ready for bed, angled the television toward the bed, turned it on, and fell asleep. Doe #13 was wakened by a gloved hand over her mouth and a voice saying, "Don't fight me." The cloth-back glove had plastic bumps or beading on the front, like bicycle or gardening gloves.

Doe #13 said she first "played possum," but the person shook her, apparently wanting her to wake up. She started to yell and fight. The man shook her head up and down, telling her to shut up, not to yell; she began to move left, making a circle as she fought. She tried to slide off the bed, but he yanked her back. The man got on top of her, and Doe #13 realized he was naked. He tried telling her not to yell or fight, asking her name, but she continued to struggle. She bit his hand, but didn't know if she broke the skin. She said her name was Joanna, and asked his name: he said "Tito." She said she was HIV positive. There was a "slight hesitation," then he said he didn't care. She asked him to use a condom.

The man picked Doe #13 up in what she called "a wrestling move" and threw her back on the bed. Her head got caught between the bed and the dresser. She told the man he was "tweaking" her neck. The man said he didn't care, and continued choking her between the furniture. Throughout, Doe #13 said she scratched her attacker with her long, "hard and strong" acrylic nails. She scratched his chest, his arms, his groin. She stuck her fingers in his left eye, scratching it, and shoved her pinkie up his nose and started yanking and ripping, to "get blood." She grabbed his penis and squeezed "hard." She hit him. She kneed him in the groin, then slid off the bed headfirst and saw that his face was covered by a shirt knotted over his head.

Doe #13 described the man's physique as "soft." He might once have "been buff, but now it just let itself go." The man had some chest hair and hair around his nipples, but not a lot. She thought he was five foot nine to five foot ten but not more than six feet. Given that the man couldn't overpower her, she didn't think he was very strong. He was in his twenties to thirties, olive-complected; his hair was dark and curly. His penis was soft, and Doe #13 told police she thought it was very small. When the man said his name was Tito, he said it with an authentic Latino accent.

Doe #13 ran to her bedroom door and opened it; the man said "Wait." She turned around, looked at him a moment, then ran out the door and on through the front door to the landlord's house, screaming. Doe #13 had abrasions on her upper lip and abrasions and bruises with redness on her body. When Doe #13 returned home, there was "blood everywhere," she said, blood that hadn't been there before the assault and that wasn't hers.

When asked by the prosecution if anyone in the courtroom looked like her attacker, Doe #13 identified Mark. But when asked by the defense if she could identify her assailant, Doe #13 said she couldn't.

Counts 63 and 64: Jane Doe #14

On November 7, 2002, Doe #14 was thirty-six years old, living alone in Long Beach. The night before, she had gone to sleep around 11:00 p.m. Sometime in the early morning, she sat up, unable to breathe, then realized there was a latex-gloved hand around her nose and mouth. She panicked; a man said gruffly, "Don't say anything." She kept struggling to remove the man's hand; when he finally moved his hand away, she said she would do whatever he wanted, that she didn't want to get hurt. The man put his hand back over her mouth and told her to be quiet and not do anything. Doe #14 asked if she could move her small, elderly dog out of the bed. The man indicated she could, she picked up the dog, went to the living room, was about to open the front door, but the man said, "No."

Doe #14 put the dog on the couch. The man wanted to return to the bedroom, Doe #14 said she needed to use the bathroom, and the man accompanied her. While in the bathroom, Doe #14 asked the man to turn off the bedroom heater. After initially refusing, he agreed. As soon as he left, she locked the bathroom door and opened the window. She noticed that the screen was off, realized this was the point of entry, and began screaming out the window. The man appeared outside the window; she tried to escape by the door, but he caught her in the doorway. They struggled, and she fell in the hall, kicking and pushing him as he tried to put his hand over her mouth. At some point, his index finger slid into her mouth and she bit him hard. She then ran out the front door to a neighbor.

Police searching the alley behind Doe #14's house found latex gloves in a trash can about three houses away. The gloves were layered, one glove inside another, so there was more than one glove per hand. There was no blood on the gloves.

Doe #14 never saw her assailant's face: he kept a dark-colored shirt over his face and head. The man was "possibly" two to three inches shorter than she, five foot eight to five foot nine. He had a medium build and seemed younger than she was.

Mark's Arrest and Confession

On the night of November 7, 2002—the same night as the attack on Doe #14—a police officer responding to the incident report stopped Mark for riding a bicycle without a headlight. He took a saliva swab from Mark because he was in the area where the rape had occurred, and noted that Mark had a fresh cut on his finger. Mark was arrested three days later. At trial, the prosecution introduced DNA evidence matching Mark to samples taken from each of the named victims: the random probability matches ranged from one in seven trillion (10^{12}) to one in forty-seven sextillion (10^{21}) to one in eight hundred and forty-four septillion (10^{24}).

As noted, Mark confessed. However, the police audiotaped only the last hour of a five-hour interrogation. Throughout the tape, Mark is heard mostly agreeing with whatever it is the detectives are saying rather than giving his account of the crimes.

So when one says, "And then you came in through the window, right?" Mark answers "Yes." When pressed to supply a detail on his own ("How did you break that pot outside?"), Mark mostly gets it wrong ("It just happened to be there. I just . . ."), and is then fed the correct answer ("Knocked it over?"), which he then adopts ("Yeah.") — or tries to ("Or stepped on it?" "Possibly."). At various points on the tape, Mark can be heard saying to the lead detective: "So you're saying to say yes?" At the conclusion of their interrogation, the detectives ask Mark why he's confessing; Mark says, "It's the truth." One detective responds, "'Cause it's the truth and I think you said you were very sorry for, to the community, the victims. Remember that?" Mark says yes. The detective says, "I mean you are very remorseful . . . And you've apologized to us for all these victims . . ." Mark: "Yes, sir." Detective: "You're almost crying, 'cause you feel bad." Mark: "Yes, sir." Detective: "You said you'd just been making bad decisions and doing hideous things to all these women." Mark: "Yes, sir." Detective #2, a woman: "You said you owed a 'great debt.'" Mark: "Yes, ma'am." Mark says he is sorry, then asks: "No BS aside . . . personally . . . What do you think of me personally?" The second detective says she doesn't think very much of him, given the horrible crimes he's committed. Mark: "What do you think of me personally besides that?"

Mark is five foot eight," hairy and stocky, half African-American and half Samoan, and very polite. He does not have a Spanish accent.

Mark's Defense Case

The defense concentrated on identification. The main tactic was scientific, vigorously attacking the interpretation and validity of the DNA test results, while hammering at the statistical possibility (as distinct from probability) that someone with the same or a similar genetic profile was running around the area raping mostly elderly ladies.[4] In the chapter on DNA evidence, I used some of the arguments and analyses developed in Mark's case, and one example lifted from one of the DNA tests. (Another DNA-based issue was whether the trial court should have given the defense access to information on other suspects' DNA profiles: the argument being that if there were other potential perpetrators with a similar profile, that would lend credence to the theory that Mark's tests were being misinterpreted or skewed to support a theory of guilt, and a theory of guilt that would conveniently close out a bunch of Long Beach rape cases.) A registered sex offender was also arrested and charged with two of the cases, but was later cleared by additional genetic testing.

There was also the commonsense matter of the contradictory physical descriptions of the rapist; though the women testified that their faces and/or the rapist's face were routinely covered during the attacks, most of the victims had a sense of their assailant and were able to provide police with at least a partial profile. As noted, these descriptions ranged from hairless white man to olive-skinned Latino, and from slender to buff gone soft.

The defense tried to present evidence by an expert on false confessions to explain generally why someone might confess to something he hadn't done, and to explain the problems with Mark's particular confession—including that most of the interrogation wasn't taped, and that most of the confession seems a regurgitation. In a circular bit of reasoning, the trial court wouldn't allow the testimony because there was no evidence that Mark's confession was false.

NOTES

Introduction

1. P. C. Hale, (1736) 635, 636.
2. *Baccio v. People*, 41 N.Y. 265 (1869).
3. *People v. Mayberry*, 15 Cal. 3d 143 (1975).
4. Susan Brownmiller, *Against our Will: Men, Women, and Rape* (New York: Simon and Schuster, 1975).
5. Andrea Dworkin, *Intercourse* (New York: Free Press, 1987). A onetime prostitute and longtime anti-pornography crusader, Dworkin once described herself as a feminist, "but not the fun kind."
6. Of course if pornography is the representation/enactment of misogyny, then it is surely protected by the First Amendment as a representation of a political viewpoint, just as the State can't prohibit neo-Nazis from using images of the Holocaust to express their particular passions.
7. Mary Ellen Ross, "Censorship or Education? Feminist Views on Pornography," *Christian Century*, March 7, 1990, 244.
8. Jean-Paul Sartre, *Anti-Semite and Jew*, trans. George J. Becker (New York: Schocken Books, 1978).

Chapter 1

1. Formerly the more prosaic Criminal Courts Building, renamed after Clara Shortridge Foltz, the first woman to practice law in California and known as the "Portia of the Pacific."
2. *People v. Mayberry*, 15 Cal. 3d 143 (1975).
3. And turnabout is fair play. No matter what goes wrong in anyone's real-world trial, unless you can show that it actually affected the verdict, you lose. The Supreme Court recognizes a very small category of error so fundamental to the system that its presence is enough to jettison a jury verdict: deep structural errors affecting the "framework within which the trial proceeds," *Arizona v. Fulimante* 499 U.S. 279, 310 (1991). Exam-

ples: not having a trial attorney at all (*Gideon v. Wainwright* 372 U.S. 335 [1963]), or having a demonstrably biased judge (in *Tumey v. Ohio* 273 U.S. 510 [1927], the judge got paid for convictions). But these are rare, the appellate equivalent of finding a four-leaf clover.

4. James R. Kincaid, *Child-loving: The Erotic Child and Victorian Culture* (New York: Routledge, 1992).

5. *Commonwealth v. Webster*, 59 Mass. 295, 320 (1850).

6. *Victor v. Nebraska*, 511 U.S. 1 (1994).

7. This raises the perfectly reasonable question: Why not use demonstrative evidence? The perfectly reasonable answer is, *what* demonstrative evidence? As the following two chapters will show, there's no such thing as Pope-pure demonstrative evidence. Priest-pure, perhaps.

8. "Even the most direct evidence can produce nothing more than such a high degree of probability as amounts to moral certainty. From the highest degree it may decline, by an infinite number of gradations, until it produce in the mind nothing more than a mere preponderance of assent in favour of the particular fact." T. Starkie, *Law of Evidence* 478 (2d ed., 1833).

9. William T. Vollman, *Rising Up and Rising Down* (New York: Ecco 2004).

Chapter 2

1. The final analysis of a single-source sample will look something like this:

Locus (genetic site)	*DNA sample* (allelic types found)
D3S1358	15,16
VWA	16,14
D18S51	16,14
D5S818	11,12
D16S539	9,13
THO1	8,9.3
CSF1PO	10,12

2. A tandem repeat consists of multiple copies of a DNA sequence ordered in succession in a particular chromosomal region (the boxcars); STRs are tandem repeats whose central repeat units involve only a few base pairs.

3. The denatured strand is exposed to synthetic primers that complement just the outside parts of the target sequence and bind with their comple-

mentary sequence on the separated strands. Polymerase enzymes can attach free nucleotides to the end of the primer; this added nucleotide is complementary to the nucleotide on the sample DNA strand already bound to the primer. Multiple additions of free nucleotides create a new strand of the targeted DNA sequence, which, again, is complementary to the sample strand and identical to the other denatured strand of the original sample. And so on.

4. National Institute of Standards and Technology studies involving forensic laboratories across the country found that problems in typing mixtures, including partial or complete minor contributor amplification failures, were intrinsic to the measuring systems used by all laboratories, and the average interlaboratory recovery in terms of DNA concentration was 66 percent of the target value. Again, the accuracy of genotyping depends on an accurate determination of the amount of DNA in the mix.

5. Databases are constructed from a relatively small number of genetic samples that substitute for a whole population; there has been some debate as to the minimum database size needed to properly represent the population, the bulk of opinion coming down somewhere over 100 unrelated individuals. In 1992, the NRC advised a minimum of 100 people; in 1996, it suggested a minimum of "several" or "a few" hundred people. This split is mirrored by other experts, and at least one author maintains even a 500-person database would be insufficient. There seems to be no immediate scientific resolution forthcoming, but some courts have approved databases that met the 100-person minimum, apparently because they can. Most forensic labs use FBI and various test kit–manufacturers' databases, typically composed of around 200 people in each major racial group culled from various "convenience samples," places where nucleated cells are routinely available, such as blood banks, research labs, etc. Databases are growing: as offender databases become larger, so do the chances of convicting the innocent. Humes, "Guilt by the Numbers," *California Lawyer* April (2009): 20–24.

6. Allele pairs at the same locus are statistically independent if they are in what is called *Hardy-Weinberg equilibrium*. As described by the NRC, Hardy-Weinberg equilibrium is the statistical condition achieved by large randomly mating populations, "in the absence of selection, migration, and mutation" (i.e., a big group that stays put and copulates according to no particular pattern). If alleles are in HW equilibrium, their frequencies will stay constant over time and there's no statistical correlation between two alleles possessed by any two individuals in the population. HW principles

are thwarted by the fact that most people don't mate randomly, at least not consensually—those in white neighborhoods tend to marry those in other white neighborhoods and Aleutian Eskimos favor Aleutian Eskimos. As a result, real-world populations are composed of subpopulations whose allele frequencies depart from equational equilibrium ("population substructure"). A calculation variable known as a theta value is used to accommodate the effect of population substructure; the more conservative the calculation, the more it favors the defendant, the less conservative, the more it works for the prosecution. *Linkage equilibrium* is the other predicate condition for proper application of the product rule. Linkage equilibrium exists when inheritance of genotypes at one site isn't affected by inheritance of genotypes at another site, leaving the alleles at each locus statistically independent, giving real effect to the multiplication of ratios. Lack of linkage equilibrium is usually the result of inbreeding (such as in small villages or among gentry) or the physical proximity of loci on the DNA strand, either of which increases the chance of combined inheritance. Minor departures from linkage equilibrium are fine, particularly if the genotype at each locus is given a conservative theta value.

7. Relevant population refers to either the whole population of possible perpetrators or a subgroup, such as Caucasians. There is a statistical difference between using general population databases and sex-offender databases, which may be negligible given the astronomical numbers involved.

8. Therefore, if the likelihood ratio is 1 in 1,000,000, and the prior odds are 1 in 10, the posterior odds are 100,000 to 1.

9. *Danbert v. Merrell Dow Pharmecuticals, supra,* 509 U.S. at 589.

10. *Yates v. Everett, supra,* 500 U.S. at 405.

11. If a case is reversed, it may or may not be retried. Whereas the appellate court may order retrial in certain circumstances, the prosecutor normally decides whether to reprosecute based on things like the strength of the case or the effect of the prior reversal on the possibility of winning a second time around. If a case is reversed for insufficient evidence, however, the constitutional bar against double jeopardy precludes retrial.

12. Though even in this idea there is the potential for overreaching, as Britain found out when the European Court of Human Rights unanimously ruled that its policy of keeping a DNA suspect database offended the human right to privacy. According to a December 5, 2008 *New York Times* article, the Court found warehousing the DNA of all suspects—without regard to whether the person had been arrested or convicted—was a violation of Article 8 of the European Convention on Human Rights. The Court said that Britain had "overstepped any acceptable

margin of appreciation" in balancing individual rights and public inter-est, http://www.nytimes.com/2008/12/05/world/europe/05britain.html.

13. Progress, like success, is often measured by its cheap imitations: a toy ver-sion of a DNA laboratory claims it "provides little scientists with a working centrifuge, an electrophoresis chamber, and a three-speed motorized lab unit to carry out the work." The *CSI* producers provide an online view-ers' handbook explaining everything from alleles ("One of the different forms of a gene or DNA sequence that can exist at the same chromo-somal locus") to Cofiler™ ("A DNA testing procedure developed by Per-kin Elmer that uses the Short Tandem Repeat [STR] system to amplify six [!] loci at a time"), although the super-telegenic Vegas criminologists are apparently still using a VTNR-based testing protocol (variable-number tandem repeats, old-school testing that involves longer strands of DNA, more accurate in some ways), and rebelliously so, given the FBI's 1999 edict that state laboratories switch to STR (PCR-based) systems.

14. *District Attorney's Office for the Third Judicial District, et al. v. Osborne* 557 U.S. ___ [129 S. Ct. 2308, 174 L.Ed.2d 38] (2009).

15. As of March 2008, the Innocence Project was reporting that 214 inmates had been exonerated based on DNA evidence, http://www.nytimes.com/2008/03/25//us/25bar.html. According to a May 2007 *Los Angeles Times* article, the Innocence Project stated that forensic testing errors caused 63% of DNA exonerations. A report prepared by the influential California Commission on the Fair Administration of Justice indicated that many wrongful convictions based on bad forensic evidence could be avoided if defense counsel "were fully competent to challenge the evidence," http://www.latimes.com/2007/may/09/local/me-forensic-9.

16. San Francisco Deputy Public Defender Bicka Barlow has been instru-mental in bringing these matches—previously thought to be statistical anomalies, if not impossibilities—into the courtroom. Since the Arizona matches were first detected, the numbers have changed: out of a database of 65,000, there were 122 matching pairs at nine loci, and 20 matching pairs at ten loci. A search of the Illinois database in 2006 revealed 903 pairs that matched at a minimum of nine loci out of a population sample of 220,000. A search of Maryland's database of 30,000 found 32 match-ing pairs at nine loci or above. Chris Smith, "DNA's identity crisis," *San Francisco Magazine*, September 2008. http://www.sanfranmag.com/story/dna's-identity-crisis. I am personally indebted to Bicka Barlow for explaining DNA analysis to me, particularly mixed-source analysis, in a way that made absolute sense. Any subsequent failures of understanding are entirely my own.

17. Maura Dolan and Jason Felch, "The peril of DNA: it's not perfect," *Los Angeles Times*, Dec. 26, 2008.

18. If only one of the ambiguous alleles was resolved, Todd would have a one in three chance of being further inculpated. If two loci were resolved, Todd would have a two in nine chance of inculpation, because he'd have to match exactly two of the nine possible combinations. If three, a three in twenty-seven chance, and so on. Extending this to include all seven ambiguous loci, Todd had a 3^7 chance of being a match—there was one chance out of 2,187 possible chances that every ambiguous locus exactly matched Todd's genotype, a .0004572 probability of an exact match.

19. Jeremy Gans and Gregor Urbas, "DNA Identification in the Criminal Justice System," *Australian Institute of Criminology*, May 2002, No. 26, http://www.aic.gov.au (italics added).

20. *Genophiler Analysis Report*, Jan. 10, 2003.

21. Nick Madigan, "Houston's troubled DNA crime lab faces growing scrutiny," *New York Times*, Feb. 9, 2003. Trouble in this case being unskilled lab analysts, including two former zoo workers; a leaking lab roof that contaminated the evidence below; and an impressive rate of death penalty verdicts and completed executions, http://www.nytimes. com/2003/02/09/politics/09; see also, Roma Khanna, "Problems persisted at reformed crime lab / DNA division called 'out of control' before shut a 2nd time," *Houston Chronicle*, Feb. 22, 2008, http://www. chron.com/CDA/archives/archive.mpl?id=2008_4518621. In 2009, the National Academy of Sciences found pervasive and systemic problems in forensic testing by crime laboratories. (See Solomon Moore, "Science found wanting in nation's crime labs," *New York Times*, February 5, 2009; Jason Felch, "Report questions science, reliability of crime lab evidence," *Los Angeles Times*, February 18, 2009).

22. Joining Justice Scalia were Justices Stevens, Souter, and Ginsberg; Justice Thomas concurred, based on his belief that the certificates were "plainly affidavits" covered by the Confrontation Clause. Justices Kennedy, Alito, Breyer, and the Chief Justice formed the dissent. (*Melendez-Diaz v. Massachusetts, supra*, 557 U.S. ___.

Chapter 3

1. TV cop shows call this "time off for good behavior." In California, this used to be half time, but for violent offenders it has been reduced to 15 percent of time served.

2. Each commitment proceeding is treated as a new commitment, even though the person is not released in the interim.

3. A second SVP hospital opened in Coalinga, California, in 2005. The new $388-million facility was designed to be a theraputic setting. Still, three-quarters of the patients refuse to participate in treatment. Even if they were willing, twenty-six of the thirty-seven staff psychiatrist positions were vacant, with hospital police providing clinician services on many wards. As of August 2007, no Coalinga patient had been released via the treatment program. Scott Gold and Lee Romney, "Treatment replaced by turmoil: A state hospital meant for sexually violent predators gets low marks after two years," *Los Angeles Times*, Nov. 15, 2007.

4. The next major textual revision of the DSM is to be published in 2011, http://www.dsmivtr.org/index.cfm.

5. Leaving open the interesting metaphysical question whether it is better to compulsively rape (rape as essence) or rape freely and voluntarily (existential rape). By way of comparison, premeditated killings get longer sentences than killings by uncontrollable impulse.

6. The ten Static-99 factors are: (1) the offender was under the age of twenty-five at the time of his first offense, (2) no two-year period of intimate cohabitation, (3) the most recent offense was violent, (4) a prior history of nonsexual violent convictions, (5) the number of prior sexual offenses, (6) the number of prior sentencing dates, (7) convictions for noncontact sex offenses, (8) unrelated victims, (9) stranger victims, and (10) male victims. All factors are scored either 0 (inapplicable) or 1 (applicable), except prior sexual offenses (factor #5), which scores from 0 to 3, depending on the number of priors, the past being the best prognosticator. In 2007, the Static-99 was statutorily authorized as the official risk-assessment tool by the State of California.

7 For an excellent article on the hazards of returning to the community— for the rehabilitated SVP—see Ben Ehrenreich's "Labels can really kill a person," in the August 2004 issue of *The Believer*. Ehrenreich chronicles the reluctance of officials to release offenders they deem rehabilitated (the SVPs call themselves "hosprisoners" in a "hosprison") and the various flaming hoops through which the released offender must jump: everything from keeping a log of activities (to the half-hour); to chemical castration; to being moved to a new location every few days, as the predictable outrage of every new community necessitates constant relocation. One released offender, unable to find a willing landlord, has chosen to live in a trailer on state prison grounds.

8. The classic pruno recipe: put a few cups of any sort of fruit (plus a can of fruit cocktail if you can get it) in a biggish plastic bag, mash it up, add a couple of cups of hot water, run the (closed) bag under hot tap water for about fifteen minutes, wrap the bag in a towel/some clothes, let ferment/fester for two days, put in six or seven packets of ketchup and about fifty sugar cubes, reheat the bag under the tap for half an hour, rewrap the bag. For the next three days, reheat the bag for fifteen minutes every other day. Skim pulp prior to drinking. In some institutions, they no longer give inmates fresh fruit, to prevent cell-stills, but yams, Jell-O, hard candies, and frosting have been used as make-do substitutes. Pruno is notoriously nasty. Jarvis Masters, a San Quentin death-row inmate, won a PEN award for his poem "Recipe for Prison Pruno." The last line is, "May God have mercy on your soul."

9. *Kansas v. Hendricks*, 521 U.S. 361, 369 (1997).

10. Ibid., 364.

11. Ibid., 356.

12. Ibid., 359.

13. For the Court: Justices Thomas, O'Connor, Scalia, and Kennedy, joined by Chief Justice Rehnquist; Justice Kennedy filed a concurrence. Justice Breyer dissented, joined by Justices Stevens and Souter, and joined in part by Justice Ginsburg.

14. *Hendricks*, 521 U.S. 372.

15. Ibid., 374.

16. Ibid., 382, 396.

17. Ibid., 411.

18. Justice Breyer quoted the DSM-IV in noting "the imperfect fit between the questions of ultimate concern to the law and the information contained in [the DSM's] clinical diagnosis." (*Kansas v. Crane, supra*, 534 U.S. at 413–414, quoting DSM-IV at xxx–xxxiii.)

19. *Kansas v. Crane*, 534 U.S. 412–413 (2002).

20. *Kumho Tire Co., Ltd. v. Carmichael*, 526 U.S. 137, 152 (1999).

21. In California, this general standard specifically cedes to a kind of nineteenth-century view of psychology, leading one court to hold the standards of scientific acceptance inapplicable to SVP clinical assessments, distinguishing between testimony involving the "learned professional *art*" of psychology and the "purported exact 'science'" of science (*People v. Ward*, 71 Cal. App. 4th 368 [1999], emphasis in original). Because SVPs are assessed by way of art, not science, scientific-evidence admissibility standards don't apply.

22. Five were considered stable factors: intimacy deficits, social influences, tolerant attitude of sexual assault, sexual self-regulation, and general self-regulation. Four were acute, meaning subject to change: substance abuse, negative mood, anger/hostility, and opportunities for victim access. For all kinds of offenders, low self-control seemed to be the most significant factor in predicting whether someone would violate parole or probation.

23. The 2004 meta-analysis underscored the need for assessment of dynamic risk factors related to recidivism, while cautioning that there was no information on whether changes in those factors would actually correlate to a change in recidivism rates. Even so, the authors noted, use of more dynamic actuarial instruments to make SVP commitment determinations would be improper, because those instruments have not been proven reliable. Meaning, for example, that by all studied accounts, a patient's refusal to participate in SVP treatment programs is not significantly related to sexual recidivism; courts that take this refusal into account are just flat wrong. And thus art trumps science, and not in a good way. R. Karl Hansen & K. Morton-Bourgon (2004) "Predictors of sexual recidivism: An updated meta-analysis (User report No. 2004-02) Ottawa, ON: Public Safety and Emergency Preparedism, Canada.

24. Accuracy rates ranged from .31 to .84, depending on the test and the crime. Accuracy rates were better for child molesters than rapists. In a disturbing new trend, Static-99 assessments have begun cropping up in probation reports, the reports prepared for the trial court to use in sentencing. That is, the government now wants to use a statistical tool designed for quantifying recidivism rates to decide how much time to give someone in prison. Does the fact that I might pose a greater statistical likelihood of reoffending mean my sentence should be peremptorily longer? How does this statistical analysis relate to the harm actually done — should I get less time because I'm less likely to reoffend?

25. A psychiatric social worker with more than thirty years' experience estimated that more than a third of the patients in one of California's SVP hospitals would pose no threat if released. Scott Gold and Lee Romney, "Treatment replaced by turmoil: A state hospital meant for sexually violent predators gets low marks after two years," *Los Angeles Times*, November 15, 2007.

26. According to the article cited in note 25 above, three-quarters of the patient population at Coalinga, California's newest SVP facility, refuse

to participate in treatment, most because they don't believe it makes any difference in their prospects for release. In the two years since the facility opened, no one has been released by way of the hospital program. Those that are willing to participate have another problem: only two of the sixteen senior psychiatrist positions, and eight of twenty staff psychiatrist positions are filled.

27. Again, the Stable 2000 looks to intimacy problems (i.e., lack of a longish-term intimate relationship, though a man in custody will have either nothing but his precustodial history of intimacy, or an intimate Big House relationship whose damned if you do/don't existence demonstrates the man's inability to conform to the rules of the institution, which prohibit such relationships), sexual deviance (proved by the crime[s]), tolerance of sexual offenses (the patient's attitude toward his crime and sex offenses in general, which may be proved by anything from "the bitch deserved it" to "sometimes men are falsely accused"), and inability to cooperate with supervision (parole history).

28. Alcoholics Anonymous—the abstinence model used by the SVP programs—is replete with stories of Doubting Thomases who stay sober by staying in AA.

29. *Lee v. State*, 854 So. 2d 709, 718 (Fla. 2003), conc. opn. by Casanueva, J.

30. According to a 2003 Department of Justice study (Patrick A. Langan, Erica L. Schmitt, Matthew R. Durose, "Recidivism of Sex Offenders Released from Prison in 1994" [NCJ-198281], www.ojp.usdoj.gov/bjs/abstract/rsorp94.htm), 5.3 percent of sex offenders are rearrested for another sex crime within three years of parole, 43 percent are rearrested for a non-sex offense. Within three years of parole, 68 percent of non-sex offenders are rearrested, 1.3 percent for sex crimes. (Rapists had a 5 percent rearrest rate; child molesters a 5.1 percent rate.) Even over a 20-year period, according to a 2004 study by Harris and Hanson, approximately 70 percent of sex offenders had not sexually recidivated. (Boy victim child molesters had the highest rate of sexual recidivism: 35 percent in fifteen years; incest offenders had the lowest: 13 percent in fifteen years.) Those who had no prior sex offenses had a 19 percent recidivism rate in fifteen years, or an 80 percent nonrecidivism rate. Statistically speaking, compared to the likelihood of a sex offender committing another sex crime, a robber is much more likely to rob again, a burglar to burgle, a batterer to bang more heads. We don't assess these latter people for additional confinement, though our world would doubtless be far safer without such workaday criminals.

31. Moreover, participation in treatment is not necessarily any indication of need to participate in treatment: in 2004, James Rodriguez, having been diagnosed with antisocial personality disorder, paraphilia NOS, polysubstance abuse, and narcissism, was released from Atascadero State hospital as one of only three patients to successfully complete treatment. Since his release, Rodriguez has been fully exonerated by one of his two accusers (the other doesn't actually remember who Rodriguez is). Though Rodriguez's treatment protocol had been somewhat hindered by his persistent "denial" of guilt, he eventually "accepted responsibility" for the actions his former accuser disavowed, and was thereby able to complete the program to the satisfaction of the state psychologists. Ben Ehrenreich, "Predator or prey?" *LA Weekly*, August 19, 2004, http://www.laweekly.com/2004-08-19/news/predator-or-prey/.

32. *Hendricks*, 521 U.S. at 372.

33. "Win" should more properly apply to games of sport and chance than to the return of a convicted sex offender to the community after a medical determination that he no longer poses a threat to the public. Boggs was released on July 27, 2006. By way of comparison, Minnesota has been civilly committing sex offenders since 1990. As of July 2006, none had been released back into the community, http://www.foxnews.com/story/0,2933,202874,00.html.

Chapter 4

1. Dante, *Inferno*, trans. Robert Hollander and Jean Hollander (New York: Random House, 2000), p. 465.

2. *Hopkins v. Reeves*, 524 U.S. 88, 96 (1998).

3. *People v. Birks*, 19 Cal.4th 108, 136 (1998).

4. James R. Kincaid, *Child-loving: The Erotic Child and Victorian Culture* (New York: Routledge, 1992), pp. 384, 388.

5. Kincaid is oddly prudish in this sense, for even as he is pointing to 1920s cartoon strips featuring Buster Brown's bare-bottomed spanking as proof of cultural pedophilia, he is playing in a morally severe all-or-nothing world, in which a drop of desire taints the whole. Kincaid argues that because this desire exists, it should mitigate criminality. But if this were the case, we'd have to modify all sorts of criminal laws to accommodate all our glass houses, for who hasn't felt the urge to pocket something not strictly yours, or to get away with murder, at least for a moment? Too, in

Kincaid's black-and-white world, smiling as one's social adversary makes a public gaffe is the same as running him through with a pickle fork, and Ambrose Bierce's epigrammatic "Happiness is an agreeable sensation arising from contemplating the misery of another" is as funny as a passage from *Mein Kampf.* But this is silly. Morality also occupies a sliding scale, and thought-crime is definitionally inchoate. More to the point, it's a fake intellectual leap to go from little Jimmy enjoying making it stand up to wanting Daddy to do him.

6. See *Préparez vos mouchoirs* (Take Out Your Handkerchiefs, 1978), where a married woman seduces a thirteen-year old. There are also movies that portray the molester as monster, *M* (1931) and *Mystic River* (2003), and those that chronicle real-life molestation cases, *Capturing the Friedmans* (2003) and *The Boys of St. Vincent* (1992, 1993). Maybe the line of demarcation is postcoital. If the adult/child relationship is seen in retrospect as nurturing, it is celebrated, as in *Voor Een Verloren Sodaat* (For a Lost Soldier, 1992), if seen as exploitive, condemned, as in *Lolita* (1962 and 1997). Put another way, it's Socrates versus Caligula, or Greek over Roman.

7. And even those two typically involve either rape or threatened rape of the younger by the older, or a faux-näif—is there any other kind?— surrounded by jaded dykes, both in *Chained Heat* (1983); or same-age-same-sex love between French girls at school, not pedophiliac desire, in *Therese and Isabelle* (1968). *Maedchen in Uniform* (1931) is a noteworthy exception (unconsummated Sapphic crush between cute student and everybody's favorite teacher). For girl-woman/middle-aged man love, American style, see *Manhattan* (1979).

8. Whereas the pervert husband/father is a stock character, molesting the maid and babysitter, the pervert mother appears to be perverted only regarding the son: *The Manchurian Candidate* (1962 and 2004), *Phaedra* (1962). This may have something to do with an obsessive reification for The Mother and The Son. Not in the Nativity sense, though there's that, but in the Freudian sense of "His majesty the baby." (I am indebted to poet/critical theorist Christine Wertheim for expounding on this notion in otherwise casual conversation.) As in *Alice in Wonderland*: The Cat: "Bye the bye, what became of the baby? I'd nearly forgotten to ask." Alice: "It turned into a pig." The Cat: "I thought it would."

9. I am being ever so agreeable in this. I am not even commenting on the requirement that the object of the pedophiliac fantasy must be flutteringly, flatteringly compliant, like Alice. Though the object of desire

might well turn out to be petulant, quarrelsome, and discontented, like Lolita.

10. According to the National Conference of State Legislatures, http://www. ncsl.org/programs/fiscal/correx07.htm#look.

11. "Offending the law," editorial, *Los Angeles Times*, October 2, 2006.

12. *Aid for Women v. Foulston*, 327 F. Supp. 2d 1093 (D. Kan. 2006).

13. The federal statutory counterpart has essentially the same provisions and has been applied to videos of girls in leotards, and Internet teen-modeling sites featuring girls in swimsuits or lingerie.

14. Typically via the arrest of a third party for molestation, finding kiddie porn on that person's computer, and tracing back the source, or through the use of police decoys/ruses in Internet chat rooms or social centers to get others to volunteer to swap images.

15. E.g., "Cuum-filled insides of UT Blond Babes, SpchoolGirl Snexy Paosing, Fist in INOSNT ASs, the SXUCKING antics of teen TRAnnies, Granny F*KD in Bathroom" and "HARDCOOR mums and dads doing their FirstTimE sons & daughters."

16. *Kennedy v. Louisiana*, 128 S. Ct. 2641 (2008) at 2646, 2658, and 2661.

17. According to a 2003 report by Britain's Home Office Research, Development, and Statistics Directorate, Britain locks up 139 people per 100,000, China 111, Australia 116, Germany 96, Ireland 86, France/Belgium/Austria 85, Japan 48, and Denmark 39. The British report further identifies the U.S. as having the highest prison population percentage in the world (686/100,000), with the Cayman Islands (664/100,000) and Russia (638/100,000) taking silver and bronze. Worldwide, we're the Man's man.

18. Another problem, too large to adequately address here, is that the racial demographics of our inmates bear no reasoned relationship to our national racial demographics: Caucasians make up about 70 percent of the U.S. general population, African-Americans about 12 percent, Hispanics about 12.5 percent; Caucasians comprise 35 percent of the U.S. prison population, African-Americans 44 percent, Hispanics 18 percent. I haven't seen any graphs that break down inmate population by class, or within class, by race, or within race and class, by crime. Anecdotally, I see as many Caucasian molesters as non-Caucasian, and, although I represent only indigent defendants, a good number of the middle-class, or formerly middle-class (private trial counsel is not cheap). I also see that some crimes—such as rape of an intoxicated person—appear to be enforced rather more regularly at house parties than at frat houses.

19. For example, certain sex offenders are classified as "special needs," meaning that they have to be housed with similar inmates in particular institutions. What makes them special is that they are especially vulnerable—old, weak, overtly effeminate. Their special need is not to be killed by other inmates.

20. Some highlights from the history of prison privatization: California's own San Quentin was built in 1852 as the first private prison in the United States. After a spate of mismanagement scandals, Quentin was permanently turned over to the state in 1861. During Reconstruction, the South replaced slave labor with convict labor by way of convict leases granted to private interests, including railroads and plantations. Frederick Douglass, among others, condemned convict leasing, writing: "The state throws off the entire responsibility of caring for her convicts, and turns them over into the hands of the lessee, whose only interest in them is to secure for himself, what profit he can for their labor." Frederick Douglass, "The Convict Lease System," in *The Reason Why the Colored American Is Not in the World's Columbian Exposition*, ed. Ida B. Wells (1893); reprint Urbana and Chicago: University of Illinois Press, 1999. The Southern convict lease system was phased out in the early 20th century, in part due to opposition from labor union and reform movements; in 1928, Alabama became the last state to stop leasing its prisoners. The convict lease system was replaced by prison work camps and the chain gang. Alex Lichtenstein, *Twice the Work of Free Labor: The Political Economy of Convict Labor in the New South* (London, New York: Verso, 1996); Anne Haw Holt, "Men, Women and Children in the Stockade: How the People, the Press, and the Elected Officials of Florida Built a Prison System," http://etd.lib.fsu.edu/theses/available/etd-10252005-172103/unrestricted/Main_Dissertation.pdf. Arizona introduced the chain gang in 1995, an all-volunteer outfit that does public works such as digging paupers' graves and weeding roadsides. The chain gangs wear old-school black and white striped uniforms, with the new day addition of female (1996) and juvenile (2004) chain gangs. In 1995, Alabama re-introduced the chain gang, complete with a hitching post: an outdoor iron post to which prisoners were hitched who claimed to be too sick to work on the chain. The hitching post practice ended in 1997, due to complaints of prisoner abuse by, among others, the Southern Poverty Law Center. The chain gang program itself was abandoned in 1999 because of budgetary constraints. (See the 1999 video *American Chain Gang*, directed by Xackery Irving.)

21. Department of Justice, December 5, 2007 press release, "One in every 31 U.S. adults was in a prison or jail or on probation or parole at the end of last year," http://www.ojp.usdoj.gov/bjs/pub/press/p06ppus06pr.htm.

22. Compared with California (pop. 36,132,147) placing at 170,676; Texas (pop. 22,859,968) to show with 169,003; Florida (pop. 17,789,864) is a distant state third with 89,768; and New York (pop. 19,254,630), a poor fourth at 62,743. And we're not dealing at all with jail (the place where misdemeanants are incarcerated, and all defendants, felony and misdemeanor, are held pre-trial) populations. For the curious, here are the top three raw jail population numbers in 2005: California 82,138; Texas 66,534; Florida 63,620.

23. To illustrate: if there is an average 3 percent annual increase in the federal inmate population, there would be an expected 787 more private federal prisoners than the year before, and 811 more the following year, and so on. The California Department of Corrections' 2006 projected increase in California's incarcerated from 172,561 (2006) to 176,088 (2007) to 179,558 (2008) means about 165 or so more privatized prisoners/year—from 2,470 in 2005 to 2,960 by 2008. But these minimums do not reflect the actual rate of exchange. In 2005, the federal system alone added 2,038 prisoners to private prisons; in 2008, California privatized 5,100 prisoners.

24. See http://www.ojp.gov/bjs/pub/pdf/pim08st.pdf. The federal government also plans to contract out immigration detention centers. As of Fall 2007, the feds expected to have 27,500 immigrants in custody every night, at an annual cost of $1 billion, exact numbers subject to increase. Profit margins are higher on detention centers (greater than 20 percent) than prisons (mid-teens) because detention centers provide no educational/vocational programming or recreational activities. Correctional Corporation of America's detention revenue rose over $25 million during the first quarter of 2006; by 2008, it was *by itself* the fourth largest correctional system in the nation. For the largest twenty state private prison populations as of 2007, see http://www.texasprisonbidness.org/lobbying-and-influence/texas-increases-private-prison-population.

25. Stephanie Chen, "Larger inmate population is boon to private prisons," *The Wall Street Journal*, November 18, 2008, http://online.wsj.com/article/SB122705334657739263.html.

26. Ibid. See also Pew Charitable Trust Report, "One in 100: Behind bars in America 2008," http://www.pewcenteronthestates.org/uploadedFiles/One%20in%20100(3).pdf.

27. A lawsuit was filed by the California Correctional Peace Officers Association and the Service Employees International Union Local 1000 to enjoin these transfers as an unconstitutional breach of traditional public duty. Transfers have been permitted while the issue is being litigated, and the California penal code has been amended to permit involuntary inmate transfers out of state. Another suit to enjoin the transfers was filed in July 2008 by the ACLU on grounds that the secret policies governing transfer decisions meant that inmates didn't know what rules applied in the decision-making process, and that decisions could be based on arbitrary criteria such as race or immigration status.

28. For example, in 2005, the governor of Hawaii announced his state was not going to build any more prisons on the island, and would simply ship prisoners to private mainland facilities.

29. *In re Americans United for Separation of Church and State v. Prison Fellowship Ministries, Inc.*, 431 F. Supp. 2d 862, 933 (S.D. Iowa 2006). On appeal, the Eighth Circuit agreed that the program violated the Establishment Clause, but declined to order reimbursement of state funds. (*Americans United for Separation of Church and State, et al. v. Prison Ministries, Inc., et. al.*, 509 F. 3d 406 (2007).

30. Anna Persky "A question of faith," *ABA Journal*, June 2008, http://abajournal.com/magazine/a_question_of_faith/.

31. Institute in Basic Life Principles: Giving the World a "New" Approach to Life, http://iblp.org/iblp/about.

32. To quote:

- 543 events conducted in communities, schools, churches, prisons, jails and juvenile facilities all over the United States and in several foreign countries;
- 87,312 Christians have been trained to share their faith in Jesus Christ through personal, individual, and small group Gospel presentations using the Four Spiritual Laws (from Campus Crusade for Christ) as the main Gospel Tract;
- 2,162,155 students, adults, and youth have seen action from Athletic Stars, music from Entertainers and testimonies from famous people. The trained volunteers then meet with them to share the Gospel with them and for prayer and encouragement;
- 454,625 lost souls have come to faith in Christ through the one-on-one Evangelism Training and techniques taught through CFL to the volunteers. The Gospel message is backed by Christ's command in

The Great Commandment, Great Commission and Acts 1:8. Through God's love for the lost, His Word, the Blood of Jesus Christ and the power of the Holy Spirit, these volunteers are used by God to lead the lost into a redemptive relationship for eternity.

(Bill Glass Champions for Life, http://www.billglasscf/.org/about.asp)

33. The Bush administration pledged $300 million for FBCO programs for 2006–2010, and in 2004 Bush's former director of the U.S. Government Accountability Office acknowledged that no direct federal grants had gone to any non-Christian religious organization. David Kuo is an evangelical Christian and former Special Assistant to the President and Deputy Director of the White House Office of Faith-Based and Community Initiatives. In his book *Tempting Faith* (New York: Free Press, 2006), Kuo wrote that the Bush administration spent $20 million less than the Clinton administration on "compassionate" social programs, privately mocked evangelical leaders, and used funds to reward the politically faithful and spread the political gospel. Money did not go to the American poor, as promised, but to Christian cultural warriors. Those reviewing grant applications simply stopped looking at applications from non-Christian groups.

34. The Alpha "recipe" for success officially includes a weekly "clean, funny" joke. Samples may be found at www.alphajokes.com and www.alphaconnected.org. The latter site links specific jokes to specific course topics. Samples include: "The little boy wasn't getting good marks in school. One day he quite surprised the teacher. He tapped her on the shoulder and said, 'I don't want to scare you, but my daddy says if I don't get better grades somebody is going to get a spanking!'" Which brings us back to Kincaid.

35. Course materials range from the basic text, *The Alpha Course—Questions of Life Book* ($9.99), to *The Alpha Course DVD*, which has the complete Alpha course—both full-length and edited versions (ideal for the workplace) ($179.99). Additional materials include The Marriage Course, The Marriage Preparation Course, Alpha for the Military, Alpha On Campus, Alpha in the Workplace, and Youth Alpha. There's also the "Alpha Course Recommended Reading" (*The Cross and the Switchblade* can be had for $4.99 for those who like their morality tales set to an ever-relevant Sharks & Jets backbeat). Those interested in running Alpha courses can prepare by buying from the "Materials to Run the Alpha Course" line, including *How To Run the Alpha Course Director's Handbook* ($19.99), the *Small Group Leaders Training DVD Eng-*

lish/Spanish ($38.99), and the *Just Beginning Kit with DVD* ($489.00). Other Course materials are available under the category "Promoting Your Course," including "Explore the Questions of Life" (Issues 1–4), invitations ($5.00 for a 20-pack), *The God Who Changes Lives DVD* ($8.99), and *Why Christmas? DVD* ($8.99). In addition to the Alpha Course, there are Alpha Conferences, including Training Events (regular registration $159.00); a typical two-day Training Event features talks on "The Principles of Alpha (I and II)," "The Practicalities of Alpha," "Model Alpha Evening," "Small Groups," "Ministry on Alpha," and "Integrating Alpha into the Church," sandwiched between coffee, lunch, and dinner breaks. The Alpha USA Web site (tag line: "Is there more to life than this?") says there are currently 8,300 "nationally networked" churches profiting from the Alpha Course.

36. According to a working paper by the UC Irvine Center for Evidence-Based Corrections, the PIA in 2006 had shrunk to 6,000 inmates in 22 prisons, with 110,000 inmates eligible for work; in 2004, the PIA produced about $144 million in revenue, and still focuses primarily on the manufacture of institutional-type clothing, furniture, signs, stationery, and some food products for public entities.

Chapter 5

1. "Governor Schwarzenegger proposes toughest sex offender laws in the history of the state of California," Governor's Official Web Site, 2005, http://www.schwarzenegger.com/news.asp?id=2084.

2. "What is GPS," 2004, http://www.trimble.com/gps/whatgps.shtml, as quoted by Niki Delson, "Using global positioning systems (GPS) for sex offender management," *The Forum* (Association for the Treatment of Sexual Abusers), Summer 2006, http://ccoso.org/GPSforumarticle.pdf.

3. "Protecting our children from sexual predators," Assemblyman Sam Hoyt Reports to the People, Summer 2006, http://assembly.state.ny.us/member_files/144/20060802/#toc7.

4. O. Kay Henderson, "Senate bill toughens penalties on sex offenders," *Radio Iowa*, 1/26/2006, http://www.radioiowa.com/gestalt/go.cfm?objectid=9EC59FC4-1707-4B94-A7CF5A546A4C915A. The Iowa state motto is, "Our liberties we prize and our rights we will maintain." North Dakota lawmakers seem modest by comparison. The Fargo police officer overseeing offender registration was "hesitant to say" if the state's laws were "the

toughest in the country." (Bob Reha, "North Dakota lawmakers to change sex offender laws," Minnesota Public Radio, January 18, 2005, http://news. minnesotapublicradio.org/features/2005/01/18_rehab_ndsexoffender/, as quoted by Delson, "Using global positioning systems (GPS) for sex offender management."

5. *Gonzalez v. Duncan*, 551 F.3d 875 (9th Cir. 2008).

6. Bob Egelko, "Court: Sex-offender law unfairly restrictive," *San Francisco Chronicle*, November 21, 2008, www.sfgate.com/cgi.bin/article. cgi?=/c/a/2008/11/21/BAER149660.DTL.

7. To see a copy of the complaint filed by the Georgia ACLU on behalf of the petitioners, go to http://www.acluga.org/docs/docket/Whitake%20 v.%20Perdue%20(Sex%20Offender)/Complaint.pdf.

8. There's also talk of repeal, partly because some 40 percent of Georgia's registered child molesters were minors at the time of the crime, and whose victims were similarly underage girlfriends, acquaintances, or siblings, and the sex was consensual. Thus far, it is still on the books.

9. Jonathan Roos, "Iowa's new sex offender law is tough—but costly," *Des Moines Register*, 2005, as cited in Delson, "Using global positioning systems (GPS) for sex offender management."

10. Monica Davey, "Iowa's residency rules drive sex offenders underground." *New York Times*, March 15, 2006, http://www.nytimes.com/2006/03/15/ national/15offenders.html.

11. Wendy Koch, "More sex offenders transient, elusive. Homeless life may increase crime risk." *USA TODAY*, November 19, 2007.

12. "Subdivision will ban sex offenders," *Los Angeles Times*, November 24, 2007.

13. David Reyes, "State denies 'shuffling' molesters," *Los Angeles Times*, May 10, 2006.

14. Jane Ellen Stevens, "Ending an awful irony," *Los Angeles Times*, January 25, 2006.

15. Peter Hong, "On his block, a molester," *Los Angeles Times*, December 5, 2006.

16. Maria LaGanga, "Megan's Law listing may be tied to slaying," *Los Angeles Times*, December 10, 2007.

17. Hong, "On his block."

18. Here's how it works: Man is convicted of molestation. Man is released, registers. Man meets a woman who has a pre-existing child. Man tells woman that he didn't actually molest former victim, that he (a) pled guilty because they told him that if he pled out, he'd get a good deal,

but if he went to trial, no one would believe him because everybody always believes the child, and he'd do life, or some chunk thereof; (b) was convicted because everyone always believes the child. Woman believes man. (Man may or may not be telling the truth.) Man moves in, is arrested for molestation of child. Man tells appellate attorney that he didn't do this new molestation either, but that woman knew of prior and knew no one would believe him because he's a registered sex offender so accused him of molesting again to get him out of house, life, etc. (Man may or may not be telling the truth.) Note inutility of registration requirement in keeping man crime- or child-free.

19. The Department of Justice estimates that about 10 percent of sexual assaults on children are done by strangers; of the yearly 60,000 to 70,000 reported sexual assaults on children, about 100 are stranger abductions/assaults.

Chapter 6

1. Code of Va. sec. 9.1-903(B)

2. Public Law 110-400 (S.431), October 13, 2008, "To require sex offenders to register online identifiers, and for other purposes"; Public Law 110-401 (S. 1738) October 13, 2008, "To require the Department of Justice to develop and implement a National Stragegy for Child Exploitation Prevention and Interdiction, to improve the Internet Crimes Against Children Task Force, to increase resources for regional computer forensics labs, and to make other improvements to increase the ability of law enforcement to investigate and prosecute child predators." http://sentencing.typepad.com/sentencing_law_and_policy/2008/10/new-federal-sex.html.

3. The Associated Press, "Virginia: Registry of sex offenders' online identities," December 12, 2006, http://www.nytimes.com/2006/12/12/us/12brfs-VIRGINIA.html.

4. Juan Carlos Perez, "NY AG pushes e-safety bill, Facebook, MySpace back it," *PC World*, January 30, 2008, http://pcworld.about.com/od/kidsteens/NY-AG-pushes-e-safety-bill-Fa.htm.

5. "State widens DNA scanning in cold cases," *San Francisco Chronicle*, April 26, 2008.

6. The U.K.'s *Daily Mail* noted that as a result of the European court's ruling, a million innocent people (i.e., individuals never charged with

a crime), including 40,000 children, would have their profiles eliminated from the nation's DNA roll, http://www.dailymail.co.uk/news/article-1091880/One-million-innocent-people-profiles-wiped-Britains-DNA-database-court-ruling.html.

Chapter 7

1. As was testified to at trial, a project resident called the cops after watching a rowdy group of mostly men and one woman outside her house on the night of the party. The woman seemed extremely intoxicated, and was hugging and kissing some of the men. The forensic nurse testified that Antoinette's bruises were consistent with either rape or consensual intercourse, particularly intercourse with an intoxicated partner, and with multiple partners. The motel housekeeper testified that she found wet sheets and towels in the bathroom, beer bottles and used condoms "everywhere." The bathroom floor was very wet, as if it had been flooded. George rented the room around midnight; another motel guest saw the SUV pull in, park, and about fifteen men get out. Five men then quickly carried a sleeping girl from the car into a room, holding her by her legs, arms, and shoulders, chair-style. People came and went from the room throughout the night; the guest did not call the police because she "thought there was a party going on."

2. CALJIC (California Jury Instructions—Criminal) Nos. 1.23.2, 10.02.

3. Mary Wollstonecraft, *An Historical and Moral View of the French Revolution and the Effect It Has Produced in Europe* (London: Joseph Johnson, 1794).

4. Years ago, I met a woman in her early thirties who confessed to me that when she was in college she liked to accuse guys of rape. She'd get someone in her room, and as soon as they started to have sex, she'd start screaming, "What are you doing?" and otherwise raise the hue and cry. The next day she would launch a whisper campaign against the young man, warning other female students that he was a date rapist. I don't think that she's a regular sort of woman or that this a common practice, but there it is. What was psychologically fascinating to me was her desire to destroy any club that would have her for its member. Legally, if any of her victims had been charged, the only way they could defend themselves would have been to find others she'd accused, and prove those were false accusations as well. Possible, but pretty unlikely.

5. "Man receives 862-year term in gang rape," Tami Abdollah, *Los Angeles Times*, February 6, 2007.

6. On November 25, 2007, the *New York Times* ran an interactive feature on the "Faces of the Exonerated," profiles of 137 men imprisoned from seven to twenty-four years for crimes they did not commit, mostly murder and rape, released by way of DNA evidence. http://www.nytimes.com/interactive/2007/11/25/nyregion/20071125_DNAI_FEATURE.html#. Accompanying stories detailed how those wrongfully incarcerated end up in roughly the same ex-con boat—post-release drug addiction, homelessness, few hopes, and fewer opportunities—as their guilty fellows. A third are able to establish themselves on the outside, a sixth return to prison or addiction, and half scrabble along trying to stay afloat. Janet Roberts and Elizabeth Stanton, "A long road back after exoneration, and justice is slow to make amends," *New York Times*, November 25, 2007.

7. Though he might be able to accuse her of rape as well, or they could each be prosecuted. Or he could try to present evidence that he was so pissed that he didn't mean to have *unlawful* sex (i.e., as sex itself is lawful, the prohibited act is *unlawful* sex). Unlawful sex is nonconsensual sex. If I can't tell whether the sex is legally nonconsensual because I'm so drunk that the drunkenness of my partner (and therefore the mooting of her consent) has totally failed to penetrate, am I guilty of rape? Perhaps not. (Though I am always guilty of worshiping at the altar of the legal technicality.)

8. *Wardius v. Oregon*, 412 U.S. 474 (1973).

Chapter 8

1. Studies of prostitutes indicate that at some point in their careers 48 to 59 percent are raped by a client, 29 to 50 percent raped by a pimp, and 27 percent raped by a police officer.

2. By way of an apologia, I should emphasize that I consistently lose the cultural argument presented in this chapter in the Court of Appeal. It is one of those arguments that is always met with stony silence. As a matter of pride, I don't believe this reflects the argument's validity. I'm right and I know it. Part of the *joie de la souffrance* of being a criminal appellate attorney lies in having legally sound arguments serially rejected. But then that day comes when one of your arguments gets through, and suddenly, all is bathed in the warm glow of constitutional illumination. This is how the *Miranda* warnings were born, and have been gradually eroded.

3. Usually incorrectly. Contrary to popular street culture, cops are not obligated to truthfully answer the litmus question, "Are you a cop?" and some will engage in varying degrees of sex before making the arrest. Though it's true that many won't kiss the prostitute.

4. Hearsay is defined as an out-of-court statement used to prove the truth of what is asserted ("I told my mother it was all her fault"). Hearsay is generally inadmissible unless it falls under a specific statutory exception, such as dying declarations ("William shot me!") and regular business records ("Widgets are always shipped on the thirteenth of the month"). Hearsay rules plague all first-year law students: the rule of thumb is that hearsay that has a very long history (pre-U.S. Constitution) of being admissible is generally admissible under the federal constitution, as long as such hearsay can generally be considered trustworthy (such as dying declarations)—which is why it's been admissible for so very long. (But see *Crawford v. Washington*, 1541 U.S. 36 [2004], holding that, regardless of reliability, out-of-court testimonial statements by witnesses are barred by the Confrontation Clause unless the declarants are unavailable and the defendant had a prior opportunity for cross-examination.)

5. Expert testimony based on hearsay typically occurs when one party has asked the expert witness a hypothetical that assumes all the facts testified to by that party's witnesses (for example, the victim says she was raped, but the sexual assault examination turned up no evidence of injury or force), and the expert has agreed that those facts would support the witnesses' testimony (there is often no evidence of injury or force after a rape). This leads to the moment during cross-examination when opposing counsel, using the steely look so favored by lawyers and bad prose writers, leans forward and hisses, "But you weren't *there*, were you? You're just *assuming* what the witness said was true, aren't you . . . *Doctor?*" And the expert has to agree.

6. *People v. Gardeley*, 14 Cal. 4th 605, 618 (1996).

7. Iceberg Slim, aka Robert Beck, started writing at the age of forty-three during a ten-month stretch in the joint. *Pimp* (1967), his first book, was a "fictionalized autobiography" that begins this way: "Dawn was breaking as the big Hog scooted through the streets. My five whores were chattering like drunk magpies. I smelled the stink that only a street whore has after a long, busy night." He recalls the words of the master pimp who turned him out (i.e., educated him): "Slim, a pimp is really a whore who has reversed the game on whores . . . A whore ain't nothing but a trick to a pimp." *Pimp* was followed by six other Afro-noir novels, which sold upward of six million copies. Beck died in 1992, a devoted husband and father of four.

8. http://childrenofthenight.org/founder.html. Many dissertations are unpublished; however, few unpublished dissertations are properly used
   as field guides for law enforcement or the basis for expert testimony. It
   should be noted that I have unsuccessfully challenged the admission of
   Lee's testimony in subsequent cases.

9. Battered wife syndrome (BWS) typically appears as a defense when the
   woman murders her partner, usually when the partner is not immediately threatening the woman, so that the usual principles of self-defense
   don't apply. Given that these murders are also often premeditated—the
   woman waiting until she has an opportunity to kill—she would normally
   be guilty of first-degree murder. BWS contextualizes the killing (and explains the woman's pre-killing behavior, such as voluntarily staying with
   her abuser), and mitigates premeditation: BWS explains that in this situation, the woman acts to save herself when she can, which may be when
   her enemy is temporarily disabled. BWS has been legislatively codified
   in most states as an affirmative defense, meaning the defense has to
   prove that the woman was battered by her victim. My all-time favorite
   BWS case involved a man who beat his wife every time he got drunk—
   and he got drunk a lot. He'd beat her, then pass out on their bed. One
   night, after he passed out, his wife sewed his clothes to the bedspread,
   with thousands of tiny stitches, all along his silhouette, like those chalk
   outlines that show where and how the body fell. In a perfect fusion of
   domestic crime and homespun retribution, she then took a ball-peen
   hammer and broke every bone in his body.

10. Ann Burgess and Lynda Holmstrom, "Rape trauma syndrome," *Ameri-
    can Journal of Psychiatry* 131 (1974): 981–982.

11. "[R]ape counselors are taught to make a conscious effort to avoid judg-
    ing the credibility of their clients. Thus, as a rule, rape counselors don't
    probe inconsistencies in their clients' descriptions of the facts of the in-
    cident, nor do they conduct independent investigations to determine
    whether other evidence corroborates or contradicts their clients' rendi-
    tions." *People v. Bledsoe*, 36 Cal. 3d 236, 250 (1984).

12. *Bledsoe* 36 Cal. 3d at 250.

13. *Kumho Tire Co. v. Carmichael*, 526 U.S. 137, 151 (1999), is also noted in
    chapter 2.

14. In California, a witness can be impeached with a prior pimping or pros-
    titution conviction. These are crimes of moral turpitude as a matter of
    law. Those who have prior convictions for crimes of moral turpitude are
    presumptively untrustworthy.

15. Destiny's End, "The Pimping Game," http://www.wmich.edu/destinys-end/pimping%20game.htm.

It seems no one should actually need to take a public stance against the sexual exploitation of children. However, adults are adults, and adults are free to make all the lousy choices they'd like, including unlawful ones and ones driven by desperation. After all, the abject subject is still a subject.

Chapter 9

1. William Blake, "Auguries of Innocence," in *The Complete Poetry and Prose of William Blake* Cambridge edition, ed. Douglas Bush (Boston: Houghton Mifflin, 1965).

2. Judith Walkowitz, *Prostitution and Victorian Society: Women, Class, and the State* (Cambridge and New York: Cambridge University Press, 1980).

3. Dickens' home for women, Urania Cottage, was a pet project of Angela Burdett-Coutts, Britain's wealthiest woman, and a great philanthropist. Dickens dedicated *The Life and Adventures of Martin Chuzzlewit*, his last picaresque tale, to her. It features Mrs. Gamp, a nurse who specializes in womb and tomb, or lying-in and laying-out. At the end of the young women's reformation, they were transported to Australia. Reintegration into society did not mean English society per se.

4. Daniel Defoe's 1722 *The Fortunes and Misfortunes of Moll Flanders* chronicles the famous and infamous adventures of a fictitious adventuress who, according to the title, "was Twelve Year a Whore," but who "at last grew Rich, liv'd Honest and died a Penitent." Crime could pay, in an Enlightenment way.

5. A. J. B. Parent-Duchâtlet, *De la prostitution dans la ville de Paris* (Brussels: Société Belge de Librairie, 1836).

6. William Tait, *Magdalenism: An Inquiry into the Extent, Causes, and Consequences of Prostitution* (Edinburgh: P. Rickard, 1840). See also William Acton, *Prostitution Considered in Its Moral, Social and Sanitary Aspects . . . and Prevention of its Attendant Ends* (London: J. Churchill, 1870).

7. Quoted in Acton, *Prostitution Considered*, 39.

8. Acton, *Prostitution*, 93.

9. "Contagious Diseases are bad, King Stork; But Tyranny's worse than disease, King Stork," read an election handbill against one Acts supporter named Sir Henry Storks.

10. Amanda Anderson, *Tainted Souls and Painted Faces: The Rhetoric of Fallenness in Victorian Culture* (Ithaca, NY: Cornell University Press, 1993).

11. "Her eye of light is the diamond bright/Her innocence the pearl/And these are ever the bridal gems/Worn by the American girl." Lydia H. Sigourney, *The Young Lady's Offering: Or, Gems of Prose and Poetry*, 2nd ed. (Boston: Phillips, Sampson, 1853), 283.

12. Barbara Welter, "The cult of true womanhood: 1820–1860," *American Quarterly* 18 (1966): 151–174.

13. "They even said it with flowers: a dried white rose symbolized 'Death preferable to Loss of Innocence,'" from Welter, "The cult of true womanhood," 154.

14. In the American West, solutions were simpler. In 1893, the *Arcata Union* newspaper of Humboldt County, California, reported that a house of ill repute in nearby Ferndale, "the cause of much trouble for several months past," had been burned to the ground one night. Noted the editor: "The Ferndalians have a peculiar method of dealing with suspected evildoers that sometimes gets them into trouble." On January 2, 1899, the Ferndale paper reported the suicide of a "half-breed" known as Rosie O'Grady, who had been rescued from a disreputable house in Eureka two years earlier, concluding, "It would appear now that after leaving the home, she had resumed her former evil life and had paid the penalty."

15. Painting a less rosy picture of the Dutch red-light district, a no-coercion campaign was launched in 2005. Many working women (sans papiers) were thought to be victims of sex trafficking, and customers were encouraged to report signs of forced sex work, including "no pleasure on the job." Too, strict codes of acceptable sexual conduct have fallen to the pressures of high demand and cheap trafficked labor, and only about 100 of the Netherlands's 25,000 prostitutes were union members as of 2004. Since brothel prostitution was legalized in Melbourne, Australia, in 1984, three times as many illegal brothels have appeared, and there are five times more unregistered street prostitutes. On a related note, Britain established a Human Trafficking Centre in 2006 to coordinate law enforcement efforts against sex slavery in that country; in 2008, the United Kingdom enacted legislation that provided for prosecution of men who had sex with women who were trafficked or pimped. Ignorance of the woman's kept situation is no defense.

16. Catharine MacKinnon, *Only Words*, reprinted in *Prostitution and*

Pornography: Philosophical Debate about the Sex Industry, ed. Jessica Spector (Palo Alto, CA: Stanford University Press, 2006).

17. *American Booksellers v. Hudnut*, 771 F. 2d 323 (7th Cir. 1985).

18. Shades of the Contagious Diseases Acts, albeit via voluntary participation. It's worth noting that during the social purification program in Thailand in the 1950s, the effort to criminalize prostitution-related activities such as trafficking resulted in systemic medical examinations and "moral rehabilitation" of the prostitutes. All roads lead to Home.

19. Contractarians, as the name implies, basically advocate for the inalienable right of a person, and all people, to freely make decisions about their lives, and freely make agreements based on those decisions. So long as these agreements are mutual, they are moral.

20. Simone de Beauvoir, quoted in her book *Philosophy of Woman* (Indianapolis, IN: Hackett Publishing, 1978).

Chapter 10

1. Iceberg Slim [Robert Beck], *Pimp, the Story of My Life* (Los Angeles: Holloway House, 1967).

2. Iceberg Slim, *The Naked Soul of Iceberg Slim* (Los Angeles: Holloway House, 2000), 95.

3. A "pimp stick" is some object a pimp uses to whup a ho. A wire coat hanger, straightened then folded over, is ideally suited to the task.

4. Chris Hansen, *To Catch a Predator: Protecting Your Kids from Online Enemies Already in Your Home* (New York: Dutton, 2007).

5. The in-house decoy was originally a real thirteen-year-old, but is now also played by young-looking adult sting volunteers.

6. There's a little media ethics in-joke here, as *Predator* has also been criticized in journalism circles for colluding with the cops; as one ethics expert told the *Los Angeles Times*, "By working with a group that has been deputized, *Predator* is essentially partnering with law enforcement. Even if the outcome is a desirable outcome, in the long run it undermines their ability to serve as watchdog." Matea Gold, "'Dateline' too close to cops?" *Los Angeles Times*, April 26, 2007. Reporters are supposed to be the watchdogs, and to be an effective watchdogs, they can't be in bed with anyone, not even the police. PeeJ can be so bedded, because it is not a news agency. But, according to Hansen, PeeJ is also a "watchdog," though a special breed: Internet watchdog. So a watchdog can partner

with a watchdog, making two watchdogs, which is obviously much better than one for watching.

7. *Sorrells v. United States*, 287 U.S. 435 (1932).

8. *Sherman v. United States*, 356 U.S. 369, 372 (1973).

9. *Jacobson v. United States*, 503 U.S. 540 (1992).

10. *People v. Moran*, 1 Cal. 3d 755, 760–761 (1970).

11. *People v. Mower*, 28 Cal. 4th 457, 480–481 (2002).

12. This standard has sometimes been called the "puke test." If the misconduct makes the judges puke, it's over the line.

13. "Disposition" evidence is also statutorily allowed in domestic violence cases, but in no other felony trials.

14. *Paris Adult Theatre I v. Slaton*, 413 U.S. 49, 67 (1973).

15. "Hey, if your place of employ (sic) asks that your shirt have a collar, you can still rock PeeJ gear!" Sample T-shirts: "Perverted-Justice.Com (American flag) Squeeze No Child's Behind," "At PervertedJustice. Com, This is What a 13-Year Old Girl Looks Like," "The Men Who Expose And Run . . . Can't Run From This Exposure! Perverted Justice (smiley face with pumping fist) Wankers," "See You Later, Masturbator. After Awhile, Pedophile."

16. I put this is in the category of the objectified self, that eyed-I that makes us look better in the mirror than in the eyes of others, where we know our intentions are good, and we would be judged by those, and not our actions, which may be more compromised.

17. PeeJ has taken up identifying registered sex offenders' MySpace pages, reporting the men to MySpace to have their pages deleted, and to their parole/probation officers for potential violation. Certainly, if the terms of someone's parole/probation prohibit a MySpace page, then he should suffer the consequences of breaking parole/probation. On the other hand, there's nothing that says a registered sex offender can't participate in an online gathering place. Many offenses subject to registration have nothing to do with predatory crimes against strangers. We also know that the registration requirements are mandatory. We also understand that sex offenders are among us in the physical world, attending ball games, parades, and hoedowns, going to nightclubs, estate auctions, and the Piggly-Wiggly. If we've no right to keep them out of one, what right do we have to boot them out of another?

18. This feature changes: in December 2007, the FAQ sheet featured "Web-exclusive clips" of experts answering parents' questions about Internet safety and how much freedom to give children online. (It should also be

noted that, according to Chris Hansen's blog, the show does not need permission to show the men involved in the sting operations because "*Dateline* is a news program *not* an entertainment program" [emphasis added].)

19. Similarly, the Arizona Supreme Court has held that the crime of "luring" can only be committed if the person solicited is either a minor or a police officer decoy; someone who solicits a non-cop decoy can only be charged with attempt. *Mejak v. Granville*, 212 Ariz. 555 [136 P. 3d 874] (2006).

20. *Jacobson*, 503 U.S. at 553–554.

21. As of March 2007, the *Predator* Web site tallied over 200 charges (not convictions; convictions total about thirty-six) as a result of "our investigations." If *Predator* isn't exactly manufacturing news, it's sure making hay.

22. See Brad Stone, "Report calls online threats to children overblown," *New York Times*, January 14, 2009; "Enhancing child safety & online technologies, final report of the Internet Safety Technical Task Force, December 31, 2008, http://cyber.law.harvard.edu/sites/cyber.law.harvard.edu/files/ISTTF_Final_Report.pdf.

23. The expert cited in Hansen's book recommends a minimum of two years active treatment and five years follow-up.

24. This is not entirely true. The Murphy sting was special in that it netted no convictions. The district attorney's office, stating there were problems with the evidence, declined to prosecute the twenty cases related to the operation. In another coda, NBC settled a lawsuit in 2008 with the family of the man who committed suicide during the Murphy sting, http://latimesblogs.latimes.com/showtracker/2008/06/nbc-resolves-la.html.

25. In this idea, I gracelessly lift the concept of "spectacular reality" from Vanessa R. Schwartz's *Spectacular Realities: Early Mass Culture in Fin-de-Siècle Paris* (U. of California Press, 1998), which chronicled how the Paris morgues were a precursor of reality television, displaying corpses for the viewing public, most popularly, corpses with salacious back stories and scandalous ends (not unlike this book).

26. On March 29, 2007, an Arts blog presented by the online edition of the U.K. newspaper *Guardian* chastised fans of Welsh actor Rhys Ifans for apologizing for his pedophile joke:

> *Who's to blame for pedophilia?*
> *Sexy kids.*

The apology was wrong, not because it's a very old joke, or because there's no excuse for making fun of such a serious phenomenon. The apology was wrong, according to blog author Zoe Williams, because it's stupid. It's stupid because it assumes that anyone who has ever been molested would be further traumatized by the joke, and because humor is very much and very often about taboo trouncing and sending up self-righteousness. I can't weigh in on the first reason: although I've known some people who've been sexually abused who make some of the best jokes ever about rape and molestation, others can't. I can't honestly weigh in on the better response. But I can agree wholeheartedly with Williams: "Who does it serve, when we demand to have everything spelt out in fridge magnets?"

The post set off a tiny flurry of responses, including several quite good pedophilia jokes, to wit:

> *What's so great about fucking twenty eight year-olds?'*
> *There are 20 of them.*

> *I was lying in bed with my girlfriend the other day when she accused me of being a pedophile.*
> *"Blimey," I said. "That's a big word for an eight-year-old!"*

> *Q: What do you give the pedophile who has everything?*
> *A: A bigger parish.*

> *The trouble with pedophilia is having to go to bed so early.*

Chapter 11

1. *In re Lynch*, 8 Cal. 3d 410, 424 (1972).
2. *Furman v. Georgia*, 408 U.S. 238, 271 (1972) (conc. opn. by Brennan, J.).
3. Legitimacy is a whole concept in legal theory, variously focusing on legitimacy as conferred by the democratic process, by legal authority, by reliability (or the ability to produce just results), and by adherence to constitutional values and promises of fairness and equality. Legitimacy is linked to, and sometimes indistinguishable from, basic definitions of "justice."
4. Of the nine justices on the court as of this writing, Justice Ginsburg is commonly considered the most liberal, though she is relatively moderate toward other branches of government. Justice Stevens is now the old liberal guard who in 2008 declared that he would no longer support the death penalty. Linda Greenhouse, "Justice Stevens renounces capital

punishment," *New York Times*, April 18, 2008. Justice Breyer favors pragmatic interpretivism, which currently makes him a liberal, although he tends to defer, like his conservative brethren, to executive interests and legislative determinations. Justice Souter has moved from the conservative to the liberal camp, in large part due to the Court's recomposition. Since the departure of Justice O'Connor, Justice Kennedy—a man of unflagging common sense—has become the bellwether of a 5–4 majority. (Says Mark Twain: "Whenever you find yourself on the side of the majority, it is time to pause and reflect.")

5. *Rummel v. Estelle*, 445 U.S. 263 (1980).
6. *Solem v. Helm*, 463 U.S. 277 (1983). Writing for the Court, Justice Powell set forth a tripartite Eighth Amendment analysis, requiring consideration of: "(i) the gravity of the offense and the harshness of the penalty; (ii) the sentences imposed on other criminals in the same jurisdiction; and (iii) the sentences imposed for commission of the same crime in other jurisdictions." The life term in *Solem* was "far more severe" than that in *Rummel* because the defendant in *Rummel* would be eligible for parole in twelve years, whereas there was no possibility of the *Solem* defendant's release.
7. *Harmelin v. Michigan*, 501 U.S. 957, 1001 (1991). The Court upheld a sentence of life without possibility of parole for drug offenders convicted of possessing more than 650 grams of cocaine. *Harmelin* betrayed a split among the justices. Two felt the very idea that the Eighth Amendment mandated proportionality in sentencing was "simply wrong." Four would have found the sentence disproportionate under the *Solem* test. Three, including Kennedy, opined that a noncapital sentence *could* be unconstitutionally disproportionate, though Harmelin didn't meet the standard, given that drugs are the scourge of society. Justice Scalia delivered the opinion of the Court only with regard to the merits of the petitioner's Eighth Amendment claim, joined by Chief Justice Rehnquist. Under Scalia's analysis, proportionality was only one "aspect of our death penalty jurisprudence, rather than a generalizable aspect of Eighth Amendment law." Justice Stevens, with Justice Blackmun joining, filed a dissenting opinion (in addition to those filed by Justices White and Marshall) underscoring that the penalty involved was "cruel and unusual in the same way that being struck by lightning is cruel and unusual."
8. *Ewing v. California*, 538 U.S. 11 (2003), produced another plurality opinion: The Court's opinion (written by Justice O'Connor, joined by

Justice Kennedy and Chief Justice Rehnquist) basically adopted Kennedy's approach in *Harmelin*.

9. See also Justice Souter's dissenting opinion in *Lockyer v. Andrade*, 538 U.S. 63, 83 (2003): "If Andrade's sentence isn't grossly disproportionate (25 to life for shoplifting less than $200 worth of videos), the principle has no meaning." In *Ewing*, Justice Breyer, writing for the dissenters— Stevens, Breyer, Souter, and Ginsburg—argued that the facts were not substantially different from those of *Solem*, and dictated the same "grossly disproportionate" finding. In a separate dissent, Justice Stevens quoted an earlier case: "The Eighth Amendment succinctly prohibits 'excessive sanctions.'" This prohibition covers everything from bails and fines to the death penalty; because sentences were once commonly indeterminate, judges historically had to exercise wide discretion in affixing punishment, discretion cabined by "a broad and basic proportionality principle" constitutionally secured.

10. *People v. Deloza*, 18 Cal. 4th 585 (1998). The California court determined the appropriate standard for imposing concurrent or consecutive terms under the three-strikes laws. The majority opinion did not address the Eighth Amendment issue.

11. By coincidence, the defendant who stole the explosives used in the 2004 Madrid train bombing also received a sentence of 30,000 years, although in Spain the maximum anyone can serve is forty years.

12. *Robinson v. State*, (Okla. Crim. App. April 1, 1996) F94-1377.

13. *O'Neil v. Vermont*, 144 U.S. 323, 340 (1892) (dis. opn. by Field, J.).

14. Sad anecdotal case: My client was a forty-five-year-old drug addict with two residential burglary priors. He bought a vial of PCP, sniffed up half, and passed out, clutching the unused portion—which is possession, a felony, which was strike three. Had he managed to sniff the whole thing before losing consciousness, he would have been only "under the influence" when the cop strolled by, which is a misdemeanor, and today would be a free junkie, recidivist burglar, or rehabbed citizen.

15. *Trop v. Dulles*, 356 U.S. 86 (1958) at p. 100.

16. *People v. Byrd*, 89 Cal. App. 4th 1373, 1383 (2001).

17. *Callins v. State*, 500 P. 2d 1333 (Okla. 1972).

18. *Fields v. Phillips*, 501 P. 2d 1390, 1393–1394 (Okla. 1972). The Oklahoma court also intuited that the jury's imposition of the aggravated term must have been due to "some additional consideration . . . such as an attempt to indicate outrage at the facts and circumstances of the case and in some way to serve as a deterrent." In fact, the victim in *Fields*

had been "raped successively by [. . .] three Negroes," including the two defendants. A concurring justice, however, felt the sentence should be modified to life imprisonment; this was the justice who dissented in *Callins, supra.*

19. *Sills v. Texas,* 472 S.W.2d 119, 120 (1971).

20. *Callins* 500 P. 2d 1336 (opn. of Brett, J.).

21. *Callins* 500 P. 2d 1337; emphasis added.

22. Again, quoting the U.S. Supreme Court: "The very purpose of a Bill of Rights was to withdraw certain subjects from the vicissitudes of political controversy, to place them beyond the reach of majorities and officials and to establish them as legal principles to be applied by the courts. Judicial enforcement of the Clause, then, cannot be evaded by invoking the obvious truth that legislatures have the power to proscribe punishments for crimes. That is precisely the reason the Clause appears in the Bill of Rights . . . we must not, in the guise of judicial restraint, abdicate our fundamental responsibility to enforce the Bill of Rights. Were we to do so . . . [t]he Cruel and Unusual Punishments Clause would become, in short, little more than good advice. (*Trop* 356 U.S. at 104, internal quotations omitted.

23. In Mark's case, I also argued a violation of the separation-of-powers doctrine, because the executive, not the judiciary, determines parole eligibility. By orchestrating millennial or multiple-hundred-year sentences, courts impermissibly poach upon executive province. More pragmatically, the executive has custody of a man post-conviction, and is best able to discern whether that man—as he proves himself post-conviction—ought ever be released into society.

24. "If pardon is equitable, the law is bad; when legislation is good, pardons are only crimes against the law." J. P. Brissot, *Théorie des lois criminelles,* as quoted in Michel Foucault, *Discipline and Punish: The Birth of the Prison* (New York: Vintage, 1995), 312.

25. *Furman,* 408 U.S. at 271 (conc. opn. by Brennan, J.).

26. *Trop,* 356 U.S. at 101.

27. Lynn Hunt, *Inventing Human Rights: A History* (New York: Norton, 2007).

28. Foucault, *Discipline & Punish: The Birth of the Prison,* 2nd ed., trans. Alan Sheridan (NY: Vintage Books, 1995) pp. 109, 133, 173.

29. California's oldest inmate was John Rodriguez, who stabbed his wife twenty-six times in 1981. In 2007, Rodriguez was 95, and he had arthritis, used a walker, was hard of hearing, was frequently forgetful, attended

Alcoholics Anonymous meetings, and slept in the prison hospital dormitory. His parole that year was denied by Governor Arnold Schwarzenegger on grounds that Rodriguez presented an "unreasonable public danger" because his crime was bad and he might get drunk and do it again. Rodriguez's lawyer thought he would be more likely to fall asleep if he ever had another beer.

30. As opposed to "official purposes," in the language of the charging instrument. This legal-ethical distinction between the intent of the photographer and the reading of the viewer mirrors Susan Sontag's discussion in *Regarding the Pain of Others* (New York: Picador, 2004).

31. Scott Horton, "Zimbardo discusses accountability for torture," *Harper's*, April 3, 2007.

32. Philip Zimbardo, *The Lucifer Effect: Understanding How Good People Turn Evil* (New York: Random House, 2007).

33. Other sociological experiments have shown that the more people who happen to be available to help, the less likely help will be rendered by any one of them. Conservation of energy, I suppose, via reduction of personal risk.

Conclusion

1. Women were bound, thumbs to toes, and tossed into the water; witches floated, innocents drowned; certain factors made flotation more or less likely, such as osteoporosis or loose-fitting clothes.

2. As far as I know, this scale has not yet been used in determining whether someone is a sexually violent predator.

3. Michel Foucault, "Discipline and Punish: The Birth of the Prison," in *On Violence*, ed. Bruce Lawrence and Aisha Karim (Durham, NC: Duke University Press, 2007), 451.

4. "Sex offenders test churches' core beliefs," *New York Times*, April 10, 2007, http://www.nytimes.com/2007/04/10/us/10pilgrim.html.

Appendix

1. This is the famous "six-pack," where a witness looks at six photos of six different individuals and identifies the suspect from among them. In order for the six-pack to be constitutionally legitimate (not unduly

suggestive), all the individuals should look generally as the witness has described the perpetrator (mustache/no mustache, bald/hirsute, Latino/Caucasian), should look somewhat the same (none appreciably fatter or older than the others), should be similarly presented (no using one color photo in a field of black and white, no photo significantly larger than another), and not suggestive in and of itself (suspect isn't the only one pictured in a jail jumpsuit).

2. The testimony of Jane Does #6 and #7 was videotaped before trial because of the victims' ages; Doe #6 was eighty-two at the time of her testimony; Doe #7 was eighty.

3. Doe #6's exclamation referred to a prior rape on August 3, 1999, charged as counts 24, 25, and 26; the jury acquitted Mark on those counts. The earlier rape was similar in detail to the later rape. During the August 3 rape, Doe #6 had to explain the purpose of her colostomy bag to her rapist several times.

4. It is perhaps too much armchair psychoanalysis to point out that when Mark's elderly mother visited him in jail, her first words were, "How could you do this to me?"

INDEX